Robert Somers, Louis Wolowski

The Scotch Banks and System of Issue

Robert Somers, Louis Wolowski

The Scotch Banks and System of Issue

ISBN/EAN: 9783337120030

Printed in Europe, USA, Canada, Australia, Japan

Cover: Foto ©ninafisch / pixelio.de

More available books at **www.hansebooks.com**

THE

SCOTCH BANKS

AND

SYSTEM OF ISSUE.

INCLUDING

TRANSLATION OF "LES BANQUES D'ECOSSE,"

By L. WOLOWSKI, MEMBER OF THE FRENCH INSTITUTE.

WITH

NOTES, REMARKS, AND APPENDIX.

BY ROBERT SOMERS.

EDINBURGH:
ADAM AND CHARLES BLACK.
1873.

GLASGOW:
PRINTED BY BELL AND BAIN,
41 MITCHELL STREET.

PREFACE.

THE Banking System of Scotland is probably the greatest and most original work which the practical genius of the Scotch people has produced in the sphere of Political and Social Economics. The proof of this is seen, not only in the fact that it has contributed more to the prosperity of Scotland than any other class of institutions within the same sphere, but equally in the observation as patent that, while placed under doubt by the Imperial Legislation of the United Kingdom, it is constantly in State inquiries into Banking and Issue, whether in the United Kingdom or in foreign countries, appealed to as an essential point of departure in all investigations of this subject, and that it is almost as invariably misrepresented from pre-conceived theory, or imperfectly expounded from want of information. In this predicament, the Scotch people have not only to guard what they have attained for themselves against a tide of innovation, which is strong enough, but also to consider that they have in their Banking System a treasure of principle that may be of value to other countries as well as Scotland, and are, therefore, bound to look both widely and narrowly into it, and see of what it consists.

Beyond this, the Author has little more to say, by way of preface, than to give some indication of the origin and scope of his present work.

The recent inquiry into the Banking Question, before the Superior Council of Commerce of France, led to animated discussions on the part of the leading economists of Paris, in which the Scotch Banking System formed a prominent topic of animadversion. M. Wolowski, Professor of Political Economy in the University of Paris, while strongly opposed in theory to "the banking principle" of issue developed by the Scotch Banks, published, in an extensive *resumé* of the whole question, a little treatise on the Scotch Banking System, in which, with such means of information as were available, and as M. Wolowski could extend by the most commendable industry of personal correspondence, a valuable and genial delineation is given of the mechanism and operations of the Scotch Banks. It occurred to the Author that by presenting a translation of M. Wolowski's work on the Scotch Banks with Notes and Remarks embodying much fuller information, as well as reflection from a more experimental basis of reasoning, a tolerably complete view would be given, not only of the Scotch Banking System, but of its differences from the banking systems and theories of other countries. There are few secular subjects on which it is more necessary, with a seemingly indisputable axiom in hand, to be wary, and to be prepared for the possible intervention of other axioms equally indisputable, than on this subject of Banking and Issue of notes, in which all the natural laws of trade and economy seem to be gathered up, as it were, into a focus. There can be no doubt, therefore, that there is an advantage in presenting what occurs to be remarked from an opposite point of view.

In the translation of *Les Banques D'Ecosse*, here given, a little freedom has been used, (1) in leaving out, in two or three parts, sentences of purely French application not bearing on the general argument, and (2) in setting aside some of M. Wolowski's appended Tables in favour of the later and more comprehensive statistics which it was necessary to compile for this work. It may be here remarked, though without any bias, on the main subject, or any intention to dwell on the question whether it arises from the flattering conclusion of a distinguished French author, nearly a century ago, that "Scotland is the country where the spirit of observation has been brought to the greatest perfection," or from the more popular and public style of our banking system, that neither England nor France could produce such an exhaustive detail of its whole banking state as is given of that of Scotland in our Appendix alone. This remark may be the more freely made, because, if the statistics of banking in England had been as attainable as in Scotland, one or two of the plain conclusions in the following pages would have been fortified by larger evidence.

The Author is conscious of objections to which this work is liable in point of form; but hopes it may be acknowledged that, considering the controversial state of the question, the object in view has been approached in not the least effective way.

CONTENTS.

TRANSLATION.

CHAPTER I.

CHAPTER II.

CHAPTER III.

CHAPTER IV.

CHAPTER V.

CHAPTER VI.

CHAPTER VII.

CHAPTER VIII.

REMARKS.

CHAPTER VII.

CHAPTER VIII.

CHAPTER IX.

CHAPTER X.

CHAPTER XI.

APPENDIX.

TRANSLATION.

TRANSLATION

OF

"LES BANQUES D'ECOSSE."

CHAPTER I.

SOURCE OF THE PROSPERITY OF THE SCOTCH BANKS NOT IN AN AGRICULTURAL DESIGNATION, NOR IN ISSUE OF NOTES, BUT IN DEPOSITS.

WHENEVER the question of credit applied to the interests of agriculture has been mooted, the Scotch banks have always been cited as triumphant examples. These have been, in fact, prosperous institutions, and in the present day they secure to an industrious country the benefits of credit upon a considerable scale; but they do not in any way resemble the fanciful type that people have attempted to cloak under a justly respected name.

They are banks that carry on all kinds of operations, and assist industry and commerce as much as they do agriculture. No one in Scotland has entertained the thought of making their action special, and we should look in vain in that country for what we call an "Agricultural Bank." The general conditions, according to which advances are made, apply to every kind of need, by means of a clever organization, whenever the necessary solvency and punctuality in the performance of contracted engagements are secured. There no one regards with a jealous eye the advantages obtained by any one branch of human activity; but, on the contrary, it is well understood that every exercise of intelligence, applied to various forms of production, helps to vivify the whole of human industry. Nor is there any privilege, any particular favour demanded for agriculture: it is treated as an industry, inasmuch as it presents the conditions that render industry capable of profiting by credit under its various forms.

In the circle of their operations the Scotch banks embrace every manifestation of labour; their results are in no way applicable, in an isolated manner, to agriculture; it is even difficult, if not altogether impossible, to calculate out of the entire transactions the separate portion that would belong to that branch of industry. On the other hand, Scotch banks are not in any way like great mints, where an abundant fabrication can be carried on of the all-happy note destined to fertilize the soil by means of paper transformed into hard money. They have no such ambitious designs: the solid success that they have obtained results from proceedings of a more reserved character. Whilst men, devoted to agricultural interests, do not hesitate among us to propose to base credit upon the multiplication of notes doing the work of ready money; and whilst they seek to depreciate the service rendered by the institutions that confine themselves to being the meeting-point between the real capital that they accumulate and the wants that they supply, the banks in Scotland have made but a limited use of their right of *issue*, and have based their operations upon *deposits*. It is this that forms the distinctive character of these establishments, and that has mainly contributed to the prosperity of the country. A single statement will suffice to enlighten every mind on this matter. The amount of notes circulating throughout the whole of Scotland does not usually exceed the total of the precious metals kept in hand in order to answer the demands for payment of the notes by more than two millions sterling, or fifty millions of francs. On the 8th December, 1866, at a time of the year when the circulation is sensibly increased, it amounted in all the notes of Scotch banks to £4,967,168, with a metallic reserve of £2,765,284, the exceptional difference for notes unrepresented by specie being thus raised to £2,261,344, or, in round numbers, fifty-five millions of francs. The average of this difference is lower by one-tenth. On the 30th March, 1867, the amount of notes issued by the banks had fallen to £4,221,024, whilst the specie in reserve had increased to £2,637,948. There was then only £1,583,074, or about thirty-nine millions of francs of notes in excess of the reserve. It is thus easy to appreciate the extent of supplementary resources that the Scotch banks obtain by the aid of issue. It is very small in relation to the mass of public wealth; it is also but a very limited fraction of the disposable capital deposited in the banks, and by aid of which they have exercised the beneficial influence that has obtained for them a legitimate reputation.

The total of the deposits entrusted to the banks of Scotland, without reckoning those in the hands of other financial firms, amounts to the enormous sum of sixty millions sterling, or one milliard five hundred millions of francs. We thus see how small a figure the result of the *issue* makes by the side of this colossal mass. It is here that we find the secret of the prosperity of the Scotch banks, and of the advantages that the country derives from them in the triple form of commercial, industrial, and agricultural credit. They work with the real capital, accumulated through saving, and not by means of a fictitious creation of instruments of circulation, the office of which is strictly limited. It is not in Scotland that the question can be asked, "Where shall we find the capital necessary to supply banks of deposit?" The Scotch find it in productive labour and in provident savings. Certainly it is not when confessing the absence of sufficient capital that we can invoke the example of Scotland, in order to construct a greater number of conveyances for the transport of this capital. To dream of multiplying bank-notes when agriculture is in want of stock, instruments, manure, and practical combinations of every kind, is to follow the celebrated example of the princess who, affected with a lively sympathy for the people that were suffering from hunger, desired to give them sweet cakes, since bread was wanting.

Let us condescend to realities instead of keeping in the cloudy regions of purely imaginary conceptions. We have often been accused of inventing theories; we think that this term, taken in one sense, applies more justly to those who are opposed to us. A great philosopher, Royer Collard, has said that a disdain of theory merely meant a refusal to understand what was said when spoken, or what was imagined when thought upon. To bring facts to bear upon doctrine is the theory that we like: to set aside facts, and to take no account of them while given up to hypotheses, is the theory of which one constantly meets the expression among those who pique themselves the most upon being practical, but who start up theories at every turn, and those of the most audacious kind, just as honest Mons. Jourdain did with prose.

Let us consult experience, and take especial care not to confound our ideas whilst employing ill-defined terms.

The fundamental confusion, from which so many mistakes arise, consists in recognizing in a bank, above everything else, the faculty of creating notes which are taken for capital. People are dazzled with this magic power, even to the point of disdaining the modest efforts of labour and saving.

For our own part, we have always said that banks should be multiplied, and that full liberty of action should be left to them, and that they should be called into existence more and more so as to excite the formation of capital by the facility of accommodation offered to the smallest funds; a body is thus given to what was but almost impalpable powder. Banks should distribute, on every side, those fertilizing waters that have been gathered, drop by drop, into large reservoirs. Such is the object of credit and its principal action, nor does it know any limit.

As to the fabrication of bank notes, it is sufficient to go back to their origin, and to follow their development, in order to appreciate in a sound manner their nature and bearing.

At a period when the variation in moneys and the alterations in specie carried trouble into all transactions, commerce, always ingenious in surmounting obstacles, conceived a mode of payment which allowed it to evade the uncertainty of the direct employment of pieces of money, badly made, clipped, or false. Banks of deposit were established; they brought about the unity of value based upon the weight of fine metal among the infinite variety of pieces exchanged into banco-money; they thus rendered a service, the extent of which cannot be appreciated too highly. Instead of a veritable confusion of tongues, corrected in an imperfect manner by the action of exchange, the unity of the commercial idiom was found. True passbooks, delivered to the depositors, declared the value of the deposits made; and clearances, effected by the help of assignments, regulated the debts. The precious metal remained immovable in the strong-room of the bank, as is still practized at Hamburg, where the "common fund" realizes with great advantages all the movement of capital between private parties. The bank operates only with what is in possession; when credit is employed, it rests upon the realized capital, and never entails a miscalculation.

The passage of assignments, transmitted from hand to hand, of the bank note, which constitutes an order at sight upon a fixed sum of money, was simple. But, instead of being contented with thus facilitating negociations, as well as accounts, and the transport of specie by means of the paper to which it was united by a direct and indissoluble bond, the banks wished to benefit by the deposits in making use of them. The permanent equilibrium between the metallic reserve, and the notes issued, was destroyed the moment that the new form of banks of circulation came into existence.

People were dazzled by this combination of instruments of exchange, extracted in some sort from nothing, and they allowed themselves to be drawn into a singularly exaggerated idea of its importance.

CHAPTER II.

NUMBER, ORGANIZATION, AND STATISTICS OF THE SCOTCH BANKS.

POLITICAL Economy is, above all, a study of facts, or "matters of fact," as the English say. We often discuss arbitrary imaginings until we lose sight of facts, and then the accumulated results of experience find themselves overlooked. More than this, we imagine, in good faith, certain mechanisms, at the effect of which we wonder, while taking simple hypotheses for reality.

However dry long columns of figures may be, we do not hesitate to produce them here before engaging in the examination of principles concerning Scotch banks. A kind communication has enabled us to compile, with this view, some precious documents completely unknown in this country, and which have had but very little publicity on the other side of the channel. Our neighbours are men of action more than anything else. They carry on affairs of great importance upon a large scale, but they rarely find time, and manifest but little taste, for detailed statements. Nothing can be more summary than the reports presented to meetings of shareholders, especially in connection with financial establishments. A great reserve presides over these communications, and those who are interested avoid all bursts of curiosity about such delicate matters. When the dividends declared are satisfactory, confidence in the directors renders all detailed investigation unnecessary. It must be some particular circumstance that produces other results. Inquiries, opened from time to time by the Parliament, have brought to light many facts that nobody has occupied himself with grouping together and bringing to the knowledge of the public. When any person wishes to be completely initiated into the management of great undertakings he must, for the most part, give himself up to personal investigation.

We have tried to enter upon this task. The relations that we have been happy enough to form with men whose intelligence equals their rare merit, have enabled us to get together some valuable information, the greater part of which has never been published. The facts are of a nature to give complete enlightenment upon the organization and progress of banks in Scotland, and it will be easy to draw instructive conclusions from them.

The number of banks in operation in Scotland at present is twelve. Each of these has numerous branches, which cover the country with a vast network of establishments of credit.

In order to have a complete notion of their actual condition, and of the changes passed through during nearly half a century, we reproduce a Table published by order of Parliament, April the 29th, 1864. It gives the names of all the banks that were in operation in Scotland on the 1st of January of the years 1819, 1830, 1845, and 1864; with the number of branches belonging to each, the amount of issue, the stock of metallic reserves, &c. The Table indicates also the time when some ceased their operations, and the union of the establishments that no longer exist separately.

The mere inspection of this document suggests observations of an incontestable gravity. It shows the number of banks diminishing, and of branches augmenting. As to the relation between the issue of notes and the metallic reserves, it is necessary, in order to make it well understood, that we should first show the spirit and the prescriptions of the law of 1845, which confined to the banks then in existence, according to the issues that they had made, the right of issuing notes, limiting the proportion that might be created beyond the amount exactly corresponding with the metallic reserve.

Amount of Specie. ...Weeks ending 3d Jan., 1846.	Last date, Average of 4 Weeks ending 5th Mar., 1864.	Dates when the Banks ceased to Operate.	CAUSES OF STOPPAGE OF OPERATIONS.
	£		
—	—	1825,	Not known.
—	—	1838,	Not known.
—	—	1826,	Not known.
—	—	1821, Oct.	Operations stopped.
—	—	1832,	Not known.
—	—	1821, Oct.	Not known.
—	—	1837, Nov.	Not known.
—	—	1838,	Joined with the Glasgow Union Bank Company.
—	—	1837,	Not known.
—		1838,	Joined with the Glasgow Union Bank Company.
—	—	1838,	Joined with Glasgow Bank Company, No. 34.
—	—	1836,	Joined with Glasgow Union Bank Company.
—	—	1843,	Joined with Glasgow Union Bank Company.
,981	—	1854,	Joined with Union Bank of Scotland, No. 44.
—	—	1833,	Not known.
—	—	1844,	Operations taken up by Commercial Bank of Scotland, No. 21.
,596	68,797	—	
—	—	1847,	Joined with Western Bank, No. 45.
,052	255,402	—	
,701	259,568		
,620	269,107	—	
,122	31,151	—	
,965	27,178	—	
,527	302,545	—	
,337	141,931	—	
,429	—	1864,	Joined with the Royal Bank of Scotland.
—	—	1844,	Joined with the Western Bank, No. 45.
—	—	1838,	Not known.
—	—	1822,	Operations ceased.
,316	—	1863,	Incorporated in the Clydesdale Bank, No. 25.
,780	—	1858, June	Incorporated in the Clydesdale Bank, No. 25.
—	—	1826,	Not known.
—	—	1845,	Joined with Western Bank, No. 45.
—	—	1837,	Joined with Ship Bank.
—	—	1842, Sept.	Placed under Sequestration.
—	—	1829,	Not known.
,346	270,391	—	
,880	76,533	—	
,426	—	1857,	Incorporated in Union Bank of Scotland. No. 44.
—	—	1836,	
,777	368,702	—	
—	—	1842, Sep.	Sequestrated.
—	—	1826,	Not known.
,574	262,764	—	
8,977	—	1857, Nov.	Suspension of Payments.
7,406	2,337,249		

hose Banks obtained a License to Issue Notes in the year 1808, when

Number	NAME OF THE BANK.	When Established.	Banks in Existence on 1st Jan. 1819: Chief Office.	1st Jan. 1819: Number of Branches.	1st Jan. 1830: Chief Office.	1st Jan. 1830: Number of Branches.	1st Jan. 1845: Chief Office.	1st Jan. 1845: Number of Branches.	1st Jan. 1864: Chief Office.	1st Jan. 1864: Number of Branches.	Authorized Issue of Notes: First date, Average of 4 Weeks ending 3d Jan., 1846.	Authorized Issue of Notes: Last date, Average of 4 Weeks ending 5th Mar., 1864.	Actual Issue of Notes: First date, Average of 4 Weeks ending 3d Jan., 1846.	Actual Issue of Notes: Last date, Average of 4 Weeks ending 5th Mar., 1864.	Amount of Specie: First date, Average of 4 Weeks ending 3d Jan., 1846.	Amount of Specie: Last date, Average of 4 Weeks ending 5th Mar., 1864.	Dates when the Banks ceased to Operate.	CAUSES OF STOPPAGE OF OPERATIONS.
	PRIVATE BANKS.										£	£	£	£	£	£		
1	Caithness Banking Company,	1812, Oct.	1	1	—	—	—	—	—	—	—	—	—	—	—	—	1825.	Not known.
2	Dundee New Bank,	—	1	1	1	1	—	—	—	—	—	—	—	—	—	—	1838.	Not known.
3	Falkirk Banking Company,	—	1	1	—	—	—	—	—	—	—	—	—	—	—	—	1826.	Not known.
4	Galloway Banking Company, or Douglas, Napier, & Coy.,	—	1	1	—	—	—	—	—	—	—	—	—	—	—	—	1821, Oct.	Operations stopped.
5	John Maberly & Co., or the Aberdeen, Montrose, Dundee, Edinburgh, and Glasgow Exchange Deposit Bank,	1818,	1	4	1	4	—	—	—	—	—	—	—	—	—	—	1832.	Not known.
6	Kilmarnock Banking Company,	—	1	—	—	—	—	—	—	—	—	—	—	—	—	—	1821, Oct.	Not known.
7	Paisley Banking Company,	—	1	4	1	3	—	—	—	—	—	—	—	—	—	—	1837, Nov.	Not known.
8	Paisley Union Bank, or Union Bank Company,	—	1	3	1	3	—	—	—	—	—	—	—	—	—	—	1838.	Joined with the Glasgow Union Bank Company
9	Ramsay, Bonar, & Company,	1807, Mar.	—	—	1	—	—	—	—	—	—	—	—	—	—	—	1837.	Not known.
10	Sir W. Forbes, J. Hunter, & Company,	1763.	1	—	1	—	—	—	—	—	—	—	—		—	—	1838.	Joined with the Glasgow Union Bank Company.
11	Ship Bank, or Carrick, Brown, & Company,	—	1	—	1	—	—	—	—	—	—	—	—		—	—	1838.	Joined with Glasgow Bank Company, No. 34.
12	Thistle Bank,	—	1	—	1	—	—	—	—	—	—	—	—		—	—	1836.	Joined with Glasgow Union Bank Company.
	JOINT-STOCK BANKS.																	
13	Ayr Bank, or Hunter's & Company,	—	1	2	1	4	—	—	—	—	—		—		—	—	1843.	Joined with Glasgow Union Bank Company.
14	Aberdeen Banking Company,	1767,	1	5	1	6	1	13	—		88,467	—	100,539		29,981	—	1849.	Joined with Union Bank of Scotland, No. 44.
15	Aberdeen Commercial Bank,	—	1	—	1	—	—	—	—	—	—	—	—	—	—	—	1833.	Not known.
16	Arbroath Banking Company,	1825, May.	—	—	1	1	—	—	—	—	—	—	—	—	—	—	1844.	Operations taken up by Commercial Bank of Scotland, N
17	Aberdeen Town and County Bank,	1825, Apr.	—	—	1	4	1	20	1	30	70,133	70,133	80,093	120,483	90,996	68,797	—	
18	Ayrshire Banking Company,	1830,	—	—	—	—	1	12	—	—	—	—	—	—	—	—	1847.	Joined with Western Bank, No. 45.
19	Bank of Scotland,	1695,	1	13	1	19	1	23	1	42	300,485	300,485	346,336	412,582	140,052	235,407	—	
20	British Linen Company,	1746,	1	27	1	26	1	44	1	50	438,024	438,024	438,340	455,097	191,721	239,368	—	
21	Commercial Bank of Scotland,	1810, Nov.	1	14	1	30	1	53	1	70	374,880	374,880	494,247	566,734	189,600	263,107	—	
22	Caledonian Banking Company,	1839, Feb.	—	—	—	—	1	10	1	12	53,434	53,434	58,947	61,793	12,127	31,151	—	
23	Central Bank of Scotland,	1834, May.	—	—	—	—	1	7	1	9	42,933	42,933	48,990	30,268	13,965	27,178	—	
24	City of Glasgow Bank,	1839, Jan.	—	—	—	—	1	10	1	78	72,921	72,921	106,169	341,380	35,527	302,345	—	
25	Clydesdale Banking Company,	1838, May.	—	—	—	—	1	13	1	48	104,028	274,321	120,828	331,396	71,337	141,931	—	
26	Dundee Banking Company,	1763.	1	2	1	—	1	7	1	4	33,451		30,681	—	7,489	—	1864.	Joined with the Royal Bank of Scotland
27	Dundee Union Bank,	—	1	3	1	4	—	—	—	—	—		—	—	—	—	1844.	Joined with the Western Bank, No. 45.
28	Dundee Commercial Bank,	1825, Aug.	—	—	1	—	—	—	—	—	—		—	—	—	—	1838.	Not known.
29	East Lothian Banking Company,	1810, Mar.	1	1	—	—	—	—	—	—	—		—		—	—	1822.	Operations ceased.
30	Eastern Bank of Scotland,	1838, July.	—	—	—	—	1	4	—	—	33,636		34,466		3,316	—	1863.	Incorporated in the Clydesdale Bank, No. 25.
31	Edinburgh and Glasgow Bank,	1844, May.	—	—	—	—	1	20	—	—	136,657		136,370		27,780	—	1858, June	Incorporated in the Clydesdale Bank, No. 25.
32	Fife Banking Company,	—	1	1	—	—	—	—	—	—	—		—		—	—	1826.	Not known.
33	Greenock Bank Company,	—	1	1	1	3	1	1	—	—	—		—		—	—	1843.	Joined with Western Bank, No. 45.
34	Glasgow Bank Company,	1809, June	1	1	1	1	—	—	—	—	—		—	—	—	—	1837.	Joined with Ship Bank.
35	Leith Bank Company,	—	1	6	1	11	—	—	—	—	—		—	—	—	—	1842, Sept.	Placed under Sequestration.
36	Montrose Bank,	1814, May.	1	1	—	—	—	—	—	—	—	—	—	—	—	—	1829.	Not known.
37	National Bank of Scotland,	1825.	—	—	1	17	1	35	1	58	297,024	297,024	294,246	429,865	69,346	270,391	—	
38	North of Scotland Banking Company,	1836, Nov.	—	—	—	—	1	27	1	34	154,319	154,319	153,993	183,920	21,880	76,533	—	
39	Perth Banking Company,	1766,	1	2	1	3	1	3	—	—	38,656	—	46,207	—	12,426	—	1857.	Incorporated in Union Bank of Scotland, No. 44.
40	Perth Union Bank,	1810,	1	2	1	—	—	—	—	—	—	—	—	—	—	—	1836.	
41	Royal Bank of Scotland,	1727.	1	1	1	1	1	6	1	60	183,000	216,451	194,069	461,903	90,777	368,701	—	
42	Renfrewshire Banking Company,	—	1	5	1	4	—	—	—	—	—		—	—	—	—	1842, Sep.	Sequestrated.
43	Stirling Banking Company,	—	1	—	—	—	—	—	—	—	—	—	—	—	—	—	1826.	Not known.
44	Union Bank of Scotland,	1843.	—	—	—	—	1	31	1	96	327,223	454,346	347,934	587,968	110,574	260,764	—	
45	Western Bank of Scotland,	1832, July.	—	—	—	—	1	41	—	—	337,938	—	381,090	[illegible]	118,977	[illegible]	1857, Nov.	Suspension of Payments.
	Total,		30	97	27	145	20	376	13	591	3,087,569	2,749,631	3,145,909	3,976,743	1,177,408	2,337,249		

NOTE.—The Dates of the Establishment of Nos. 2, 3, 4, 6, 7, 8, 11, 12, 13, 14, 15, 27, 32, 33, 35, 42, and 43, are not known for certain, but these Banks obtained a License to issue Notes in the year 1808, when a Tax for such License was first imposed.

The subjoined Table contains details relating to the six Banks of Issue which have ceased operating since 1845, the number at that date being 18.

Names of the Banks.	Date of the last Statement of Accounts	Authorized Issue of Notes.	Actual Issue at the time of the last Statement.	Gold and Silver reserve at the time of the last Statement.
		£	£	£
Aberdeen Banking Company,	Mar. 23, 1850,	88,467	91,426	37,763
Dundee Banking Company,	Feb. 6, 1864,	33,451	41,545	25,325
Eastern Bank of Scotland,	Jan. 10, 1863,	33,636	41,345	21,404
Edinburgh and Glasgow Bank,	June 5, 1858,	136,657	136,603	35,544
Perth Banking Company,	Aug. 1, 1857,	38,656	45,247	18,144
Western Bank of Scotland,	Oct. 24, 1857,	337,938	454,983	182,522
		668,805	811,149	320,702

The Banks of Issue in operation at present are:—

At Edinburgh,	5 Banks.
,, Glasgow,	3 ,,
,, Aberdeen,	2 ,,
,, Perth,	1 ,,
,, Inverness,	1 ,,
Total,	12* ,,

The Dundee Banking Company, which carried on operations in January, 1864, and which was the thirteenth bank then in existence, has since been joined to the Royal Bank of Scotland.

* The number of Scotch Banks is now eleven. The Central Bank, with head-quarters at Perth—included in M. Wolowski's enumeration—has been joined to the Bank of Scotland.—*R. S.*

CHAPTER III.

THE ANCIENT RIGHT OF ISSUE IN SCOTLAND, ITS ABUSE, AND MODIFICATION BY THE ACT OF 1845.

THE ancient constitution of the Scotch banks allowed the issue of notes without any limit. It has been often asserted that this permission had produced no inconvenience; but this is an error into which, as far as regards a former period, the reading of Adam Smith alone ought to have kept people from falling, and which has been frequently exposed by facts of a more recent date.

Adam Smith, in his admirable "Chapter on Money," has described the dangers and embarrassments caused by the too extensive circulation of the notes of the Scotch banks, the faults of which he has severely blamed. "The banks of Scotland," he says, "all pay very dearly their own want of prudence and attention; but the Bank of England paid very dearly, not only for its own imprudence, but also the much greater imprudence of almost all the banks of Scotland." Another passage is still more significant, and involves a lesson, the utility of which is always the same. "Persons engaged in commerce and other undertakings," Adam Smith said, "having drawn so much help from banks and bankers, sought to obtain still more extensive assistance. They imagined that banks could extend their credits to any amount whatever, according to their necessity, without being exposed to any other expense than that of a few reams of paper. They complained of the narrow views and the cowardice of the directors of those banks (in Scotland) who, they said, did not know how to extend their credits in proportion to the extension of the commerce of the country,—meaning doubtless by the extension of commerce the promotion of their own projects beyond what they were in a condition to undertake with their own funds, or with what their credit permitted them to borrow from private parties in the usual way of bond or hypothec. They seem to have figured to themselves that the honour of the bank compelled it to supply this deficiency, and to furnish them all the capital they required for their enterprises."

These lines appear to have been written yesterday; the error that the good sense of the Scotch philosopher puts in such strong relief still prevails and excites similar complaints, but every time that it has been yielded to a severe penalty has been paid. It is necessary sometimes to stop in so dangerous a course; sooner or later credits have to be restrained and the circulation lessened; then a crisis takes place, and failures are multiplied.

The banks in Scotland, severely tried by the necessity of cashing, at sight, an excessive number of notes, conceived the plan of inserting a "clause of option," by which they promised to pay at the time of presentation *or six months afterwards*, with lawful interest for the delay. In consequence of the uncertainty of payment, notes fell below the value of gold and silver money. By the Act of 1765 Parliament suppressed the clause of option, and at the same time prohibited the issue of notes below one pound sterling. The great Bullion Report of 1810, which threw so clear a light upon questions relative to circulation on trust, recalled the example of the reverses suffered and the faults committed by the banks in Scotland. They have been no more free from similar mistakes in our time than in a preceding age, and the suspension of payments by several of their establishments should moderate the too absolute adhesion given to their mode of operation.

We are the first to recognize the useful action of those institutions of credit, whose progress has been so regulated by the prudent spirit of Scotchmen, that their advantages have more than counterbalanced the disadvantages. It is a fact, however, that the reform accomplished in England, under the powerful direction of Sir R. Peel, had its necessary consequence in Scotland. The Act of 1844, which limited to a fixed sum the issue of the notes of the Bank of England, led, in 1845, to regulations, if not identical, at least analogous for the banks in Scotland and Ireland. Scotland had never had a central establishment like the Bank of England. The Act of 1845, which came into vigorous operation on the 6th December, confines itself to limiting the right of issuing notes to the bearer, and at sight, to the establishments that were in existence on the 1st of May in that year; and the amount of the circulation of each of them, at the average of the year, ending with that date. These banks were permitted to increase the issue of their notes only on condition of keeping the counter-value of the surplus in specie. This is a right that the provincial banks in England do not possess. The Scotch banks return every week to the Stamp Office a statement of the notes in circulation, as well as of the metallic reserve, one-fourth of which may consist of silver. These statements are published every four weeks in the *London Gazette*.

The Table that we have published shows that at the time when the Act 8 Victoria (1845) was put into operation, there existed eighteen Banks of Issue in Scotland, having a total of notes of about £3,150,000. The authorized circulation was stopped at that amount; since then, successive insolvencies or fusions have reduced the number of banks to twelve, and the amount of the [authorized] circulation to £2,749,271. The same Table enables us to state that the diminution in the number of banks had already, since 1819, been going on in a similar way, so that it was not the law of 1845 which promoted that result. The failures of the banks of Ayr, East-Lothian, Stirling, &c., are long anterior to that date.

The amount of the circulation of notes has been higher

in our time than in the eighteenth century; but it has never been beyond the following sums:—

In Aug. 31,	1833,	£2,489,000
In January,	1834,	3,000,000
,,	1835,	3,000,000
,,	1836,	3,200,000
,,	1837,	3,100,000
,,	1838,	3,000,000
,,	1839,	3,300,000
,,	1840,	3,100,000
In March 28,	1840,	2,400,000

The last statements prior to the application of the Act of 1845 give the following amounts:—

	February.	November.
1842,	£2,700,000	£3,000,000
1843,	2,500,000	3,100,000
1844,	2,600,000	3,500,000
1845,	2,900,000	3,700,000

Far from causing any drawback upon the employment of notes, the Act of 1845 helped to increase it, while augmenting at the same time the metallic guarantee. In fact we find—

	February.	November.
For 1846,	£3,000,000	£4,000,000
,, 1847,	3,500,000	3,700,000

The amount of notes has increased still more since the last-named period.

The *maximum* to which the circulation had risen gave in November, 1836, the round sum of about £3,700,000, and the *minimum*, on 30th December, 1837, had fallen to £2,100,000.

In the month of January, 1867, the situation of the Scotch banks was as follows:—

	Authorized Circulation.	Notes of £5 and Upwards.	Notes below £5.	Total of Notes.	Reserve of Gold and Silver.
Bank of Scotland, . .	£300,485	£173,942	£336,657	£510,599	£315,565
Royal Bank of Scotland, .	. 216,451	195,229	364,702	560,151	458,760
British Linen Company, .	. 438,024	180,881	328,518	509,399	230,970
Commercial Bank of Scotland,	. 374,880	211,175	411,650	622,825	347,820
National Bank of Scotland,	. 297,024	169,400	328,605	498,005	302,815
Union Bank of Scotland, .	. 454,346	204,165	414,485	618,050	280,932
Aberdeen Town and County Bank,	70,133	67,875	89,134	157,009	101,355
North of Scotland Bank Company,	154,319	103,840	123,164	227,004	96,045
Clydesdale Banking Company,	. 274,321	149,795	258,049	407,844	200,978
City of Glasgow Bank, .	. 72,921	144,107	223,696	367,804	345,928
Caledonian Banking Company,	. 55,434	26,698	56,337	83,036	43,461
Central Bank of Scotland, .	. 42,933	28,780	39,893	68,673	43,559
	£2,751,271	£1,655,887	£2,974,890	£4,630,399	£2,768,188

CHAPTER IV.

INSIGNIFICANCE OF THE ISSUE OF THE SCOTCH BANKS IN COMPARISON WITH THEIR DEPOSITS, AND OTHER GENIAL MODES OF ACTION.

THE issue of notes has never furnished Scotland with more than a feeble contingent of resources. In the 18th century it was very limited, and it is only during the last fifty years that this contingent has been developed. It has grown especially under the favourable arrangements of the Act of 1845, without, however, exceeding a moderate proportion, whether we compare the amount of notes not covered by the metallic reserve with the deposits placed at the disposal of the Scotch Banks, or whether we contrast it with the usual results attained in other countries.

Those who represent the fiducial [credit or paper] circulation of Scotland as the indication of the assistance rendered to agriculture, commit a serious error. They do not make the distinction of the advances consented to for various commercial, industrial, or agricultural uses; and the information that has been given to us leads us to believe that the numerous branch banks, spread through the country districts, rather perform the part of a suction-pump towards the realized savings which go to feed the wants of credit in the manufacturing and trading cities, than they serve to carry back to the fields the excess of the accumulated capital. Farmers use cash accounts, which are credits opened under the condition of a guarantee provided by at least two solvent sureties, much more than they do the discount of bills. Now, cash accounts form by no means the most important of the operations of Scotch banks.

The mechanism of these is very simple. The legitimate success that they have obtained does not depend upon any wonderful receipt: it springs entirely from the moral qualities of the population—from a spirit at once enlightened and full of foresight, which sets to work the facilities that are offered, and sustains them both by savings and by the punctual regularity observed in fulfilling the obligations agreed upon. What predominates here is not an artifice of finance: it is men whose power of action is manifested just as intelligence increases and good habits are developed. The Scotch Banks are merely a means of advancement open to laborious activity, and to the spontaneous efforts of the inhabitants. The individual reserves feed these great reservoirs with funds placed at the service of every enterprise, at a rate of interest that is enough to encourage the economy that is destined to touch a notable portion of the receipts effected. This rate of interest varies according to the general conditions of the market: it is regulated, in a normal manner, by the course of the market in London.

The very reduced rate at which advances may be obtained in Scotland should be consigned to the region of fantastic notions that have been so long worked upon in matters concerning these establishments. They possess a character sufficiently serious, and their influence is quite beneficial enough for them to be admired for what they are in reality, without attributing to them artificial qualities that are only good for deceiving those who complacently repeat accredited errors, without taking the trouble to study and examine the facts. These dangerous friends of the Scotch Banks have helped a great deal to mislead minds by putting them on a false track. If, instead of giving free course to these imaginations, and drawing a chimerical picture, they had confined themselves to presenting the actual situation of these Banks, describing the springs they set in action, and placing in relief the powerful force that is the soul of this great and useful movement, they would, doubtless, have hastened the desirable moment when similar institutions shall be called upon to operate in our country.

Let us take a rapid survey of the manner in which the genial action of the Scotch Banks is exercised. Let us notice the energetic lever they employ, and the phases they have passed through. A singular mistake has been committed in wishing to attribute the services rendered by these establishments to the faculty of issuing notes doing the work of money. Bank notes have never performed but a secondary part in these services. Their proportion was feeble in the 18th century; and they were the first cause of the disasters incurred, of suspensions of payment, depreciation of the instrument of exchange, and of all the evils so well described by Adam Smith, those evils that afflicted the banks in Scotland during a long period of their existence. Whence comes the respect inspired by the banks both in that country and among the most distinguished thinkers? From the character they were able to assume very early, and which corresponds with the most important part of the service performed by them, that of intermediaries between the saving encouraged by the facility of deposit and the spirit of enterprise animated by the concurrence of the disposable capital. The Scotch Banks organized the system of deposits and the employment of open credits; they supplied the necessary meeting-point between the realized economies and productive labour; and they have caused to be set to work the two distinctive qualities of the population—prudence and activity. Do not look upon them for grand stage effects which dazzle, but are dissipated in smoke; you will only find a patient man by initiative, proceeding with prudence, creating instruments of labour by economy, employing them incessantly, and arriving by persevering effort at a success so much the greater and more solid from having borrowed nothing from fiction, but from having known how to neglect none of the substantial elements capable of being made useful.

At a time when the banks established in England afforded to their depositors no other advantage beyond that of collecting the scattered sums, while promising for them a security too often deceptive, and facilitating transactions with them, the Scotch Banks soon created the true mechanism of a *Bank Office*, as understood in a wide acceptation of the term. They organized, under an ingenious form, the system of deposits and open credits, and combined the increase of disposable resources with the most profitable and the safest employment of the accumulated reserves. Their mode of operation is as follows:—They receive deposits under a double form—first, the *deposit receipt*, which consists of the placing of money in the bank, at a fixed interest, under the condition that the sum inscribed can only be drawn personally, and not disposed of *to order*, or by means of a cheque; and second, the *operating deposit account*, which constitutes, on the contrary, a veritable *account current*—the banks undertaking to allow an interest, which, since 1863, varied according as it is applied to *daily balances*, or to *minimum* of the monthly balances.

On the other hand, the Scotch banks have the *cash credit account* at the service of the party credited, under the valid guarantee of two or more sureties accepted at the time the credit is opened for a fixed sum of 100, 200, 300, 500, and sometimes 1,000 pounds sterling.

The deposits are not made for fixed periods. In a country where the variations in commercial movements might be more frequent and more considerable, this system of deposits, withdrawable at will, might present some dangers, that are in a great measure avoided by the calm spirit of the Scotch and the more regular course of their undertakings.

The operations of deposit and cash accounts form the distinctive features of the Scotch Banks, and have been the principal source of the prosperity they have enjoyed, as well as of the services they have rendered. In the judgments pronounced upon these excellent establishments, there has been a confusion produced which it is of the utmost importance to clear up; nor can we insist too much on this point. All the writers who have spoken of them with great eulogy, have rendered homage to the *banks* without distinguishing between the action exercised by the *notes* and that exercised by the *deposits*. Their admiration is perfectly justified, but it requires to be explained.

Notes render incontestible services by their facility of transport and their rapidity of account, and they save the loss incurred by the wear and tear of metallic money. As to the economy resulting from the employment of notes, that is small, for it is limited to the interest that might have been claimed for the service of the metallic capital, replaced by notes issued over and above the reserve in gold or silver. It is trifling in comparison with the total of the capital and the mass of the deposits. We have shown how, for the whole of Scotland, the economy thus made does not, at the most, exceed fifty millions of francs. If we take into calculation the sacrifice made in the shape of interest allowed on the capital received in deposit, assuming here an average of three per cent., the benefit will be limited at the *maximum* to 1,500,000 francs per annum, a total from which the manufacture of the notes must be deducted.

What is the amount of deposits? We have already said that throughout Scotland they amount to sixty millions of pounds. The following is an abstract made in August, last year (1866), for the twelve banks of issue. The total is increased by the amount of deposits effected in other establishments:—

Bank of Scotland, ...	£7,014,915
Royal Bank of Scotland, ...	8,127,791
British Linen Company, ...	7,322,095
Commercial Bank of Scotland, ...	7,088,834
National Bank of Scotland, ...	7,000,266
Union Bank of Scotland, ...	8,258,927
Clydesdale Bank (Glasgow), ...	4,578,710
City of Glasgow Bank, ...	4,446,365
Aberdeen Town and County Bank, . .	1,164,264
North of Scotland Bank (Aberdeen), .	1,280,000
Central Bank of Scotland (Perth), . .	835,000
Caledonian Bank (Inverness), ...	400,000
Total, ...	£57,517,167

By what rate of interest are deposits paid, and what is the interest received upon advances (cash accounts)? Through an obliging communication we have been supplied with the movement of *deposit accounts* and *deposit receipts* since 1789, and of *cash accounts* since 1822, in the Royal Bank of Scotland, which was the first that adopted (in 1729) this ingenious system of advances. We are consequently enabled to furnish a decisive element for the solution of many questions rather ill understood or falsely interpreted.

From a long time back a general understanding has been established among all the banks in Scotland for the periodical fixing of an uniform rate of interest allowed for deposits or received upon advances throughout the entire country. At the chief offices of these establishments, as at all the branches, this is an essential point. It shows how vain is the idea of the competition of *free* banks in Scotland. That country has no *free* banks, in the meaning that has been attempted to be given to that term, and the competition is in no way exercised in fixing the rate of interest. When the rate adopted for one of the Scotch Banks is known it is known for all. It is useful to remember that since 1863 the Scotch Banks have established a difference as to the interest allowed for *operating deposit accounts* between those that are paid according to *daily balances* and those for which *minimum monthly balances* are taken.

[Here follow four long Tables of Royal Bank of Scotland:—

Rate of interest allowed upon Deposit Receipts, 1789-1867.

Rate of interest allowed upon operating Deposit Accounts—daily balances.

Rate of interest allowed upon operating Deposit Accounts—minimum monthly balances.

Rate of interest received upon operating Cash Accounts, 1822-1867.]

Deposit Receipts, which always receive the best treatment, as they are much more stable and fixed, and do not entail those expenses of management caused by the action of *cheques* and *current accounts*, have obtained an allowance of interest varying from 2 to 5 per cent.

Operating Deposit Accounts, with interest made good upon daily balances, have seen the rate reduced to 1½ per cent., without ever rising above 4 per cent., while those for which interest has been paid since 1863 upon the *minimum monthly balances*, the figure has oscillated between 2 and 4½ per cent.

Nothing has been more instructive to us than to follow, through the long series of sixty-eight years, both the successive modifications of the conditions made by the Scotch Banks with the capitals that sustain them, and the changes that have occurred in the rates of the *Cash Accounts*, the principal source of the credits accorded to agriculture. *Never since* 1822 has the interest upon advances descended below 4 per cent. For a long time it oscillated between 4 and 5 per cent.; extended in 1847 (it was 5¼ from the 1st March, 1847, to 1st June, 1849), it reached 6 per cent in 1856; 6½ in 1857; 7 in 1863; 8 and 9 in 1864, and the same figures present themselves in 1866. The rate of discount has pursued a parallel course; it has been down to 3½ per cent. only in 1853 and 1863, and since February, 1867.

Notwithstanding this, have not some distinguished writers, and amongst them quite lately the Marquis Trioulz, in a work inspired by a good sentiment (*la Banca patriotica*), but incorrect as to the data collected, and singularly hazardous in its conclusions, boasted of the moderation of the interest received by the Scotch Banks? Have they not contended that they had never exceeded the rate of 5 per cent.? Scotch banks are not in possession of any magic wand that permits them to avoid the natural conditions of the supply and demand of capital.

CHAPTER V.

CONSTITUTION, LIABILITY, AND RESOURCE OF THE SCOTCH BANKS.

THE Scotch banks are fed by the fertile spring of savings; they derive a profit from the difference between the interest that they allow upon deposits and that which they receive upon advances and discounts. The notes that they issue serve rather to facilitate transactions than to procure a benefit. The benefit thus gained does not upon an average reach the annual amount of $\frac{3}{4}$ per cent. upon the combined capital. According to the actual value of the shares, which represent a value more than double the amount of issue, the return thus obtained scarcely reaches $\frac{3}{8}$ per cent. This is something without doubt; and thanks to the multiplied precautions by which the issue of notes is surrounded in Scotland, this supplemental benefit is scarcely at all counterbalanced by any serious inconveniences. But it must be confessed that it does not furnish matter for loud admiration. The advantage is a modest one, and should be spoken of in a modest manner.

With the exception of the Bank of Scotland, the Royal Bank of Scotland, and the British Linen Company, which, having charters of incorporation, are placed under a system analogous to our *Sociétés Anonymes*, the other Scotch Banks are subject to the severe rule of joint and general liability, and the unlimited responsibility of the shareholders.* They

* This is a somewhat meagre and incorrect statement of the question of liability of shareholders in the Scotch banks. The Bank of Scotland was constituted by Act of Parliament, which, since unlimited liability was the sole principle recognized by the mercantile law of the country in joint-stock as well as private partnerships until of very recent years, would appear *prima facie* to be the only form of authority competent to give to any company the privilege of limited liability. But the Act of

must deposit the personal list of their partners between the 1st and 15th of January every year. This list is published on the 1st of March following in the newspapers of the localities where the chief offices and branches are established. The partners are all responsible to the extent of their entire

Parliament incorporating the Bank of Scotland does not give this privilege to its stockholders. There is literally no mention of such a concession in the Act. The Royal Bank and the British Linen Company Bank were founded subsequently by Royal Charters, in which also there is no mention of limited liability; and while Parliament, including the Crown with other Estates of the realm, had undoubtedly the power of giving the exceptional privilege of limited liability in special cases, it is not so undoubted that the Royal Authority alone could traverse the common mercantile law of the kingdom in any such way. Neither the Act of Parliament founding the Bank of Scotland, nor the Royal Charters founding the Royal and British Linen Banks, bear any literal trace that such an exception to the general law of the kingdom was in either case designed or intended. The Commercial Bank and the National Bank, both of still later origin, were incorporated by Royal Charters, in which the distinction occurs that limited liability is expressly excluded; and so in the case of neither of these two Banks can any doubt or dispute as to the unlimited liability of shareholders arise. This distinction might be used in forensic argument either way. It might be held, on the one hand, that since the Charters of the Commercial and National Banks expressly exclude limited liability, it may be inferred, however loosely, that the Charters of the Royal and British Linen Banks were meant to include what they do not in like manner expressly exclude; or, on the other hand, with greatly more strength, that the Royal Authority, incorporating the Commercial and National Banks, on reviewing its own constitutional power, and on seeing that the Parliament of Scotland, with greatly more constitutional power than its own, did not convey to the Bank of Scotland this privilege of limited liability, put the clauses excluding limited liability into the Charters of the Commercial and National Banks as a settlement of the whole question. This is the exact state of the case in its general outline. But it remains to be observed that there is a theory of law, countenancing the distinction drawn by M. Wolowski in the case of the three Scotch Banks he has named, to the effect that incorporation of a company, whether by Act of Parliament or Royal Charter, creates *per se* a separate entity distinct from the individuals and fortunes of the individuals of which it is composed, and that the liability of the com-

fortune; and sad examples—such as those of the Ayr Bank and the Western Bank—have shown that the responsibility is real and not nominal.

The issue of notes obtains a considerable guarantee in the joint liability of the partners, both as regards the management of business and the limitation of engagements subscribed under the form of bank-notes, payable to the bearer and at sight. The *solidarité* of the engagement constitutes an essential feature of the Scotch Banks, and has singularly maintained their regular action. Small capitalists, unable to become partners, or unwilling to incur a menacing responsibility, have gone to increase the number of depositors, while augmenting the disposable capital of the banks. They have profited by the facilities of the deposit accounts and deposit receipts, which procure for them a modest but safe interest, and which keep their pounds at their own disposition. These reserves, the fruit of labour, are employed by the banks in credits, opened with the guarantee of two solvent sureties, under the form of cash accounts, so profitable to the farmer, the artizan, and the dealer, and so convenient for being set in work, for they admit of fractional repayments, while taking account of the interest. The Banks give great attention to the paying of regular and frequent sums on account; and as they perform the office of cashier for all the customers, they are able to watch over them closely, and to restrain, or, in case of need, withdraw the opened credits. The sureties, who are generally landed proprietors, have a right of inspection over the accounts of

pany thus incorporated is determined wholly by the capital and the conditions named in the Act of Incorporation itself. The value of this theory we do not presume to judge. It is a theory which has happily not been—is never, indeed, likely to be—put to the test in the case of any of the three Banks named; and which, were it more than a theory, they would probably be the first to renounce. There are, however, some practical differences of privilege betwixt chartered and unchartered Banks in Scotland, and betwixt chartered banks themselves, as compared with each other; for which see Appendix.—*R. S.*

those whom they have guaranteed, and they have also the right of closing their accounts by withdrawing their security. We may add that the publicity of hypothecary charges, and the promptitude with which possession may be taken, very much increase the security of Scotch banks, which often cause bills of sale to be given, so that, in the event of engagements not being regularly fulfilled, they may sell the property. The guarantee upon which the security of the Banks rests, is, then, very strong; but they find themselves subjected, besides, to severe conditions, that prevent all excess in the issue of notes. They have been able, without waiting for the intervention of the law, to conform to rules faithfully applied, which, however, have not been sufficient to keep off all danger. Thus, twice a week, the Scotch Banks interchange the notes that they have received, and settle the balance in Exchequer bonds or drafts on the Bank of England. In this manner, the average of the circulation of Scotch bank-notes is reduced to a few days. Their re-imbursement in specie is protected by a metallic reserve that generally exceeds the half of the *(fiducial) paper* issue, which, moreover, after deducting the amount of gold and silver in reserve, constitutes but a small fraction —*less than one-fourth*—of the combined capital.

In presence of these incontestable data, what becomes of the singular pretension to establish among us Agricultural Banks, with a circulation in notes equal to three times the capital. It is not, certainly, upon the precedents of the Scotch Banks that so rash a plan can be based. Let us add that these Banks have always a portfolio well supplied with bills of exchange, at short dates, discounted in the course of industrial and commercial operations. This is the foundation upon which the optional conversion of notes into gold is principally fixed; whilst agricultural enterprises profit chiefly from prolonged credits, which are based upon the deposits, and which have nothing to do with the payment of *bank notes to the bearer and at sight.* It suffices to make this position known in order to put an end to many chimerical notions.

In all time the Scotch Banks have relied upon the Bank of England, in order to obtain, in case of need, the precious metals necessary for the payment of their notes. The withdrawal of gold, induced by this cause, has more than once contributed to produce, or to aggravate, the crises suffered by the metropolis of the United Kingdom. This is one of the reasons why it was urged that the notes of the Bank of England should have the "legal course" throughout the United Kingdom, as they have had since 1833 in England and Wales. In the latter they constitute a legal tender, nor can they be refused for any transaction stipulated for in pounds sterling, so long as the Bank pays for them in gold at an open office. The recourse had to the Bank of England from time to time by the Scotch Banks, in order to recruit their reserve of ready money, would exercise a less sensible influence on the London market, if the English bank note became a legal tender beyond the Tweed.*

It is, however, always the case that the security of the circulation of Scotland has its main prop in the monetary market of London. It is necessary not to lose sight of this circumstance when speaking amongst us of the creation of local Banks.

* The author falls into mistake here, from overlooking the condition on which notes of the Bank of England are issued, which is that of equivalence to the deposits of gold in the issue department. The increase and decrease of the Bank's total issue of notes is an exact expression, beyond the limit of the authorized issue on the basis of securities, of the increase and decrease of the stock of bullion; but it is the reserve of notes which forms the index of the banking resources, and by which the rate of discount is regulated. Were the Scotch banks, therefore, to withdraw Bank of England notes, the same effect precisely would be produced on the London money market as when they withdraw gold. M. Wolowski, indeed, misapprehends the whole operation of what he calls "the recourse of the Scotch Banks to the Bank of England to recruit their reserve of ready money." The

Scotch Banks withdraw and send gold to London at certain periods of the year; but when they withdraw, it is not "to recruit their reserve of ready-money," but simply to fulfil the legal deposit of gold required of them by the Act of 1845 in proportion as their note-circulation rises above the authorized amount. The gold is brought down to Scotland, not because it is in demand, or is wanted for any commercial purpose, but only because an unwise statute compels it to be brought. It is locked up for a few weeks in the coffers of the Banks, and, after performing this idle ceremony, is sent back again. Moreover, when the Scotch Banks withdraw gold from the Bank of England, they do not have recourse to or obtain aid from the English Bank. They simply withdraw a portion of the funds which they have already placed in London, and which they always keep there.—*R. S.*

CHAPTER VI.

EXAMINATION OF THE VIEWS OF THE GLASGOW CHAMBER OF COMMERCE ON THE ACT OF 1845.

THE Act of December, 1845, in no way modified the essential features of the constitution of the Scotch banks. It confined itself to fixing the contingent of the issue to the amount reached six months before the Act acquired the force of law; the average of the circulation of each bank of issue during the year preceding the 1st May, 1845, was taken as a basis. The Banks of Scotland obtained the faculty, refused to the private banks and joint-stock banks of England, of issuing over and above the authorized circulation as much in notes as they should possess of a reserve in gold and silver—that is to say, of creating metallic warrants. No disturbance can result from this as to the circulation, which secures the advantages offered by the notes without running the evil chances of a hypothetical re-imbursement.

It has been said that Scotland made energetic reclamations against the Acts of 1844 and 1845. There should be a distinction drawn between the limit imposed upon the *legal tender* put in circulation by the Bank of England and the fixing the credit circulation of the Scotch banks.

In reality every complaint is summed up in a noisy demonstration of the Chamber of Commerce of Glasgow, upon which M. Michel Chevalier has sought to build as a stroke of good luck in the midst of the almost unanimous agreement of opinions by which his doctrine is condemned on the other side of the Channel,

Let us clear the ground of this too-often recurring argument before we conclude what we have to say about the constitution of the Scotch Banks.*

The memorial addressed last year by the Glasgow Chamber of Commerce to Mr. W. E. Gladstone, Chancellor of the Exchequer, attacks the Act of 1844 as the prime cause of the frequent and extreme variations of the rate of discount. We shall not return to this question after what we have said in speaking of the Bank of England.

But we cannot leave unanswered the arguments put forth prominently to cry up the right of free issue, which is confounded with that of freely conducting banking operations. "The advantages that result from the perfect freedom of issue and the entire freedom of the banks," says the memorial, "are proved in an irrefutable manner by the experience of Scotland since 1695."

History, carefully studied, hardly confirms this hazardous conclusion. The indications that we have multiplied prove, on the contrary, that the *free issue* caused more than one

* The Glasgow Chamber of Commerce, it should be observed, is a very numerous body, and, consequently, not harmonious in the views which its members entertain on the subject of currency and banking. The directors, who are the most operative part of the Chamber, have usually discovered a disposition, while conscious of existing defects, to abide by the arrangements made by Sir Robert Peel in 1844-45; and the misfortune has been, that the general voice of the Chamber has only been evoked on this question in periods of crisis and excitement, when the opinion of the majority was apt to be neither measured in expression nor consistent with what had been expressed before. But M. Wolowski misses the point of the particular memorial which he dissects, namely, that, under Sir Robert Peel's innovations on the freedom of the Scotch Banks, recurrences of excessive speculation, extreme rates of discount, financial panic, and commercial distress, have been as frequent as before, and quite as marked and disastrous in their results—a position which M. Wolowski does not contest, and is in reality incontestable. If so, *cui bono?* What good in elaborate trifling by Acts of Parliament with respect to the issue of bank-notes? This has been the general view of the Glasgow Chamber, whether directors or members, since 1845, the legislation of which year was universally unpopular in Scotland.—*R. S.*

disaster in Scotland in the last century—it injured the development of *deposit accounts* and *cash accounts*, instead of coming to the aid of these admirable instruments for augmenting wealth and the impulse which they give to production.

The *bank note* goes for nothing in the service that consists in collecting the savings and the floating money of the people, so as to employ them with benefit for the depositors, for the banks themselves, and for the public in general. We are always compelled to dissipate the same ambiguity; the partizans of free issue rely upon the advantages that belong exclusively to the operations of banking, properly so called, —that is to say, to the accumulation and employment of *deposits*. Herein consists the true secret of the prosperity of the Scotch Banks.

The Glasgow Chamber of Commerce commits a serious error, when it asserts that the Scotch issue alone enables banks to operate in that country. According to it those banks would cease to work profitably, and would wind up, to the great detriment of the country, if they did not profit by the benefit they enjoy from the creation of bank notes. We know what this argument is worth; we have shown how insignificant the profit is that the Scotch Banks derive from the *issue;* almost all the benefits that they derive arise from the difference between the rate of interest that they pay to depositors and that which they receive for advances. In estimating this difference at only 1 per cent. (it is much more) we arrive, upon 1,500 millions of francs of deposits (£60,000,000), at a gain of 15 millions (£600,000). The profit realized from the issue is not more than one-tenth of this sum. The dividends paid by the Scotch Banks vary from 6 to 11 per cent. upon the paid-up capital. It is then easy to show that the diminution even of a tenth would but little affect the prosperous existence of these establishments. Moreover, there is no question of withdrawing from them the right that they possess at present, a right sufficiently extensive, since there always exists a notable difference between the *authorized circulation* and the amount of notes issued beyond those that agree with the metallic reserve.

The assertion of the Glasgow Chamber of Commerce is, therefore, without foundation.

That free association of merchants (indeed, the Chambers of Commerce of Britain have no official character, they represent only the members that compose them; the similarity of name must not confound them with our Chambers of Commerce)—that association sought to make something of the principle laid down in 1844 by Sir Robert Peel, when the great Minister drew the fundamental distinction between the creation of notes, destined to perform the office of money, and the natural functions of banks, such as discount, the account current, the clearing, deposits, &c. Sir Robert Peel said, with reason, "that there could not be a competition too free, and *too unlimited in the industry of the bank. The principle of competition ought to govern banks.*" This is what Mr. Gladstone also maintains; such is the conviction of which we have always been the interpreter. What do these words signify? They mean, that so long as it is a question only of private industry, banks ought to be entirely free—they ought to profit fully by *free trade.* It is otherwise when—by the manufacturing of notes payable to the bearer and at sight, which are to serve as money, and which would be worth nothing if they were not admitted under that character into circulation—banks encroach upon the domain of public interest, and may exercise an influence upon the security of transactions and upon the fidelity of contracts made between citizens who have nothing to do with the banks themselves. It is then that the State, charged with watching over the sincerity of social relations, is compelled to intervene.

The doctrine of Sir Robert Peel, and the meaning of the Acts of 1844 and 1845, agree with this fundamental truth. Far from contradicting the principles of liberty, they strengthen them by preventing abuses that would be prejudicial to all.

The well-merited praise of Adam Smith and the approbation of Lord Liverpool apply to the solid and substantial system of the Scotch Banks, which rests upon the principle of the joint and unlimited liability of the partners. It is this principle that has made bankruptcies more rare, by awakening the attention of those interested, and by making their entire fortune a pledge for the operations performed. The *deceitful and dangerous* system of which Lord Liverpool spoke was that of England, where the freedom of issue prevailed, deprived of the absolute responsibility of all the interested parties. This necessary complement, demanded in Germany by the economists who incline to the side of the multiple creation of notes payable to the bearer and at sight, would scarcely be acceptable to the greater part of those amongst us who have sought to apply a similar mechanism to the agricultural districts.

The sad mishaps that occurred in the last century, and the suspension of payments by the Western Bank and the City of Glasgow Bank, two establishments, one of which was utterly shipwrecked, and the other suffered severe embarrassments, ought to have made the Glasgow Chamber of Commerce more cautious: it had witnessed the disasters experienced in that city; how then could it speak of the absolute security of bank-notes? As to the limitation of these, it was the fruit of experience dearly bought, before being formally expressed by the Act of 1845; it brings back the benefit derived from the issue to an almost insignificant amount, when placed face to face with the profits derived from deposits.

It is not sufficient to assert that Scotland traversed without danger the long period of free and unlimited issue, it must be proved. The merest knowledge of actual facts shows the contrary.

Neither does it suffice to say that it is of the highest

importance to associate the liberty of issue with the freedom of the Banks, when these two distinct principles are ruled by considerations of a totally different order, and when the right of creating documents, intended as monetary instruments, but wanting the metallic guarantee, belongs to quite another order of ideas than that of employing existing money, and giving one's-self up to the operations of credit. We think we have more than abundantly cleared up these points, so that we shall not return to them.

A monopoly that it does not possess in any manner is wrongfully attributed to the Bank of England. As to the limitation of the issue of notes, the rapid and immense development of commerce does not require the basis of monetary security to be weakened, but quite the contrary. This development has profited by the immovable fixity acquired at present by the instrument of exchanges. When, moreover, we compare the enormous growth of public wealth to the light sacrifice entailed by the solid constitution of money, we acknowledge how insignificant would be a fresh economy of 50 or even 100 millions (of francs) upon the metallic security. The several millions of interest that the portion of real capital devoted to giving the circulation an unshakable guarantee costs, what are they in presence of the tens of milliards of production and annual exchanges thus preserved from fatal shocks? There can be as many bank-notes as they desire, by increasing the reserve of gold: the facility and convenience of circulation have nothing to lose by a prudent system, and the sincerity of relations, as well as the extension of credit, have everything to gain by it.

The authorizing the establishment of *joint-stock banks* in England has completely silenced the reproach against the system of *private banks.* Is there anything to be vain of in the fact that Scotland no longer has one of the latter, and that all financial operations are concentrated among a small number of shareholding banks? We are far from thinking so; and, besides, it would be a singular application of an absolute principle of freedom.

The Glasgow Chamber of Commerce lays a good deal of stress on the fact that only *twenty-one banks* have suspended payment in Scotland. If we do not forget how small the number has always been of these institutions, we shall find that these disasters have been relatively very frequent. The Chamber has only presented assertions without any serious foundation: it is sufficient to recall the fact that it put forth prominently the pretended *perfect security of the absolute freedom of issue and of banking*, as shown by the history of one hundred and seventy years, in order to judge of the value of the arguments produced. Let us add, however, that it does not, at least, commit the error of believing that the banks can influence the rate of interest; it acknowledges that the rate of discount rises and falls according to the natural law of supply and demand. A distinguished writer (Mr. James Stirling), whose work, *Practical Considerations on Banks and Bank Management*, published in 1865, has obtained the assent of the most distinguished men in the United Kingdom, does not spare the opinions of the Glasgow Chamber of Commerce, to which he belongs. But he renders it this justice, that it clearly recognized, in 1858, during a *lucid interval*, so far as ideas upon the system of banks are concerned, the cause and remedy of crises. In the report upon the crisis of 1857, after having expressed the opinion that that disturbance was caused by the giving way of a credit unnaturally excited, the Chamber indicates as the only efficacious remedy the *maintenance of a high rate of interest and of large reserves*. The rate of interest is to be increased with a *peremptory* firmness, as much as is necessary for sustaining a reserve proportioned to eventual demands. It is not the increased rate of interest, but the fear of not obtaining any advance, no matter what conditions may be imposed, that excites general alarm. As long as the Bank of England shall keep a sufficient *reserve* there will break out no panic, whatever may be the rate of interest (Report of the Directors of the Glasgow Chamber of Commerce, 1858, p. 14).* It is in acting with this prudent security that banks may be spared from spasmodic efforts, and not expose the whole country to terrible suffering.

We have under our eyes the reports of April, 1865, and April, 1866, of the Edinburgh Chamber of Commerce. It is far from participating, on the subject of issue, the radical opinions of the Chamber of Commerce of Glasgow. Its wishes are limited to demanding the examination of the question, so as to know whether there might not be reason to lighten the limit imposed upon the total amount of *authorized circulation*. As to the fundamental bases upon which the Acts of 1844 and 1845 rest, there is no proposition whatever to modify them. The other Chambers of Commerce in the United Kingdom are singularly divided in opinion as to the limitations admitted in 1844. Several would, like the Edinburgh Chamber, merely extend the fixed *contingents*. The greater part declare for a system analogous to that of the Bank of France; whilst others demand the most complete application of the absolute principle of division between the banking operations and the issue of notes, the latter to be entrusted only to a Commission of the Treasury under the surveillance of the House of Commons. This has been particularly the opinion expressed in a remarkable memoir drawn up last year by the Chamber of Commerce at Bristol.

Concerning the real opinion of Scotland upon the subject of the Act of 1845, the inquiry of 1857 contains some valu-

* The Chamber was no doubt right enough here, and yet not inconsistent with its declaration on other occasions. The evil is that the Bank of England, under the system of 1844, is unable by the highest rates of interest to maintain a "large reserve"—that its reserve undergoes periodical exhaustion under the Act, and only begins to recover when, after much mischief to industrial interests, the Act is suspended, and trade, deposit, and public confidence are allowed to return to their normal action.—*R. S.*

able information. Sir George Cornewall Lewis, then Chancellor of the Exchequer, asked, in 1856, the opinions of the Scotch Banks themselves; but of the ten principal banks that then existed in that country the five oldest had their principal office in Edinburgh, whilst the five later ones were established at Glasgow. The first five pronounced in favour of the Act of 1845. The *Bank of Scotland*, it is true, declared that that law had exercised no influence upon the operations, that it had been *inoperative*. But the opinion of the others is much more decided. The secretary of the Royal Bank of Scotland affirms, in the name of that establishment, that experience did not allow of any doubt being raised upon the wisdom of the principle admitted; nothing had occurred to give support to the opinion of those who pretended that the Act had restrained the facilities of credit. The manager of the *British Linen Company* said that the Bank regards "all the arrangements of the Act of 1845 as perfectly judicious and salutary. They are well calculated to keep, in Scotland, a moderate quantity of specie, only sufficient to be in suitable proportion to the circulation of notes. The experience realized had brought no inconvenience to light, either for the Banks or for the public, and it is permitted to express the hope that no modification or rule less severe will come in to lessen the efficacy of this system." The *Commercial Bank* of Scotland "manifests a complete approbation of the Act as a whole, and does not see that there is any change to be introduced into the arrangements admitted." The *National Bank* of Scotland says:—"Some persons have imagined that the Act of 1845 imposes useless restrictions upon the action of banks, and impedes their power of answering the demands made upon them. We have experienced nothing of the kind." On the other hand, the five Banks of Glasgow were of one accord in condemning the law, and the restrictions imposed by it.

The ten principal Banks in Scotland were thus divided into two camps, equal in number. But, as Mr. James Stirling remarks, there is an infallible touchstone that reveals the real authority attached to the respective opinions. A few months after these opinions had been procured, the crisis of 1857 desolated the country. The five old Banks of Edinburgh sustained the shock of the tempest without giving way. It was not the same with the Glasgow Banks, that were newer and more enterprising. One of them, and the most considerable, fell without recovering; a second suspended its payments for a time; and a third had to sustain a *run* excited by public mistrust. A fourth also, it is said, experienced serious difficulties. To resume everything, among the protests directed against the rigorous restrictions of the Act of 1845, the one that was the most developed and the most vehement emanated from the Western Bank of Scotland, and bore the *ominous* signature of John Taylor. The Western Bank failed, and the principal cause of the disaster was the rash impulse given by John Taylor to operations worthy only of condemnation.

It is necessary always to return to this fundamental truth, that the limit of notes can alone prevent a deep disturbance in the progress of transactions.* They argue wrongly about a factitious lowering of the rate of interest; that diminution is impossible, unless it corresponds with the normal situation of the market, which alone determines the price of capital. Formerly the natural relation between supply and demand was disturbed by the laws on usury. Thence arose the apparent permanence of a rate of interest varying only from 4 to 5 per cent. But it is useless to attempt to force the

* M. Wolowski here gives intense expression to what one can only be sorry to find his dominant idea. The only efficacious limit of bank-notes is to issue them, and maintain them, payable at sight. Any artificial limit of notes is worthless, and has no effect on the limitation of credit, which rests not on the issue, but on the deposits, unless its effect be to aggravate the "deep disturbance" of abuses of credit, when these have been committed on a large scale by the Banks and the commercial public.—*R. S.*

nature of things. Numerous subterfuges and troublesome feints disguised the actual rate, which often rose to 7, 8, 9, 10, and even 12 per cent., according to the irrefutable testimony of M'Culloch, Macpherson, Lord Overstone, and Mr. Chapman. The last established, in the course of the Inquiry of 1857, that, according to the table of operations compiled by the powerful and celebrated firm of *Overend & Gurney*, in the ten years preceding the Act of 1844, there had been *seventy-three variations of the rate of interest*, the average of which amounted to £4, 2*s.* 9*d.* per cent., while, during the ten succeeding years, the number of these variations was reduced to 70, and the average rate to £3, 7*s.* 11*d.* per cent. Thus, instead of multiplying the fluctuations and aggravating the rate of discount, the Act of 1844 had produced the contrary effect. If we extend our investigations to twenty years before the Act of 1844, we find that the annual average of the minimum interest was £2, 3*s.* 4*d.* per cent., while since 1844 this average has fallen down to £1, 15*s.* per cent. In presence of these instructive facts, what becomes of the accusations of the Glasgow Chamber of Commerce?*

* M. Wolowski, in this passage, rather confirms than shakes the memorial of the Glasgow Chamber, the drift of which was that the rate of discount had touched wider extremes, sinking lower at one period and rising higher at another, and had been subject to more violent changes since the Act of 1844 than before. There can be no question that this is true, for the averages of £2, 3*s.* 4*d.* per cent. in the twenty years before 1844, and of £1, 15*s.* since 1844, prove it. The violence with which, under the present law, speculation is encouraged by low rates of discount at one time, and repressed by extremely high rates, increased once or twice a-week, at another, cannot be disputed. But as no one is so unwise as to wish either an extremely low or extremely high rate of discount, or to expect as possible an uniform rate, the only question is, whether the Act of 1844, in swelling by a purely mechanical arrangement the reserve of issued but unemployed notes in the Bank of England, when bullion is coming in from the mines, and diminishing this reserve of notes as swiftly when a market is being found for this access of bullion, does not induce more rapid changes and more extreme rates of

Banks can only conform to the situation of the market; they have no serious power of imposing a rate of discount. The variations that occur are the inevitable result of the freedom of transactions; Banks place in opposition to fluctuations the only useful corrective. Murmuring against the remedy is fit for children, but not for reflecting men. " Modern science," says Mr. James Stirling, " consists, so far as commerce and finance are concerned, in obeying the natural laws, and mistrusting the influence of arbitrary regulations. When we feel the sting of necessity, it is vain to call in the aid of the legislator. What is then necessary to be done, is to increase the reserve of capital, by keeping that which we possess, and attracting a surplus by means of favourable conditions. In fact, we ought to apply to financial difficulties the principle applied to *free trade* by commerce, and pay the natural rate for the use of capital, as we pay the natural price of products and merchandise."

Far from affording any help, the issue of notes (when it exceeds strictly drawn limits) increases the confusion and aggravates the losses. We have felt obliged to dwell upon

discount than, without excluding the element of bullion as an essential postulate in the problem, would be induced under a broader and more adequate consideration of all the conditions of the market. The commodity in question is loanable capital—capital available for ordinary usance in commercial and industrial purposes—which commodity finds its strongest manifestation in the deposits of the Banks; and M. Wolowski, who has attained such a clear perception, in his study of the Scotch Banks, that deposits are the great matter, must be acute enough to see that there is something anomalous in the rate of discount for loanable capital not being ruled by deposits at all, but by an issue of notes in the Bank of England. The introduction of deposits as an element of the question would not radically change the regulation of the rate of discount; but recognized on such a basis for the whole kingdom as the Scotch Banks supply as regards Scotland, and not confined as now to the deposits of a few great capitalists, chiefly engaged in sending parcels of bullion from one capital to another, the effect would certainly be to modify the regulation of the rate of discount considerably, and to render it more consistent with reason and the public good.—*R. S.*

these questions, often misunderstood, and to examine closely the manifesto of the Glasgow Chamber of Commerce, about which a great noise has been made. History, experience, solemn inquiries, the enlightened opinion of men, who, like Mr. James Stirling, were in the best position for forming a judgment upon the matters, and also the opinion of the Scotch Banks themselves, forbid us to accept conclusions as unreasonable as they are without motive.

We merely add here, what was written lately to us by a director of one of the principal Banks in Edinburgh. "The rate of discount in the Scotch Banks is regulated entirely, and in an almost constant manner, by the rate of the Bank of England. During the recent period of elevated rates, the Scotch Banks, however, did not exceed the interest of 9 per cent., whilst the discount was raised to 10 per cent. in England."

Inquiries show that the rate of discount by the Scotch Banks, for half a century, has been—

From March, 1817, to 8th July, 1822, . .	5 per cent.
,, 8th July, 1822, to 19th December, 1825,	4 ,,
,, 19th December, 1825, to May, 1828, .	5 ,,
,, May, 1828, to 17th November, 1836, .	4 ,,
,, 17th November, 1836, to 12th Feby., 1838,	5 ,,

We have a complete Table of the variations of the rate of discount in these establishments from 1838 to the present time. It shows with what regularity the rate follows the direction of the market of London, without ever descending below 3½ per cent., and rising as high as 9 per cent.

CHAPTER VII.

THE RATE OF DISCOUNT IN SCOTLAND.

We have said that the rate of discount depends upon the position of the market; but a great deal has been advanced as to the happy influence exercised upon the price of the use of capital by the competition among the Scotch Banks. One word is sufficient to dissipate this kind of phantasmagoria, and to show that no competition in this respect exists in that country. We have mentioned the fact already; it is necessary to prove it in a decisive manner. *Every Bank or Branch Bank receives the same rates upon advances made, and pays the same interest upon sums deposited.* Each fortnight the directors of the Banks hold a meeting, at which the rate for every operation is established by common consent, and a circular acquaints the branches with the decision with which they have to comply. We have been favoured with a copy of one of these *official circulars*, dated Edinburgh, 8th February, 1867, since which time no notable change has taken place. In these circulars the Bank directors announce the uniform rates of discount and interest, and all the establishments in Scotland must conform to them so long as they receive no orders of a contrary nature.*

* It does not follow, because the Scotch Banks adopt the same rates in all their common transactions, and require these rates to be the same in their branches as in their head offices, that there is no competition, or no advantage to the public of competition. The rates are fixed by a conference among all the Banks, in which there is the free play of a various judgment. There is no dictator among them. A syndicate of this kind establishes itself in all trades, however free and competitive. As regards the rate of discount on bills of exchange, the Scotch Banks are compelled to follow at some close distance the minimum of the Bank of England, whether they think it a fair and necessary average or not; because, if they were to discount at 5 when the Bank of England

Like the Bank of England, the Scotch Banks only give the *minimum* rate of discount. It was from 3 to 4 per cent. on the 8th February; and was raised to 4½ for bills exceeding four months' currency. The rate of the Bank of France was only 3 per cent. in February, 1867.

Current accounts, under the form of *cash accounts*, paid 4½ per cent.: this is the form that is most convenient for the

has declared say 7 per cent., this would only bring upon them, under some disguise, an avalanche of bills which did not lie within their sphere of business. In point of fact, however, the Scotch Banks allow their rate of discount neither to fall so low as the Bank of England sometimes decrees when gorged with bullion, nor to rise so high as the "Old Lady" puts it in periods of panic. M. Wolowski will find this fact in his own text. There is no doubt ample reason for this variation of the Scotch Banks from the Bank of England rates. The English Bank is required, by the Act of 1844, to study only its stock of bullion and corresponding issue of notes in declaring its minimum rate of discount, whether that may be down to zero or up to phrenzy; and it sometimes, therefore, happens that the Bank of England, under this whimsical law, especially since it pays no interest on deposits itself, reduces the rate of discount so low—it has more than once been 1½ per cent.—as not to suit the condition of Banks which do pay an interest to their depositors, without whose funds all the gold ever accumulated in the Bank of England would be but a gilded toy. The Scotch Banks have never followed the Bank of England in this descent. They have always maintained a rate of discount which gave an interest, however small, to their depositors, with some margin of brokerage to themselves. And so, at the other extreme, when the Bank of England raises the rate of discount from 8 to 9 and 10 per cent., and is prepared to advance another per cent. twice every week, in the vain hope of attracting some consignments of bullion, while spreading only alarm and discredit through the whole commercial world, the Scotch Banks have not followed these frantic efforts, but have continued to discount bills of exchange 1 and 2 per cent. below the Bank of England minimum. So far the Scotch Banks do vindicate their liberty, and do act on a theory of rate of discount differing materially from that of the Act of 1844. But it is inconsistent on the part of M. Wolowski, who gives his whole support to the law of 1844, and to a formal metallic restriction of issue, to turn the bad effects of his own system to account in the argument, and complain that there is not competition enough in the Scotch Banks.—*R.S.*

agricultural interest. Advances made *on overdraught* bear also the name of "*overdrawn account.*" They constitute a current account with the use of *cheques*, so that the customer of the Bank obtains the means of drawing for some particular enterprise, or for a time agreed upon. The interest in this class of operations was paid at 5 per cent.

As to the interest allowed upon deposits, it was 2½ per cent. upon *deposit receipts* for deposits exceeding a month, no interest being allowed by the Banks upon sums withdrawn within that time. The interest was 2 per cent. upon current accounts, when it was calculated upon the *minimum monthly balance*, and 1½ per cent. for *daily balances*. The banks agreed to restrict to *five* days the currency of bills, which they cash to each other free of charge. The agents of all the establishments are to take notice of this arrangement, and act accordingly. We have before us a previous circular, dated 28th September, 1866. It is identical in form, but the final arrangement is different. The interest was fixed—

On London bills not exceeding 3 months' currency,	4½ per cent.
On London bills exceeding 3 months' currency,	5 ,,
On other bills not exceeding 3 months' currency,	4½ ,,
On other bills exceeding 3 and not exceeding 4 months' currency, ...	5 ,,
On other bills exceeding 4 months' currency, .	4½ ,,

The interest upon advances upon *cash accounts* was then 5½ per cent. and 6 per cent. for *overdraughts*. As to the price allowed for deposits, it was 3 per cent. for *deposit receipts*, 2 per cent. on current accounts (minimum monthly balances), and 1½ per cent. for current accounts with daily balances.

We think it useless to dwell on this subject. Many illusions are dispelled by contact with the fertile reality that takes the place of fantastic descriptions of the manner according to which the Scotch Banks operated, and of the enormous reduction of interest that they were to procure.

But the serious services rendered by them in encouraging the formation of capital, and in placing the means of work, under reasonable conditions, within the reach of those who are able to make the most of them, must grow in public esteem by a profound study. They supply to Savings Banks, of which they form the "crowning," a valuable complement. They pay, in fact, interest upon deposits of £10 and upwards. Savings Banks, which have been so well styled "the primary school of capital," receive funds shilling by shilling; and when they have reached ten pounds, they go to swell the reservoir of the Banks that are destined to give an impulse to agriculture, industry, and commerce. The patient economy of labour thus feeds the intelligent industry of the nation. The mass of united capital, in increasing the amount offered, contributes to render the price of its use lower; but, we cannot repeat too often, this result is not due to any artifice of fiducial (or credit) creation; it proceeds from the regular growth of real resources. The Scotch Banks do not possess a magic wand to make capital with paper, but they prevent small reserves from being lost, or from fading away in sad expenses; they encourage their formation, they accumulate and remunerate them, while vivifying the spirit of enterprise by the morals-encouraging spirit of economy.

CHAPTER VIII.

THE LARGE INVESTMENTS OF THE SCOTCH BANKS IN PUBLIC SECURITIES A LESSON TO FRANCE.

LET us touch upon another question to which a certain importance has been attached. Among the criticisms raised against the Bank of France, the principal attack has been made against the employment made in *rentes* of part of its capital. We have examined this objection in the part of this book devoted to the *debates* on the Bank of France; but it will not be out of place to notice a curious fact. Those who have denounced in the most lively manner the wrong done to commerce by devoting a portion of the disposable resources to an investment in stocks, have not failed to quote the Scotch Banks, the whole of whose credit was, as they said, placed at the service of industry and agriculture. Here, again, facts answer badly to such assertions. There is not a Bank in Scotland that does not possess *consols* for a portion of the capital, superior relatively to that which the Bank of France utilizes in this way; *and the greater part of them have invested in this manner sums beyond their capital.* "The Scotch Banks," writes the honourable director, whose assistance has been so valuable and useful to us, "consider it necessary to possess *securities* of this solid kind." The guarantee that they find in them is also that which the Bank of France seeks after.*

* There is little parallel betwixt the sums which the Scotch Banks voluntarily place at London in consols and other securities; and the advances wrung from the Bank of England and the Bank of France by the respective Governments, and re-constituted in consols or rentes which the Banks are required permanently to hold as a guarantee of the note circulation, the real security of which has to be provided for all the same by the reserves of "coin and bullion." In the one case, the Government securities are a real banking reserve, which the Scotch Banks can operate upon at any moment; in the other they are what the French call "immobilized."—*R. S.*

The statements published by Banks in Scotland are not any more explicit than those of the English Banks; the divers "heads" are not clearly distinct; the information supplied, however, is sufficient to edify us upon the principal object that we are now aiming at. The investments in stock and other shares absorb, in each of the Banks, a sum superior to the paid-up capital. Nothing compels the various establishments to place sums in the public funds; they simply seek in this way to have the productive consolidation of part of their resources; frequently they do not limit themselves to employing their capital in this manner, but they also make a similar use of their deposits.

In his classic work, *A Practical Treatise on Banking*, Gilbart recommends the placing in public funds, and *especially in consols*, as the best use a banker can make of a portion of the resources at his disposition—a placing not dependent upon uncertain events in order to speculate in the difference in the price of buying and selling, but permanent, and offering at once both a solid guarantee and assistance in extreme cases. Such is the system pursued by the Scotch Banks upon an extensive scale. Inquiries have made this fact known many a time: "large investments of their funds in national paper and Government securities." Such is the result constantly indicated by accumulated evidence.

CHAPTER IX.

USEFUL SERVICES OF THE SCOTCH BANKS UNDER RESTRICTED ISSUE.

UPON the whole, the Banks of Scotland have rendered great and inestimable services to that country; but notes payable to bearer and at sight have had but a small share therein: the merit belongs above all to the gathering together of small capitals by means of deposits at interest, and their employment by means of cash accounts.

The proportion of notes issued has always been restrained within narrow limits: whenever the Banks have departed but a little from the rules of a rigid prudence, they have suffered severe punishment. Instead of trebling the capital by the issue, they have only in fiducial *paper circulation* about one-half of the combined capital, and the *metallic reserve* exceeds the half of that circulation. The supplemental resources furnished by the excess of notes above the metallic reserve do not amount to fifty million francs, whilst the deposits supply a disposable capital thirty times larger. The benefit derived by the issue of notes constitutes a small part, not even the twelfth of the profits reaped in the form of dividends. The constitution of Scotch Banks and their existence are in no way dependent upon this element, but rather upon the capital of savings placed at their disposal with an abundance encouraged by the general security founded upon the solidity of the instruments of exchange.

Far from diminishing the amount of bank-notes, the Act of 1845 has increased it, while giving a more secure guarantee to the circulation. Recriminations raised against the Act have principally borne upon the proportion of the *authorized circulation*. That proportion is sufficient for business, as it compasses the co-operation of perfect means of credit—

means that are so much the more active, as the market is placed more completely above all suspicion as to what fulfils the office of money. Any extension of the authorized circulation could only bear upon a very small sum in relation to the mass of collected deposits, and still smaller relatively to the total of public wealth. Far from being barren, the portion of the social capital devoted to keeping up the regular play of a solid monetary mechanism produces more than it costs by establishing security in relations, and fidelity in the fulfilment of contracts. Instead of a profit, a more relaxed organization of the issue would only bring a loss.

The liberty of issue, such as certain writers have demanded in our country, does not exist in Scotland. That right is strictly limited to a proportion that no one of the twelve Banks, alone authorized now to create bank-notes, can exceed. That proportion, it cannot be too often said, is hardly equal to the half of their capital and to twice their metallic reserve. The Banks exercise a mutual control upon the notes issued in interchanging them twice a week, and paying the balance in specie or exchequer bonds. In this way the duration of the circulation of the notes does not exceed, on an average, ten or twelve days. The material advantage that they yield to the Banks is very limited. Convenience and facility of transport are in accord with the solidity of the offered guarantee; but we must give up all hope of finding in the *issue* that fruitful mine of paper money which many inventors of fiducial plans look for so ardently. In attempting to rely upon the example of the Scotch Banks they distort their proceedings, which are at once simple and governed by a strict prudence.

Scotland possesses but few Banks—twelve altogether—which have instituted numerous *branches*. These Banks constitute a real *confederation*, animated by an unchangeable spirit of brotherhood. They thus arrive, by another road, under a different form, at those results that elsewhere are produced by *unity*. No competition exists in Scotland as to the rates of the various banking operations, the small number of Banks facilitating this perfect understanding. These rates are periodically fixed at the meeting of the directors of these establishments, and are applied uniformly by all the branches throughout the entire territory.

So far as the agricultural interests are concerned, the most useful instrument is found in the *cash accounts*, which procure for industrious men, who are exact in the performance of contracted engagements, and endowed with intelligence and morality, prolonged credits, that permit of protracted undertakings being assumed. But the rate of interest for cash accounts, almost always a little above the rate of discount, follows, like the latter, the fluctuations of the market. It has never fallen lower in Scotland than 4 per cent., whilst it has risen to 7, 8, 9, and 10 per cent. It is always the market of London, as shown in the rate of discount received by the Bank of England, that serves as a regulator of the rate of interest fixed, with common consent, by the Banks of Scotland.

It is a remarkable thing, and one that proves how much empire *custom* exercises over the forms of credit, that cash accounts extensively employed in Scotland have never been able to get naturalized in England. On the other hand, Scotland is very rebellious against the system of *cheques*, which entails multiplied entries. The attempt has been made in vain to establish a Bank operating according to the English model, with a *halfpenny* [*sic*] of commission for each entry and each payment of funds. The use of *deposit receipts* has remained predominant, the custom being, in all current accounts, that customers take out in one sum the amounts of which they make use in the course of the day.*

* The issue of cheques upon deposit accounts is quite common in Scotland. The Banks may have wished to charge 5s. per cent., like the English Banking Companies, on drawings by cheque, but this practice has not been introduced. A bank depositor in Scotland,

Thus, whilst desirous of the introduction of *cash accounts* into France, we do not wish to be under any illusion as to the facility with which the system might be adopted amongst us. If it succeed, so much the better: it will be a striking proof of the progress made in the prudent intelligence of our rural populations. It appears, however, useful to us not to confine ourselves to this attempt, but to organize, as we pointed out at the commencement of this work, another mechanism quite as efficacious, and better adapted to established customs. The *local Banks*, which would be established by personal initiative, and with a guaranteed capital, might issue bonds, the currency of which at six months, or one, two, and three years, would agree both with the term of contracted engagements, and with the necessities of agriculture. These engagements might borrow from the Scotch institutions the excellent system of joint securities up to a fixed amount; such an organization would have great chances of success, and would render a serious service to agriculture without any fiducial artifice.

We have seen that the Scotch Banks do not attempt any special operations: they act for the benefit of human industry in the widest acceptation of the term, whether it is applied to the field or to the workshop, to manufactures or to commerce. In that country there never has been the idea of isolating the agricultural interest; it is well understood that such a course would weaken it under the pretext of giving it protection. It is good to notice here that the 40 or 50 million francs worth of notes issued beyond the metallic reserve furnish but a small portion as a resource applied to agricultural enterprises. The operations of commerce and industry profit by the most considerable portion of the advances that can be made under the form of discount

while enjoying marked advantages both as to rate of interest and freedom of lodging and drawing on operative accounts, as compared with the sister kingdom, draws by cheque *free of charge*, as customarily as a bank depositor in England draws by cheque *under charge*.—*R. S.*

with the guaranty offered of bills at short dates. People deceive themselves doubly when they talk of capital in Scotland placed at the disposal of agriculture through the *free issues;* the Scotch Banks do not possess the faculty of issuing at will notes payable to the bearer and at sight; and the great majority of those that are created without corresponding with a metallic pledge (at the maximum only up to 50 million francs), rest upon bills arising from industrial and commercial undertakings.

The proved stability of the Scotch Banks attracts and multiplies deposits, obtaining the benefit of a modest profit, and the *cash accounts* give rise to the custom of continued relations that help to make the smallest reserve productive by causing it to participate in the advantages of the *common fund,* which prevents the weaker resources from going astray in dangerous employments, or from disappearing altogether through various temptations. Capital increases at the same time that moral ideas are strengthened.

All the Scotch Banks employ at least the equivalent of their capital in public funds; they thus augment the credit that they enjoy both for the circulation of their notes and the multiplication of deposits. A guarantee in stock subscribed by a part of the founders of the local Banks would facilitate the placing of obligations at short terms that would incessantly supply the funds required for turning over. The payments to be made by these institutions, always squaring with the expiration of contracted engagements, they would develop themselves with a force analagous to that with which the *Credit Foncier* has proved the demand for loans contracted at long terms and redeemable by annuities.

The experience realized by the Scotch Banks presents a subject of study that is every way profitable, but, especially, in order to cure those minds that are permeated with the weak chimera of paper money, and of a *freedom of Banks* that is badly understood, if it is confined to the very secondary faculty of issuing notes payable to the bearer and at sight. That faculty only allows the handling of a too short lever, whilst the organization of deposits and the creation of obligations by the medium of solidly constituted bonds furnish the fulcrum by the aid of which credit may exercise the most fertile influence in our rural districts. But in order to succeed, it is not sufficient to instil a more or less perfect mechanism: there must be habits of order, of foresight, and of intelligent activity to give impulse to the springs: without these, all would be abortive.

The organization of the Scotch Banks is simple, but powerful by its very simplicity; the pretended magic sound of fiducial paper issue plays but a very small part, and one that is singularly kept in the dark. Those who have allowed themselves to be seduced by what seems to be the bright prospect or the apparent facility of creating new resources with a few reams of paper, will be convinced by any slight reflection of the truth of the popular saying, "All is not gold that glitters." It is folly to seek for wealth in the crucible of modern alchemists; its only real source is intelligent labour and patient economy. The thought of being able to contribute in bringing back to a practical ground the generous efforts that are too often led astray by false lights, has sustained us in our researches.

Scotland has not trusted to a lifeless mechanism—she has called forth living strength. Of what use would facilities opened up for credit be, if the people did not know how to set them to work? What we want among us is the spirit, at once enterprising and practical, that distinguishes Scotchmen, and their intelligence as to the results that are to be obtained from the concentration of savings and the employment of instruments offered to labour. If we succeed in introducing them, the institutions will multiply of themselves, for they will encounter what constitutes the vital element of their existence. It is not with bank-notes, of which she uses very few; it is not by means of a competition among institutions of credit, which does not exist; it is not by the great number of Banks, for, when distinguished from mere branches, the number is small; nor is it by employing the paid-up capital for advances; nor by reducing the interest by means of financial artifices, for the interest is paid upon a normal condition determined by the abundance with which capital is offered and by the intensity of the demand. None of these dazzling chimeras has enabled Scotland to employ a wide organization of credit. In order to arrive at that, it has only been necessary to comprehend the value of the bringing together of capital, amassed bit by bit, and labour constantly developed. When this is once understood in France, all will be done, without sudden efforts, by the energetic application of individual initiative and the rapid accumulation of private resources. Let the results of previous labour, preserved from immediate destruction, be united with present efforts and plans for the future, and agriculture will find infinite resources in the wide reservoir of Banks, without having recourse to the dangerous creation of a sort of paper money, stripped of a metallic guarantee.

Instead of empty discussion we have quoted facts, produced figures, and scrutinized the causes of the power of the Scotch Banks. Several of the data given here are published for the first time, but we have endeavoured to present them in their true light. Without making a sacrifice to any illusion, and in seeking only the spring of this vast mechanism, we think we have justified the admiration inspired in us by the Banks of Scotland, devoted to the service of an enlightened and industrious population.

CHAPTER X.

THE MORE BANKING COMPANIES CONFORM TO THE ACTION OF LOAN SOCIETIES THE BETTER, AND RIGHT OF ISSUE UNIMPORTANT.

THE partizans of a *pretended liberty of Banks*, that would consist in the right of free issue of notes, have largely to profit from the spectacle furnished by the Scotch Banks. These show by the most profitable teaching, that of actual experience, how necessary it is to embrace, over and above the interest of the institution of credit and that of the parties who make engagements with it, a third element—the indirect and to some extent involuntary custom or support of the public who receive and give the notes as money. The force of things has introduced into Scotland measures of severe restriction that have removed danger by enclosing within a narrow limit a right of issue strictly regulated. It is only by the aid of either perverted or ill-understood facts that people have been led to suppose that the bank-note performs an important part in Scotland. The brilliant success obtained by the institutions of credit in that country rests upon a different basis, though wide and solid—that of the enormous effective capital accumulated by deposits. The bank-note, on the contrary, more than once caused them to run a serious risk and to suffer considerable loss, both in the eighteenth century and in more recent times. A confusion that we cannot labour too much to dispel has caused the real question to be slighted.

The illustrious Macaulay was right in saying that her *schools* and *banks* had transformed Scotland. We are quite of the same opinion; but we make a distinction between *Banks* as active intermediaries between the capital, whose formation they encourage, and the labour that they nourish, and the *bank-note*, a secondary instrument, that produces but a very slight economy in the circulation, and that is more valuable by its facility of transport and convenience of using, than by the slight saving effected by it in the metallic mechanism of exchanges.

The advantages of *loan societies*, banks for advances, the true popular banks that Scotland has possessed for more than a century, are incontestable; but, like the *popular Banks* of Germany, that have never sent out one note payable to the bearer and at sight destined to circulate in the form of money, these useful creations owe nothing to the *issue*. Our honourable friend, Mons. Battie, has himself recognized this in his work, *Le Credit Populaire*. The following is a passage from it:—"The Banks of Scotland are real popular Banks; herein is their characteristic feature and the secret of their healthy influence upon the economic development of the country, as well as of their continued success—they have for customers the entire productive population of the country, and they render immense services to it by the *cash credit*." He also explains very clearly all the machinery of this system. But in all this the bank-note plays no part; it does not set at all in movement the lifting and forcing action of Banks that gives life to credit. Forty years ago the deposits in the Scotch Banks were estimated at thirty millions; this amount is more than doubled at present. Does this arise from the notes? Not in the least. It is the fruit of an intelligent economy. If applied to France, it would put more than 15 milliards of francs at the constant disposal of a serious and regular credit. We will say, in our turn, that this parallel is eloquent, and needs no commentary. Whoever takes an account of the colossal amount of deposits in Scotland forms a correct judgment of the exaggerations entertained on the subject of bank-notes, to which a skilful trick of discussion endeavours to attribute the merit of the wonderful development of Scotch credit.

The joint and mutual liability of the shareholders that

operates in all the establishments of the country, except in the three oldest Banks, which are *incorporated*—that is to say, subject to the system of our "Sociétés Anonymés"—has, as we have already remarked, increased in a striking manner the solidity of the Banks, and, at the same time, given more regularity to their operations. It is not only an important accessory; it is the very principle that an attempted intervention of *men of straw* could not alter, for the list of partners, published periodically, makes the credit of each company depend upon the known position of the parties interested.

The relative elevation of the capital excludes the easy benefits of an abundant issue of notes; and as to the exclusive employment of the resources of the Banks in the operations of credit, that is a pure and simple illusion that is dispersed by a contrast with official figures. All the Scotch Banks devote to investment in consols and other stocks much more than the paid-up capital. As to the mutual control that they exercise, the one over another, it limits the fiducial paper circulation to small proportions. This result, obtained in an unanswerable manner, shows the reliance that should be placed upon the pretended trebling of the capital by means of the notes. This control would not be sufficient by itself, as sad examples have proved more than once, if the complete absence of competition between the Banks in fixing the interest on advances and the legal limit imposed upon the fiducial paper contingent of each Bank (a limit that not one amongst them ever reaches) did not restrain the circulation of notes within a narrow circle. The Act of 1845 has imposed no gratuitous difficulty in the way of a circulation that does not even make use of the margin that the law opens to it.* The

* M. Wolowski, in other passages, has shown such a full acquaintance with the legal mechanism of issue in Scotland, under the Act of 1845, that it is difficult to see how he has fallen into the idea expressed here. The "margin" of circulation allowed by the law to the Scotch Banks,

most devoted partizans of the system that they decorate with the attractive, but inexact, title of "*liberty of the*

save on a metallic equivalent, has long been much exceeded in the case of every one of the Scotch Banks. M. Wolowski may have been glancing at the case of the Bank of Ireland, placed by the Act of 1845 under precisely the same conditions of issue as the Scotch Banks, and, in a momentary phantasy, may have transferred the conclusion there found to the Banks in Scotland. The circulation of the Bank of Ireland, authorized by the Act of 1845, is £3,738,428. The total average circulation of the Bank of Ireland, according to one of the latest *Gazette* returns (September 7), is £3,109,125, largely within the "authorized" amount, and answering perfectly to M. Wolowski's idea of a legal "margin" not made use of. But the case of the Scotch Banks is very different. The total "authorized" circulation of all banks of issue in Scotland is £2,749,271, and the actual average circulation of the Scotch Banks, according to the same official return (September 7), is £5,313,560—this expansion beyond the authorized issue having its co-relative under the Act in the metallic reserves held by the Scotch Banks, amounting on the whole, at the date named, to £3,324,893. It is sadly against "the currency theory," translated into Acts of Parliament in 1844-45, that it has left a state of things in which there is no equality or intelligible ratio of issue and metallic reserve—its cardinal point—either in the three kingdoms, as compared with each other, or in the banks of issue in any of the three kingdoms as compared with themselves; but, on the contrary, a growing inequality and unreason, which is simply intolerable as a legislative solution. The Bank of Ireland may not only issue its whole attained circulation at the present time, but half a million sterling more, without any obligation, under the Act of Parliament, to hold a single sixpence in coin; while the Banks in Scotland, since 1845, have been compelled to adjust their issue of notes, month by month, to a metallic reserve which, though always advancing, is now by the quoted returns (September 7), in the proportion of 3 to 5. This is not an international grievance, but only a point of illustration: and, taking the broadest view of the question, it is enough, not only in correction of the error of M. Wolowski in the immediate text, but of much of his general reasoning as to the small part of issue in banking operations, to state that the issue of notes by the Scotch Banks is, at certain periods every week, three or four times more, and by the Bank of Ireland no doubt in like proportion, than the monthly *minimum* circulation recorded in the *Gazette*.—*R. S.*

Banks," acknowledge that the notes in their existing proportion supply, largely, the wants of Scotland. Of what, then, should they complain?

As to the number of branches, that does not in any way imply more considerable resources. The foundation of "comptoirs interessés," like those that are in operation in Belgium, and the creation of local Banks, fed by private initiative, and setting to work the energetic lever of deposits, will endow France with quite as fertile means of action, from the moment that, instead of running after the deceptive chimera of a creation of resources by means of issue, we shall content ourselves here, as they have done in Scotland and Belgium, with placing the result obtained from labour, converted into money, at the service of the spirit of enterprise.

Some folks fall into ecstacies before the notes of many Banks. Why? It is not that they give either more guarantees or more facilities, nor is it that they multiply more than the notes of a single Bank radiating through the whole country. As for the idea that the Bank of England finds itself embarrassed more frequently than the *free and equal Banks* of Scotland, it errs in the very foundation; for it is the Bank of England that, alone, bears the weight of the monetary edifice of the United Kingdom; it is upon it that the Banks of Scotland lean for support; thanks to it, they can enjoy a security that is sometimes attained at the expense of that of the metropolis. Moreover, concerning the *issue*, the Scotch Banks are not *free*, and the epithet of *equal* belongs to them only in one sense that it is necessary to explain—in excluding all possibility of competition they proceed upon an *equal footing*, both as to the amount of interest allowed for deposits and the rate imposed upon advances.

Where, then, has Mons. Horn found that the system of plurality in Scotland secured a credit and a circulation of notes that the single right exercised by the Bank of France could not give among us? We have, in reality, as many bank-notes as the Scotch, and nobody suspects the value of a circulation that is well received everywhere. The phantom of paper money may be left at rest, for our Bank has no inclination for that fatal expedient of Governments at the last extremity. We felicitate Mons. Horn upon the holy horror that he has of paper money; but, to be just, he ought not to have forgotten that if events stronger than human foresight and strength caused the introduction of the forced currency after the revolution of 1848, the amount of notes, instead of being left to the facilities of excessive issue, was strictly limited to a proportion that is not equal to the half of the existing circulation. He ought to have remembered also that the Bank of France insisted for a long time upon the withdrawal of the forced currency, because the circumspection of that establishment very soon reduced the right of not paying the notes in specie to a purely ideal one. The example selected by Monsieur Horn condemns him: as for the abuses committed in Austria and Russia, they belong, not to the system of Banks, but to an actual fabrication of assignats. Italy, if she has allowed herself to be led into decreeing the forced currency, follows, at least, the example of France in 1848, by limiting the issue. In short, Monsieur Horn ought also not to be silent about what occurred in the eighteenth century, for it was the Scotch Banks that introduced the *famous optional clause*, afterwards interdicted by Parliament—a clause that put off the payment of the bank-note, while placing it under the category of the *fictitious note*, which Monsieur Horn declares he abhors. He is not, however, fanatical for the bank-note; he merely looks upon it as a panacea, which we state with real satisfaction. But why, with such just ideas, should he give himself the appearance of swelling the ranks of those who proclaim the issue to be the source of an increase of capital. When one understands as well as Monsieur Horn does that the note is but a *vehicle* for circulation, and that it is not the number of vehicles but the use that is made of them which secures a sound and productive circulation, he should leave to dreamers any incorrect interpretation of the mechanism of Scotch Banks.

Nevertheless, Monsieur Horn denounces the limited number of notes issued by the branches of the Bank of France, without thinking of the cause of this difference from the Scotch system. The note of the Bank of France circulates equally everywhere, and therefore renders the local issue useless in a great measure. The fiducial paper-circulation, so far as it renders serious services, is not concentrated in our towns; it penetrates also into the rural districts, and the *unity* of the note has singularly advanced the education of the inhabitants on this point.

The formation of banking establishments in our departments would utilize the energetic lever of deposits, and this lever will act with an efficacy so much the greater if it be not crossed by the mistrust that might be excited by the fractional circulation of notes performing the office of money. In this latter respect Scotland possesses secular customs that are not formed suddenly. The result, moreover, that she has gained can be easily obtained in a somewhat different way, and the issue of notes does not present any advantage of sufficient extent to allow of trusting to chance. Mons. Horn acknowledges that the deposits exceed almost ten-fold the issue in Scotland; he might have said that, deducting the metallic reserve from the amount of notes, the sum added to the circulation by bank-notes does not reach the *thirtieth* part of the capital supplied by deposits.

The argument relating to deposits without interest in the branches of the Bank of France fails, from the moment that it is a question of organizing the system of deposits with interest by means of local Banks, solidly established and sheltered from all danger by the absolute separation of that which is really the function of Banks—the accumulation and distribution of capital—from that which constitutes an irregular accessory, the issue of notes called upon to do the work of money.

Doubtless, the confidence gained by the Banks for the capital that they draw from the locality will prevent the withdrawal of the deposits at the moment of a crisis, especially if the fear of not seeing the notes paid in specie has no foundation. Monsieur Horn ought to know that the unshakeable power of the Banks of England and France causes the accumulation by them of deposits, which increase instead of diminish in times of difficulty.

To pretend that Banks cannot fulfil the office of collector and distributor of credit if they are not armed with the right of issue, is just simply to take no account of the most important fact, the immense affluence of resources in the *joint-stock Banks* of England, which would take good care not to employ the dangerous instrument of notes, while they derive enormous benefits in their character of intermediaries between economy and labour. One of the most important institutions of credit in the United Kingdom, the National Provincial Bank, gave up, of its own accord, an *authorized issue* of £448,371 that was reserved to it by the Act of 1844, nor did it obtain any indemnity from the Bank of England. It attached little value to the right of issue in presence of an *amount of deposits* that exceeded £13,000,000 sterling.* We may add that this Bank, like all the others, has invested in Consols much more than its paid-up capital: £2,248,476 have been expended by it in *Government securities*, and

* M. Wolowski misapprehends the motive of the National Provincial Bank of England in giving up its authorized issue of £448,371, which was not exactly a voluntary act on the part of the Bank. With the help of the right of issue, this Bank, established in the provinces, became a really great and almost national Bank. But in the magnitude to which its business had attained, it was found necessary that the Bank should get into London; whereas the law said that it could not establish itself in London and remain a Bank of Issue. The Bank, availing itself of Mr. Gladstone's Act of 1865, gave up the right of issue—thus choosing what had become, in its own opinion, the least of two evils.—*R.S.*

£1,222,525 in other available securities at a fixed rate of interest.

By a singular contradiction Monsieur Horn, after having said with reason that the issue of notes does not create an atom of fresh resources, and that the most perfect system of credit does not increase by one halfpenny the previously existing capital, asserts that the benefit arising from the difference between the interest that the Bank pays and that which it receives upon the funds placed at its disposition, is not sufficiently *enticing* to induce excessive operations of that nature, and that it is necessary to add the profit of a certain *supplement of capital* that pays no interest. Fortunately this is a purely imaginary hypothesis; if the perspective of *future credit* attracts deposits, the notes count for nothing. A gratuitous error is committed in pretending that the local Bank, in order to obtain considerable funds, should be able to dispose of a surplus of capital, and that it can only find this in the fiducial paper issue. A man in the rural districts, who is naturally prudent and timid, will not trust his savings to an institution that is always threatened with a crisis through the active presentation of notes to be changed (for money).

The free multiplicity of Banks of issue exists no more in Scotland, and has disappeared in America. To do away with the natural conclusion to be drawn from the facts as stated would require something more than puerile arguments and sweeping assertions, that are contradicted every moment by irrefutable experience. The community has nothing to gain by these games of chance, that are intended to enrich a few speculators to the injury of the general security. From the moment that all the profit to be expected rests upon a fictitious currency, the danger is great and the advantage extremely limited. Inexact assimilations of institutions, attempted in the normal track of credit and liberty of exchanges, will not succeed in doing away with the fundamental distinction between that which stops within the region of private interests and that which affects the entire domain of public interests.

To urge a dangerous experiment is to make too little of the principles of stability and sincerity in agreements; to reproach the *metallic system* with the crises that are quite foreign to it, is to deny those which it has prevented from recurring, and it has never pretended to employ an universal panacea against financial and commercial disturbances; in short, to attribute to the right of issue a system of discount and advances at a cheap rate is to forget all the precedents of the Scotch Banks, and to call up a veritable phantom.

The multiplicity of banks of issue that have been able, by means of a strongly-bound *confederation*, to escape the danger of competition, exercises no sway over the price of lending capital, which, instead of lowering, it would tend rather to increase.

The study of the Scotch Banks demonstrates once more that no more can be lent than is possessed; the most ingenious combinations cannot enable us to employ over again a capital that has once been disposed of. The Bank is merely the medium that dispenses the supply and demand of capital, and that facilitates their junction. The power of disposing of capital, which the owner either cannot or does not know how to employ, is placed temporarily in hands that employ it usefully. Banks succeed in multiplying capital, but it is by drawing in the instalments of savings in order to transform them into active instruments, without making fixed capital of them in too great a proportion. It is not the Banks in Scotland alone that render this service; the Joint-Stock Banks of England are quite as successful without any fiducial paper issue, for that machinery is foreign to the functions of a Bank soundly understood.

Attempts have been made to reproach the Banks that concentrate the issue with having the strongest dividends at critical periods. It is sufficient merely to examine the results obtained by every prudently administered Bank, in order to prove exactly similar effects.

The system of *a plurality of Banks* is good, so long as there is no question of the fabrication of a real monetary instrument that influences the measure of value and the measure of all contracts. Far from contradicting this truth, the financial history of Scotland confirms it in a striking manner; it shows, in fact, how, in order to avoid the viciousness inherent to a right of fractional issue, it has been necessary to restrain this right, to confine it in an exclusive and limited manner to a small number of establishments, and to weaken competition. Agriculture, industry, and commerce have been fortified, and their prosperity has increased with the disappearance of a serious element of disturbance that some have attempted to ornament with the pompous and illusive title of "*liberty of Banks.*" This does not exist in Scotland in the sense put forward by our pretended reformers—forgetful, at once, both of what is required by the democratic idea, taken in the highest acceptation of the term, and of what equity in social relations demands, namely, the greatest fixedness in the monetary instrument that is used to interpret all engagements and stipulations. That is the grand side of the question as to Banks, and which interests the whole State; the free issue concerns only the secondary side of private benefit, that should never be placed in opposition to the public interest. This is the last word of instruction supplied by Scotch Banks.*

* M. Wolowski, in this passage, sums up his whole preference for some form of national issue of notes, responding perfectly to the metallic standard as the public measure of value, without considering by what means any national issue of notes can possess or maintain this character. It is a remarkable fact, boldly to be stated, that the convertibility of paper currency into specie, and the maintenance of its current value in equivalence to the metallic standard, have never been realized save in the notes of responsible banking companies under the simple legal obligation of payment to bearer at sight. There is now a sole national issue of notes in the United States; but it is an inconvertible issue, and is under

A few remarks will suffice to make known the information supplied by a decisive experiment. The small circulation of bank notes in Scotland shows how narrow is the limit of the wants of the public as to this instrument of exchange, even where *cheques* are only used exceptionally, and where specie and bank notes alone serve for transactions. As many notes as are desired can be obtained in exchange for the gold that is brought; there can, therefore, be no question as to any deficiency of these commercial *instruments*. Everything is thus brought back to the question of the existence and increase of the *capital*. Now, multiplying the documents of credit does not increase capital; to do so, disposable wealth must be accumulated.

The creation of notes does not exercise any influence upon the price of borrowing capital, which depends upon the relation between the supply of disposable resources and the intensity of the demand. The Scotch Banks have understood these truths. Instead of running after the shadow, they have strengthened the reserves destined to be fertilized

large and daily fluctuating discount in its relation to gold. The notes of the Bank of France are not equivalent to the standard of value, because they have been under suspension of specie payment since the late Franco-Prussian War, as they have been more than once within a very recent period of history. The paper currency of the United Kingdom has been uninterruptedly convertible during half a century; and it does no injustice to the Act of 1844 to add, that this result has been attained through the credit and resources of banking companies alone. The idea of an exclusively national or State issue of notes has many advocates besides M. Wolowski; but when they and he come to consider how the nation, or the Government in its name, is to provide for the payment of the issue in specie on demand, all the difficulty or impossibility of the scheme will appear. It is also wide of the truth to say, as M. Wolowski says here, that it has been found necessary in Scotland to restrain the right of issue, and to confine it to a few establishments, in order to maintain bank-notes at standard value; for the consolidation of banking companies, with right of issue, and the perfect equivalence of the issue to the standard money of the kingdom, had been attained in Scotland under entire freedom long before 1844.—*R.S.*

by labour, and they have encouraged the fruitful results of saving.

Credit adds nothing to capital; it can only transfer the use of it; it delegates the power of dispensing it, but the capital must first be in existence; that is to say, the fruits obtained by man's labour must have been preserved in order to serve for the future production. Such is the *magic of saving*, which is real and productive in a sense quite different from that of the *magic of credit*—a figure of speech that has been too often abused.

The notes and specie constitute only a very small fraction of the wealth of countries that are advanced in civilization; nothing can be more fallacious or more dangerous than to confound the function of the instrument of exchange with that of capital, and to believe that the power of *labour* is increased by merely multiplying the *signs*, by the side of which transactions are accomplished.

END OF TRANSLATION.

REMARKS.

REMARKS.

CHAPTER I.

INTRODUCTORY.

THE Banking question, whether discussed in London or Paris, always reverts to the history of the Scotch Banks as a fragment indispensable to the controversy, and is always found to centre in the issue of bank-notes, of which Scotland presents an example at variance in some degree with prevailing system and theory.

The issue of bank-notes has thus come to be invested with a relative importance among the many not less difficult problems in the administration of capital, which could hardly be predicated from the simplicity and naturalness of the operation itself, or from the well-ascertained and definite conditions by which it is regulated. If those who constantly assail the issue of bank-notes not only attribute to this source the most fanciful evils, but are blind to its manifest advantages, as well as to its necessary place in the banking system, it may not be astonishing that others who take up the defensive should not only exaggerate in the opposite direction, but sometimes fail to see wherein the chief virtue of a banking currency consists. It may reasonably be inferred from this contention and exaggeration on the subject of bank-issue that it forms in reality an important and salient part in the mechanism of monetary and banking institutions.

The constant appeal to the Scotch Banks on all sides may thus be accounted for, the more especially since their history and experience, as regards the issue of notes, are not only unique, but, though untouched till of late years by Imperial legislation, have been crowned with complete success, and present a model which, if not everywhere imitable, can never be bereft at least of the lessons it conveys.

M. Wolowski not unjustly complains of the want of information as to the history and principles of the Scotch Banks. It may not be very creditable to our economists, bankers, and *literati*, that more pains have not been taken to display the progress of these great companies, to unfold the rich experience through which they have passed, and to exhibit all the springs and manifestations of the marvellous stability and prosperity they have attained. But there is much truth in what M. Wolowski says, viz., that the Scotch are men of action: they do not trouble themselves in these days with principles or recondite history or observation, and are quite satisfied with a favourable balance-sheet, showing that all for the time being is going on well. It is only when their banking system is attacked—as it was in the days of Sir Walter Scott without avail, and as it was in 1845 with partial effect—that the literary genius of the country comes to the rescue, and then only with an evanescent and periodically declining flash. Scotland, while materially prosperous, is undergoing a centralization that drags both her mind and body more and more into the general movement of the Empire; and so small is the sympathy betwixt her men of business and men of thought, and so commonly are the two classes shooting outward on parallel lines from home studies, that when an attack comes which may be vital to the prosperity of Scotland, so far from having a history prepared for the crisis, she may possibly have neither voice nor pen adequate to express the inarticulate experiences and convictions of her men of business. M. Wolowski may forgive the Scotch for their lack of banking literature. The most complimentary return for the research he has made into our banking institutions is to produce a faithful translation of his work; and if a supplement be in our opinion necessary, it is less with the view of combating his opinions than of inciting inquiry—of stirring up our banking and mercantile people to study and reflection, and perchance securing from some more competent authority such a history of banking in Scotland as Mr. Gilbart has given, with persevering assiduity, of banking in England.

The study of banking as practised in England and Scotland presents a somewhat different point of view. As regards the issue of notes, the two systems are practically irreconcilable; and though the one, in the solidity of institutions, may not soon absorb or supersede the other, yet, as the tendency is all against the smaller country in favour of the larger, it follows that if there is any good in the Scotch system, that good can only be preserved for the Scotch themselves, and for the guidance of other nations, by means of a full understanding and delineation of its peculiar features.

M. Wolowski does not disguise, while contributing ably to a needful and interesting inquiry, that he is a controversialist—that he has opponents to encounter and refute—and that he is the advocate of a system with which the Scotch does not correspond. Hence the quiet thrusts and the occasional throbs of triumph in which he seems conscious of being in the act of doing summary execution on his foes. A rash assertion, a statement of principle exaggerated in a not too friendly rendering, a trivial misapprehension, or, let us admit, some extravagance or error of opinion at one point or other of the controversy, may be exposed to a crushing refutation at the hands of so cool and painstaking a critic as M. Wolowski. Some of his opponents may have laid themselves too open to rejoinders of this kind: the discussion of the monetary question in France may have been as prolific of illusions as elsewhere; but as M. Wolowski counts as his chief antagonist M. Chevalier—than whom there are few more enlightened economists in Europe—it is difficult to resist a suspicion that our French author may have been tempted to create some of his giants for the pleasure of slaying them. At all events, such ideas as that of basing credit on the multiplication of bank-notes instead of capital and savings—that the chief virtue of banks consists in the creation of a fictitious and illimitable paper credit, and that the beneficial results of bank-notes are in any sense to be measured by the quantity of such notes forced into circulation—are too crude to enter into any rational discussion of the merits of the Scotch system and experience of banking issue.

There are few subjects in the range of economic science on which there is more need of guarded statement, or on which it is more easy to fall into extremes on one side and the other, than the issue of bank-notes as a part of the general mechanism of banking business; because it is itself not only governed by natural laws, and by conventional adjuncts arising out of natural laws, requiring only intelligent recognition in order to give it everywhere a free and safe operation, but is interlaced with other banking processes, such as deposit and discount, that have a category of their own, in which the bank-note appears on the foreground as an instrument, but of which they are the substance. When this complexity is not understood and carefully studied and observed, the whole question of issue is apt to fall into chaos, and to give rise to the most divergent conclusions. Thus, when we contend for liberty of issue, it is with full consciousness that no operation of commerce is under a more strict dominion of natural law and fact than the issue and circulation of bank-notes payable at sight. And thus, also, when we raise our voice for the free development and extension of institutions of credit, it is with a painful conviction of the too common abuse of credit, of the sometimes insufficient though always powerful motives by which credit is restrained, and the inevitable reverse that attends its abuse or excess. If there be any despotism, tempered only by the care and judgment exercised in its administration, it is the system of natural law which governs the use of money and the movements of capital, and consequently, also, the issue of bank-notes, so unnecessarily apt to be confounded with money and capital, though in reality only a subordinate and professional instrument in circulating and utilizing both. The prevailing tendency is to exaggerate and misunderstand the exact place of bank-notes in the monetary system. It is too often found, whether in the pages of M. Wolowski, who has a dread of the issue of bank-notes, or of other writers who hold it in inordinate esteem, that paper currency is a substitute for money and capital, and that it is expected in some way to supersede both with the most magical effects. But this is a grievous error, from whatever point of view entertained; since there is the danger that, in arguing on a purely conjectural hypothesis, the real utilities of bank-note issue, its natural function in the business of banking, and its practical though not the less marvellous results in the development and organization of money and capital, may be altogether overlooked.

The French economists have tersely comprehended the question of bank-notes under the terms of "freedom and plurality of issue," as opposed to issue from some singular or specially authorized source under restrictions and conditions external to, or not inherent in, the nature of the commercial document called a "bank-note" itself. "Freedom of Issue," not that issue can be practized by all, or that it can be delivered from the restraints of legal obligation and professional fitness, but because it shall be open to all for whom it is competent to be undertaken, on the same conditions, like any other legally recognized financial or commercial function: And "Plurality of Issue," not by any means that the greater the number of sources of issue in any country the better—for this may not be the natural tendency or expediency of the operation even when most free — but because two, three, or as many sources of issue as, in the development of banking, may be found adequate and *solidaire*, are more just, more expedient, and more conducive to the public interest, than to select one Bank as the sole source or medium of issue, and place all other banking companies of equal usefulness and solidity under a functional disability.

It would be idle to permit any doubt to exist as to what is contended for on the one hand, or opposed on the other, in this question. The matter under consideration is the issue of bank-notes, of a convenient but not too small denomination, *payable on demand* in gold or silver in the specie or standard money of the country, by banking companies of adequate means and responsibility to give acceptance and currency to their paper. Of this form of issue, at once free and plural, the history of the Scotch Banks affords the rarest, if not the only practical example, extending over a long period of years, over a tract of time, indeed, as extended as the history of the Bank of England itself; and has thus acquired an importance which renders it impossible of being overlooked, or deemed unworthy even of the most careful study, in any attempt to solve the controversies that have arisen on this subject.

CHAPTER II.

ACTION OF THE SCOTCH BANKS ON AGRICULTURE—CONNEXION OF THE RIGHT OF ISSUE WITH THE DEVELOPMENT OF BANK DEPOSITS—SUPERIORITY IN THIS RESPECT OF SCOTLAND TO ENGLAND OR FRANCE—TENDENCY OF RIGHT OF ISSUE TO CONSOLIDATE BANKING COMPANIES WHILE INCREASING BRANCH OFFICES.

It is probable that, in following M. Wolowski, it will be necessary to execute a series of surprises—to be in flat contradiction with him at some points, to catch him unawares at others, even to rise from under the ground and take possession of his works before he knows that there is any danger. But it is not desirable to indulge any strong antagonism in these remarks. The main object is to explain the Scotch system of issue, and its relation to the development of banking and of general prosperity in Scotland—matters of information which are probably not too well understood among ourselves. However, without departing from this simple *rôle* of description, we shall presently have to controvert M. Wolowski in some measure on these points:—(1.) His *quasi* refusal to allow the Scotch Banks to be in any sense Agricultural; (2.) His total misunderstanding of the intimate connexion betwixt the issue of notes in Scotland and the accumulation of deposits; and (3.) His halting interpretation of the Parliamentary returns which he gives at the end of his second chapter.

It is difficult to admit, as M. Wolowski seems to demand in his opening paragraph, that the Scotch Banks may not be cited in France, or indeed anywhere else, as signal examples of the application of credit to agriculture; for it is certainly one of their peculiar qualifications that they are Agricultural as well as Commercial Banks, and that they fructify the country as well as the towns.

Superabundant proof might be adduced of the direct and beneficial action of the Scotch Banks on the progress and enrichment of Scotch agriculture. Merchants and manufacturers, after having acquired wealth in the large towns, have bought estates in the country, to lay out capital on them and improve them; and Scotchmen who have gone to India or other parts abroad, and made their fortunes, have returned to embellish their patrimonial acres, or render productive the moor or morass where they had the honour simply of being born. One must not circumscribe the various causes which, in a century and a-half, have converted Scotland from a barren into a fertile country. But the relation of landlord and tenant prevails over nearly the entire surface of Scotland; the landlord gives his tenant a lease of nineteen or twenty-one years, on condition that each shall contribute a part to the reclamation and improvement of the soil; and both landlords and tenants have been largely enabled by the Banks to carry out these wholesome covenants. Not only do most young farmers, on entering on a lease for the first time, fortify their position by cash credits in one or other of the Banks, but farmers generally, who need financial aid, obtain advances in Spring when seeds and manures have to be purchased, or in Autumn when wages are heavy, to be repaid when their crop or stock is brought to market. The consequence is, that, notwithstanding all disadvantages of soil and climate, nowhere are there more prosperous landlords and farmers, a more advanced or elaborate agriculture, better implements of husbandry, or more productive and well-stocked farms than in Scotland. So far from the direct agricultural operation of the Scotch Banks needing to be set aside, this is precisely one of the phenomena of banking in Scotland which strikes attention at the outset, and solicits inquiry.

The fact being, that the Scotch Banks, without any special agricultural designation—of a purely commercial origin, having their headquarters in the capital and large cities, with a full play in the manufactures and foreign trade of the kingdom—have nevertheless extended their operations into the rural districts, and almost into the smallest and remotest hamlets of the country, the question naturally arises to what virtue in their constitution or administration, or to what force and vitality springing from the liberties they have enjoyed, is this quite unwonted result to be ascribed? Wherever one goes in Scotland, the practice of depositing in Banks, and of obtaining loans, credits, and discounts on personal and commercial securities, is found to be in operation. How comes it that the Scotch Banks have this distinction? How does it happen that they not only embrace the interests and command the confidence and custom of greater masses of people than Banks anywhere else, but that they are equally as operative in the rural districts as in towns and cities? An endeavour to follow up these questions to a conclusion would show that this result of banking in Scotland is much more attributable to the right of issue possessed by the Banks than may appear on the surface, as will, indeed, be manifest immediately we proceed to touch on the question of deposits.

M. Wolowski says that it is not their notes, but their deposits, that the Scotch Banks operate upon. Very true; but how have their deposits been obtained? M. Wolowski can answer this question in a fashion; for, farther on, he compares the branches of the Scotch Banks to "suction-pumps," which draw supplies of capital from the rural districts to keep the wheels of discount moving in the centres of commerce. M. Wolowski does not add that these streams send back a fertilizing influence to their fountain-heads, wherever these may be, in the form of interest, and in the support and stimulus which trade and manufactures impart to agricultural industry and agricultural products.

The depositors in Banks are a very miscellaneous body. They belong exclusively to no particular class of society; they are not found exclusively in the country or in the towns.

They are scattered everywhere, and they follow all occupations, and in some instances are engaged in no industrial pursuit. Yet there can be little doubt that this mixed and various body have a general character. They are persons who, over and above their fixed investments and ordinary pecuniary obligations, have certain surplus funds to spare, which it is their advantage to utilize if possible, but which it is necessary or desirable that they should hold in command—that while formally parting with them for sake of some moderate return, they should feel that they still have them on hand, and that they can call them up at any moment, or within some brief period of time. It is obvious that it is only a very peculiar organization which can hope to search out people in this position, supply the exact convenience they require, and command their implicit trust—in short, which can develop, for general economic applications, funds of this description. It is a distinguishing merit of the Scotch Banks that they have developed Bank deposits to a magnitude, and with a universality as regards both locality and classes of individuals, which are unexampled by any similar institutions in the world. Until the wherefore of this result be examined, it is only rashness to pronounce judgment even on so small—and as M. Wolowski, in one of two favourite though contradictory moods, would have it—so microscopic, and almost immaterial a function as the issue of bank-notes.

Let us glance at some of the facts.

Scotland has a population, to take only round numbers, of three millions. She has eleven Banks, and these Banks have altogether 600 branches. There is a Bank office in Scotland for every 5,000, young and old, of the population—a population which, though dense in a few spots, is widely and sparsely distributed over a mountainous and naturally poor country. The advantages and the rarity of this banking development are equally conspicuous.

In the great seats of commerce, in the shipping ports and

the central marts of business, there will always under any system be banks and bankers. The necessity of exchange and credit in such places is too vast and incessant not to call into existence, whatever the law or policy of the State may be, whatever form may be given to or whatever restrictions may be placed by statute on banking institutions, the intermediary agency of dealers in money. But to disseminate this agency, as in Scotland, over all parts of the country, to introduce it into the agriculture and petty trade as well as the grand commerce, and while placing it at the service of the large towns to establish it on the soil—this is a result which is not always nor even customarily attained.

France, which, by the way, is more agricultural than commercial, and has therefore all the greater interest in the distribution of banking agency,* has a population of 40 millions, and in the same proportion as Scotland, should have 80,000 banking offices.

The Bank of France has 60 branches, which is almost six times more than the Bank of England;† and has besides various features in favourable contrast, in our opinion, to the great Bank of our own country. The Bank of France has the monopoly of issue, but it enjoys a freedom of judgment in the exercise of this monopoly, which is impossible under the mechanical rule of the Bank Charter Act of England. Yet withal, it is not in the power of any one Bank, however freely endowed and privileged, to spread itself over

* Recent official documents show that the town population of France is gaining slightly on the rural; but while the larger towns are increasing, the smaller are on the wane. In 1861 the rural population of France was 75.58 per cent., and the urban 24.42 per cent. While the town population of England is computed at four-fifths of the whole population, the town population of France is no more than two-fifths. According to the census of 1871, the proportion of town and rural population in Scotland, including those in the latter "villages," is 57.10 and 42.90.

† The branches of the Bank of England are 11 in number—viz., West End of London, Birmingham, Bristol, Hull, Leeds, Leicester, Liverpool, Manchester, Newcastle, Plymouth, and Portsmouth.

all parts, and to embrace all the various interests of a whole country. Statesmen and financiers lose themselves in the glory of building up a great national Bank (sure enough, without their anxious care, to be established in the capital of every compact commercial country), and of surrounding this national institution with a solitary *prestige* that cripples and prevents the rise of banking companies on a common national model, from which a Bank of England or a Bank of France would only derive additional strength and importance. The monetary resources of a country are only dissipated, neglected, and sterilized by this idea of one Bank, that will direct and absorb all. The object of banking can only be effected fully by a plurality of Banks, exercising the same functions, and established on the basis of an equality of privilege. Banks, like other commercial establishments, acquire a certain *clientelle;* they make for themselves, in the course of time, a certain position; and satisfied with the field which they command, they are apt to care but little for the region, always extending beyond their own circle. The new ground can only be occupied, and all its resources collected and developed, by banking companies sufficiently numerous to incite competition, and by a remaining freedom to institute new companies on a legal equality with existing ones, when the want becomes great and obvious enough to command the necessary capital, co-operation, and responsibility for so important an undertaking.

Scotland, indeed, no longer enjoys the liberty of forming new banking companies. This liberty was struck down by an insidious stab in the Act of 1845. But our Banks had happily been so far multiplied and consolidated ere this prohibition was covertly established as to neutralize for a time its evil consequences; and Scotland may still, therefore, be adduced with propriety as an example of the safe operation and wholesome results of free banking and of a plural issue of bank-notes. The contrast presented by this small corner of the world, in virtue of its banking institutions, to much greater and richer nations, is in some respects very striking.

In the rural districts of France, the attorney, the wine merchant, the private money-lender, and the Jew, still occupy the place of the regular banker ; mortgage is all that exists in lieu of the cash credit; and rude barter still keeps at a distance monetary and civilized exchange.

Napoleon I., on his return from Austerlitz, stopped a little while at Strasburg, where he heard many and loud complaints against the Jews, to whom it was said more than half of the land in Alsatia was mortgaged, and who crushed to the earth proprietors and farmers under claims far beyond the sums which had been lent to them. These complaints became the subject of animated proceedings in the Council of State, and a commission was issued from which the Jews derived at once pecuniary loss and ecclesiastical gain. Jewish creditors were restrained within the limits of the common law of France, but Jewish rabbins were recognized, and a grand Sanhedrim was constituted. Religious equality soothed the appetite of Jewish usury. Some short while after, the eagerness of the Jews to serve the French army in Poland gratuitously caused the French Emperor to exclaim, "See the benefit I have got out of the grand Sanhedrim!"* The Jews, it is to be hoped, have moderated their usury in France since the days of the great Emperor; but the pall of mortgage still covers and sterilizes the soil of that country. The difficulty, cost, and legal perplexity by which pecuniary accommodation is obtained in the rural districts, and the primitive and clumsy form in which much rural business is conducted, are well known. On the other hand, every one can testify that in Scotland the barbarisms of usury and barter, the intervention of legal functionaries, and the class of men who used to be known as "10 per cent. bankers," have disappeared in proportion as the Banks have extended their agencies, and have increased the number of their branches.

* M. De Barante: A Memoir, by M. Guizot.

Nor is this contrast confined to France. Take England, where both private and joint-stock banking are more generally diffused than among our neighbours across the Channel. The inferiority of England to Scotland in banking organization is apparent both in town and country. London, with the Bank of England and its great Joint-Stock Banks, has always great monetary strength. The London Joint-Stock Banks hold vast sums in deposit. But go into the great provincial cities of England, into Manchester or Liverpool, and there see how small are the local banking resources compared with their immense trade and world-wide commercial operations. When a Bank, with only one or two millions of capital and deposits, fails in Liverpool, a great void is felt, which there is no means or resource on the spot to fill up. The reason of this is that the local Banks in England have their seats only in the towns where they are established. They undertake to provide capital where immense capital is in constant demand, without penetrating into districts where capital is in superabundance, and where the number of those who are able to deposit greatly exceeds the number of those who are eager to borrow. The banking system of England, in short, fails to combine town and country as the banking system of Scotland combines them.

The extent to which the Scotch Banks have brought within the circle of mutual advantage the most remote and unpromising districts, and directed the savings of the whole population, on the one hand, into productive relation with its trade and labour on the other, cannot but appear worthy of special notice, as well as of some care in tracing so remarkable a development to its sources.

Any person in Scotland who has a sum, either large or small, £5 and upwards, for which he has no present use, can deposit it within a few miles at most of his dwelling-house, at interest, and at call. It will be paid to him on demand at the same office where he lodges it. He may choose a more permanent form of deposit, and obtain higher interest; but he may also make a cash account of it, and draw and lodge from day to day such sums as may be convenient, and still have interest for the balances daily or monthly at his credit. The capitals thus placed in the Bank offices, though payable where they are deposited, are not sealed to these localities, but are transmitted in part to the great centres of trade, where they are employed in discounting the bills of the merchants and manufacturers. Yet the lending action of the Banks is not confined to the great towns, but is as wide-spread as their system of deposit. The landowner, the farmer, the country shopkeeper or tradesman who requires to equalize the current of his income and his outgoings, finds it easy to obtain the necessary advances. Without any surplus capital to deposit, yet by the admirable contrivance of the cash-credit, and on the strength of good character and of personal securities, a Scotchman can draw and lodge money in small sums, economizing the interest to be paid, and, as Adam Smith remarks, be thus enabled to keep a larger stock of goods, to cultivate a larger farm, or employ a greater amount of labour than an Englishman or Frenchman of equal means could hope to do. A countryman coming into town to replenish his stock of goods does not require to carry money with him. His banker's letter or cheque-book is enough. So also a townsman going into the country to buy corn, cattle, or dairy produce. The business of a cattle market or wool fair in one of our rural villages is conducted with the same facility as the business on the Exchange of the largest city. The confidence and intelligence felt in Glasgow or Edinburgh are communicated to the most distant provinces by a mere sign. A sum of money or fund of credit is equally as powerful hundreds of miles distant as at the place where it is lodged. Wherever there are transactions going on the Scotch Banks push their outworks. At our great country fairs, held on moors or hills at some distance from a town or village, they open tents or booths; and sheep, lambs, or cattle sold are paid for within a few paces of where they stand, without the handling of money by buyer or seller. Such is the elasticity of the Scotch Banking system. Fifty or more years ago country people entrusted their savings to some neighbouring proprietor or large cattle-dealer, who had the advantage of being known to them, while the Banks were as yet too far away to be known. But this irregular banker, of course, often failed, and money then came dropping in forty or fifty miles to the nearest town, where there was a Bank, by the hands of the common carrier. As such contributions increased, the Bank bethought itself of opening a branch in these virgin fields; and where one banking company went another followed. Nearness to depositors is absolutely necessary to confidence. If you seek the custody of people's money, and more especially the money of the shy saving class, you must be known to them, and be seen by them in flesh and blood.

The Scotch Banks, according to their latest annual reports (1872), have £66,727,805 of deposits. The exact population of Scotland by the census of 1871 is 3,360,018—so that the Bank deposits amount as nearly as possible to £20 per head of the population. In the same proportion to populasion, England and Wales should have 450 millions, and France 800 millions sterling of Bank deposits. The amount of Bank deposits in England or France cannot be so exactly discovered as in Scotland. The number of private bankers, and of banking companies which make no public or official return, is considerable in both the former countries. The Bank deposits of London, which are on a gigantic scale, include a large element of foreign capital; and the same may be said of the Bank deposits of Paris. The practice, moreover, of investing spare funds in public securities is more prevalent in England and France than in Scotland, and absorbs in this form much floating capital which in Scotland goes to the Banks. But the fact remains, that England has certainly not attained the same proportion as

Scotland in this particular development of national wealth; while it will be admitted by M. Wolowski, as well as the ablest of his opponents, that 800 millions sterling of Bank deposits utilized, yielding interest to the depositors, and acting fruitfully on all the springs of national production, as in Scotland, would make France a new country, and a greater country relatively than she has probably ever been.*

M. Wolowski never wearies of telling us that it is the amount of their deposits, and not the issue of notes, which explains the utility and success of the Scotch Banks. He sees that these institutions have the custody of immense funds, of actual capital, the product of laborious industry and saving, and that they use them discreetly; and there he stops. He inquires no further. But there is surely the fundamental question, what peculiarity in the constitution, functions, or polity of the Scotch Banks has given them this pre-eminence in the number of their branches, the elasticity of their organization, and the amount of their deposits?

It is unsatisfactory to treat merely with derision the notion that the issue of bank-notes has anything to do with these results. It is still worse to adduce these results as a conclusive proof that the issue of notes is nothing. On the contrary, it is demonstrable that the issue of notes, common to our banking companies, is a prime source of all this solid magnitude and prodigious extension. That which M. Wolowski thinks at once so insignificant, and yet so full of danger, is a mainspring of the machine. It is not only the scaffolding by which the tower of deposits has been reared,

* The vast amount of Bank deposits in Scotland has not hindered a development of the smaller deposits of the working classes in Savings Banks fully equal to the rest of the United Kingdom. Thus the total capital in the National Security Savings Banks in 1871 was £38,905,746, of which £4,119,319 was due to Scotland, considerably more than one-tenth, with one-tenth only of the population. The National Security Savings Banks, moreover, were several years later of being introduced into Scotland than into England.

and which it were unwise to contemn, even were it no longer useful, but which actually keeps the tower always standing and growing. Without the right of issue the Scotch Banks could neither have established so many branches nor afforded such facilities to depositors, and without the branches and these facilities they could never have had the deposits.

M. Wolowski leaves us to infer what lessons he imagines to be conveyed by the Parliamentary return which he has reproduced, showing the number of banks and branches in Scotland at various periods since 1819, &c.; but it is the custom of those who take the same view of the banking question to dwell on the tendency of a general right of issue to multiply Banks to excess, and to reduce Banking to a baneful struggle betwixt a multitude of weak and competing companies. Yet there are two facts plainly written on the face of that table, and these are, that during the last fifty years the number of Banks in Scotland has decreased, while the number of branches only has multiplied. There has been a vast progress in the accumulation of banking resources and the extension of banking agency and operations, which would be more apparent had it been the practice at the earlier dates for the Banks to publish returns of their capital, circulation, and deposits; while at the same time there has been internally, and, as regards the organization of the Banks themselves, an equally great change towards consolidation, and towards the emergence of a few great companies of large capital, and almost national magnitude, in the room of a greater number of local and necessarily weaker Banks. On the 1st of January, 1819, there were 39 Banks in Scotland, and only 97 branches; the same date, 1830, there were 27 Banks, and 145 branches: in 1845, the number of Banks had further diminished to 20, while the branches had increased to 376; and in 1864, this movement had made still further progress, the number of Banks being 13, and the number of branches 591.

This great change, in which our banking system gradually

and spontaneously strengthened itself at the centre, in order to act with greater vigour over the circumference, was brought about partly by the cessation of certain firms, and partly by mutual amalgamations. It appears that since 1819, seventeen banking companies have disappeared, from causes for the most part returned as "not known." One only, the Leith Banking Company, was "placed under sequestration." The Western Bank of Scotland suspended payments in 1857, and was liquidated under voluntary arrangement, every creditor having been paid in full. Since 1819, nearly as many Banks, viz., 15, have joined with other Banks. The Union Bank of Scotland represents the Ship Bank, the Thistle Bank, the Paisley Union Bank, and we know not how many Banks, which had at one period a separate and thriving existence. The Royal Bank, the Commercial, and the Clydesdale have all opened their ranks to other companies. The Banks thus merging in others were either personal firms, such as Sir William Forbes, Edinburgh; Carrick, Brown & Company, Glasgow; and Hunter & Company, Ayr, or small Joint-stock Banks established in provincial districts, or having only a single town as their field of operations. The banking history of Scotland, on the whole, has been singularly free from disaster, and disaster, when it has come, has fallen chiefly on the companies, very slightly on the public. We will show by and by the extent of Bank failures in Scotland; but it must here be observed that the unions and amalgamations shown in this Parliamentary document were, in most instances, carried out on terms advantageous to the companies that were merged in others, their partners receiving stock of the united Bank, and participating in its ampler and richer business. It was not a convulsion, it was not the shock of a wrong or disordered state of things which produced these changes, but the natural growth and tendency of a free system, adapting itself to the progress of the country, to the improvement of communications, by which towns and districts once distant and isolated were brought near the great centres, and to the views of practical men as to the arrangements best fitted to promote stability, economy, and profit.

It is so much the fashion to attribute everything good or safe in banking to legislation, that it ought, perhaps, to be specially pointed out that it was not the Act of 1845 which introduced this process of consolidation among our banking companies. It will be observed that it was in full progress a quarter of a century before Sir Robert Peel began to "amend" the Scottish Banks, and that the fear so often expressed that freedom to form Banks, with right of issue, would cause a multitude of weak banking companies to spring into existence, and deluge and vitiate the circulation with an excess of paper-notes, is entirely chimerical. The reverse of this is what is taught us by the experience of Scotland, where liberty wrought out its perfect work, giving us joint-stock for private Banks, a few large and strong banking companies for many small and weak ones, and unlimited liability for limited. The more the Banks were thus consolidated, and the more they extended and improved their organization, the prompter became the check upon the issue of notes, and the more strictly was the amount of paper in the hands of the public reduced to the level of the essential circulation. So that if there be any danger in freedom and plurality of issue in its inception, it is a danger which always grows less, and very soon disappears.

CHAPTER III.

ORIGIN OF BANKING COMPANIES IN SCOTLAND—CHARACTERISTIC PRINCIPLES ON WHICH THEY WERE FOUNDED—AND THEIR PROGRESS.

It is necessary, before proceeding to consider closely the main question, which seems to us to be raised by the remarks of M. Wolowski—viz., the relation betwixt the function of issuing bank-notes and the development of bank deposits—to follow this distinguished critic on certain points in the history of Scotch banking.

The history of banking in Scotland may truly be described as "philosophy teaching by example." The Scotch Banks had to throw themselves, at their origin, on the lessons of experience. They had to pursue their course under the light of such science as existed, but with the certainty of evolving knowledge and rule at every step in their career. They had no official chart to guide them; they were happily exempt from that State patronage which usually imposes a more than equal weight of State control and State appropriation; and as they were free from all embarrassing relation of being creditors of the Government, so they had no ground of appeal to the factitious aid of the Government in the hour of need. They had to stand or fall from the first by their own merits, by their own ability to pay, and to weather whatever storms of adversity might befall them. In this critical adventure of dealing in money, in loans and credits, and pecuniary obligations, the Scotch Banks come before us simply as other commercial establishments which enter upon any new and untrodden path of industry or commerce.

That their course in these circumstances should be entirely free from mistake or loss is a result not to be expected; but M. Wolowski, in deprecating "the too absolute adhesion" given to the success of the Scotch Banks, seems to overlook the fact, that it is their success, in comparison with similar institutions in other countries, which above all other things distinguishes the Scotch Banks, and which has drawn to them, at various periods, the attention of the world.

England, Ireland, and the United States of America have been devastated time after time by Bank failures. The Banks of Scotland alone, though within the same sphere of commercial and financial influence, have stood firm.

There are two ways of accounting for this fact, one of which is that the Scotch are a superlatively prudent, saving, and industrious people—and on this solution M. Wolowski lays much stress; while the other is, that the system of banking in Scotland must have merits of its own, which are not unworthy of observation and study. Nothing could be more flattering to the proverbial vanity of the Scotch than to have it understood that they have administered an essentially bad banking system with incomparable success by the force of their extraordinary virtue of character alone. Indeed, this view may harmonize only too sweetly with a deep-rooted conviction of our countrymen. But, after giving the utmost credit to the industrial and economic virtue of the Scotch people, it must still be very interesting to know the *modus operandi* of their success in banking.

There are at least three incidents, involving important principles, in which the Scotch Banks differ in their constitution and history from the Banks of most other nations of Europe. In the first place, banking in Scotland was free in its origin and progress from the taint of monopoly. The exclusive right of the Bank of Scotland, our first Bank, was limited to twenty-one years. The Parliament of Scotland appears to have contemplated the formation of more Banks than one, and to have desired only to give the first adventure in banking a fair and reasonable start. The limitation of the period of sole possession of the field by the Bank of

Scotland to twenty-one years, shows conclusively what was in the mind of the Legislature. In the second place, banking was treated in Scotland as a matter of commerce—a matter in which the State was only indirectly concerned—and accordingly was left for its regulation and control to the ordinary commercial law of the country. The object of Banks was deemed to be the promotion of trade, agriculture, and manufactures; their business was among the people; and on the people they were thrown with all their resources, and for all their hopes of success. No attempt was made by the Government to appropriate the capital of the Banks; no restriction was placed on the right of association for banking purposes; nor was it decreed that all Banks but one or more should consist of only six or any other number of partners as in England. Having started with the idea that banking should not be a monopoly, the Parliament of Scotland left the right of banking association open, and was content to let the form and extent of banking association adapt themselves to practical expediency. Its policy was tentative almost to a fault. It did not even distinguish betwixt private bankers and banking companies. The same position which was accorded without question to the Bank of Scotland was left open and available to any individual banker. In the third place, the only trace of legal prohibition to be found in our early banking statutes is that the Banks were required to confine themselves to the business proper of banking, in which business the issue of notes was tacitly, if not expressly, *included.*

These ideas, which are clearly to be read in the Act constituting the Bank of Scotland, had been fermenting, for some time prior to that Act, on the north side of the Tweed. Mr. Paterson, the projector of the Bank of England, which preceded the Bank of Scotland by one year, was a Scotchman; but though in such favour at home as to be elected M.P. by the Dumfries Burghs, the practical initiative had to be made in London. Yet it is doubtful whether

Mr. Paterson's enthusiasm for the founding of Banks would have had a successful response in England save for its lucky coincidence at the moment with urgent necessities of State.

The Bank of England, in point of fact, originated in a Government loan.

The revolution had disorganized the system of taxation and revenue, and, moreover, amidst the troubles which prevailed, had impaired confidence in the stability of the new Government. In this emergency a number of private capitalists had advanced £1,200,000 to the State, and these gentlemen were constituted the Bank of England, with 8 per cent. interest on their loan, and the right of banking and issuing notes. In two years the capital of the Bank, which was really all lent to the Government, and therefore unavailable for the proper business of the corporation, was increased to £2,201,171. In 1708 the Bank, having circulated a million and a half of Exchequer Bills, agreed to withdraw them, with interest due, and also to allow £400,000 to the Government for the renewal of its charter, by which the debt of the Government to the Bank was increased to £3,375,028. The capital of the Bank had, of course, to be increased, and was increased to £4,402,343; but this increase, it will be observed, was not to promote commerce and agriculture, or to carry out the proper and legitimate purposes of banking, so much as to cover amply the debt which had been contracted to the Bank by the Government, and which the Government had spent. What, in these circumstances, could the Government do to reinstate the Bank but increase its privileges and extend its monopoly? It does not appear that things were yet ripe for giving the Bank of England an absolute right of issuing legal tender notes to the extent of the Government debt, but this was the object aimed at indirectly. In the same year, 1708, the Act was passed which prohibited any banking company exceeding the number of six partners from issuing notes payable on demand or in any less time than six months. No banking company or firm in London ventured to issue notes under this Act. Only in the provinces, where the competition of the Bank of England was not felt, did any banking company even of six or fewer partners issue notes. The effect of the Act, therefore, was to secure a practical monopoly of circulation to the notes of the Bank of England. In order to make this creation of the State strong, the English Legislature went out of its way to make all other banking companies weak, and to place the issue of notes, other than that of the Bank of England, on the most narrow and precarious basis. It must add to the astonishment of present times at such a law as this to remember that it actually survived to so very recent a period as 1826, and was only then repealed because the English provincial issues which it had fostered, and which it had alone permitted, had proved in some measure unsound, and especially prejudicial to the issue of the Bank of England! It is unnecessary at present to trace the history of the Bank of England farther; for, as it proceeds, it is the same story repeated and re-repeated—the Government borrowing all the spare funds of the Bank, and, unable to replace its loans, requiring the Bank to increase its capital on the condition of some new privilege. It is curious, however, to remark, and, as contrasted with the different fortune of Scotland, significant of the want of any native and original policy in the sister island, that precisely the same distortion was given to Irish banking as to banking in England. In Ireland a national Bank was also bolstered up, and all other Banks discouraged, even to the application of that most scandalous restriction to six partners, and of course with the same accompaniments of outcry against the unsoundness of paper issues, and of many actual and lamentable banking failures with all their bitter consequences of widespread distress and ruin.

The Bank of France—while we must admit the admirable skill with which its affairs have been conducted, and the wonderful escapes it has made from the political convulsions of the country—labours under the same unhappy destiny of having been regarded and used as an engine of the State. Napoleon I. gave it the monopoly of issue, and required that it should always be ready to discount bills at 4 per cent.! Successive Governments have equally deemed it their right to pounce upon its funds. The advances it was called upon to make to the Provisional Government and to the city of Paris necessitated its suspension of cash payment in 1848; and though it was able in a short time to recover this temporary insolvency, yet, as a permanent feature of its condition, the capital of the Bank is absorbed by the Government, while its privilege and monopoly are an obstacle to the creation and development of other banking agencies.

This catalogue of mingled banking monopoly and disability might be much extended. It has become, indeed, a European system, and has tended to distort the views with which some of the greatest minds approach the treatment of this question. It has given rise to the notion that one great Bank of issue is necessary in every country "to manage the circulation" alone—a notion which, we venture to say, has no foundation either in monetary science or in banking experience. The circulation is always competent, under reasonable conditions, to manage itself, and indeed spurns and defeats every attempt "to manage" it.

Banking in Scotland, then, was happy in its exemption from the impecuniosity of Governments, and in its freedom from the weakening effects of the monopoly and exclusive privilege by which Governments, deeply indebted to their Bankers, have pretended to give compensation in public rights for liabilities which they were unable or unwilling to discharge. The issue of notes, and the presumed preference claim of the State to the profits of paper circulation, have always been eagerly pledged, and have formed the equivalent that has commonly been tabled against the sums which the Government had drawn from the coffers of the

Bank, and from their legitimate purpose, according to the Scotch statutes, of "promoting agriculture, commerce, and manufactures."

The Bank of Scotland, which, constituted in 1695, had been debarred by a clause in the Act from employing its funds in any other way than that of banking, and whose capital was not only preserved intact from State loans, but temporarily exempted from public burdens, began to issue notes and to establish branches in 1696. In 1704, as soon as it had time to become popularly known, it issued notes of the humble denomination of £1. The idea that issue and banking were distinct affairs had not then been conceived. The one followed the other as naturally and inseparably as if they had been parts of the same operation. And so what the Bank of Scotland did, other Banks, which arose, upon the lapse of its monopoly of 21 years, did also. The issue of notes was not even confined to Banks constituted by Act of Parliament or Royal Charter. The private banker deemed it as much a matter of right to issue notes, if he thought proper, and if his customers were willing to take them, as the joint-stock company, created under public sanctions. The issue of notes had neither in theory been blown into the critical importance which has since been attributed to it, nor were its practical advantages in the conduct of banking business so lightly esteemed or blindly ignored as is now the fashion. The issue of notes was in the Scotch mind, and in the eye of the Scotch law, a simple commercial act, which, like buying or selling, requires only the necessary freedom and concurrence of the transactors to render it legitimate. In the absence of the elaborate philosophy that has since been reared on the subject of bank-notes, the law of Scotland a century or two ago could only think of interfering when in any case it should become necessary to enforce the obligation of the issuer. As long as Scotland had a separate Legislature, and for more than a hundred years after its Legislature was united with that of England, and, in short, until 1845, when Sir Robert Peel, on the slender plea of assimilation to English legislation, introduced a different order, all experience in the northern kingdom had only taught the necessity of legislative regulation on three points: (1.) That the note should represent and be resolvable into a certain sum of the standard money of the kingdom; (2.) That the denomination of notes should be limited to £5, as was at one time contemplated, or £1, as has become, with many advantages and without any disadvantages, the established custom; and (3.) That the payment of the notes should be to the bearer on demand.

Simple as all this may seem, it becomes us, in the presence of the undoubted success with which the issue of notes has been conducted in Scotland, to inquire into the reason of the matter before condemning it.

What is a bank-note?

It is a promise to pay a sum of standard money on demand. If such a promise, more especially on the part of great monetary companies established under legal sanction and regulation, is to be prohibited, it is difficult to say what act in the conduct of a banking or commercial house may not fall under an equal ban. May the manager of a bank give an order for money on the cashier? Should the cheque of a merchant on his bank account be allowed to circulate? The payment on demand reduces the credit of the note to the briefest limits. The bank-note does not supersede the money of the realm. On the contrary, it bears a fixed and constant reference to it, while in so far as it becomes a substitute for money in the circulation it takes nothing from the State, seeing that the State does not gain, but only loses by the coinage, and wear and tear, of gold and silver money. Moreover, the bank-note as known in Scotland receives nothing from the State. It is not a legal tender. No one is compelled to take it in payment. Any one may refuse to take it. The credit which puts it in circulation is a property solely of the issuers and users of the note. It has sometimes been said that this freedom to take or refuse bank-notes is more imaginary than real, and that in practice they have a species of forced currency; but we have yet to learn that if the bank-note were not rendered completely acceptable by the established certainty with which it is paid, and with which it sustains its full monetary value, any class of men, however humble or dependent, could be induced to accept it in satisfaction of their just pecuniary claims.

The promissory note-on-demand of the Scotch Banks is thus, in every point of view, an unexceptionable commercial document, peculiarly independent of all State attribute, and presenting no tangible feature *prima facie* to justify State interference, except in the form of necessary legal definition and judicial enforcement.

It was with clear and distinct views in regard to the legal *status* and obligations of the document itself that the issue of bank-notes began in Scotland; but the practical principles which govern the circulation of notes could only be found out from experience; nor was it to be expected that the free use of an instrument of this kind, an experiment hitherto so novel, could be attempted without some mistakes and some failures.

The Bank of Scotland, in its early history, suspended payment three times, and on one of these occasions the suspension lasted six months. These were but the halts and jibbings of a steed yet unused to its traces. Both bankers and people had to be educated to the proper use of bank-notes, and to learn the limits imposed by the sternest facts on their issue. Abuses also arose. Not only banks and bankers, but proprietors of public works issued notes, and issued them for very small sums. These were errors of detail, which required only to arise to be corrected, either by enactment or by a movement of public opinion. They were accordingly effaced, but the principle of banking issue remained. The public have a direct interest in freedom and plurality of issue; but it is not necessary to this interest that everybody should issue notes, or that notes should be of any, however small, denomination.

M. Wolowski quotes Adam Smith as a witness in evidence of the great evils which arose from the ancient constitution of the Scotch Banks; but he does not give a quite fair interpretation of the passage adduced from the "Chapter on Money," while he overlooks the conclusion in which the economist sums up his whole inquiry and argument on the subject, viz.,—"If bankers are restrained from issuing and circulating bank-notes, or notes payable to the bearer, for less than a certain sum, and if they are subjected to the obligation of immediate and unconditional payment of such bank-notes as soon as presented, their trade may, with safety to the public, be rendered in all other respects perfectly free."

The "Chapter on Money" gives a most faithful description of the errors of opinion and practice, and the illusions which arose in regard to the administration of credit in Scotland. But that description applies to the experimental stage of Scotch banking. It was while the Scotch bankers and mercantile classes were groping their way to the light of knowledge and experience that the errors referred to were manifested. The introduction of the "optional clause," by which the payment of bank-notes might be put off for six months, with interest, was a gross innovation which the Legislature very properly prohibited, and which has never been revived. At a time when banking capitals were small in amount, and before deposits, by their very magnitude, had put notes in their proper light and place, it was a natural, but still in any circumstances a very hollow, mistake for a newly-formed bank of issue, or its customers, to imagine that it might go on discounting bills by means of notes. But it was a mistake which could not, in the nature of things, survive. A bank of issue soon learns, if it has not already learned, that the parcels of its own notes which lie behind its counter are not a part of its assets—are not even in any sense banking funds—and that the portion of its notes in circulation belong to its liabilities. When these very elementary facts are mastered, there is an end to all illusion as to what may, and may not, be done by the issue of notes.

CHAPTER IV.

RECORD OF FAILURES OF BANKS OF ISSUE AND NON-ISSUE IN SCOTLAND FROM MIDDLE OF LAST CENTURY TO PRESENT TIME; AND COMPARISON WITH BANK FAILURES IN ENGLAND.

M. Wolowski, it must be confessed, does not rest much on the record of banking failures in Scotland. He admits the general merits and remarkable success of the Scotch Banks; and if he adverts to the errors and dangers which marked the early days of notes-issue in Scotland, not without intent probably to raise suspicion against the system, these form, nevertheless, an invaluable part of the Scotch experience, which has determined so precisely the exact function of bank-notes, and shown so clearly, when this is fully understood, with what safety and utility they may be employed. But we are enabled to supplement largely the detail of banking misadventure in Scotland.

The following Tables, compiled under competent authority, exhibit the whole extent of Bank-failure in Scotland during the reign of free issue. The Imperial Parliament could not obtain this information when it called for the return that has been reproduced in M. Wolowski's work, and that was all he had to guide him as to banking mishaps in Scotland. It will be remembered, of course, that the fall of the Western Bank, the greatest banking disaster that ever befell Scotland, occurred twelve years after the passing of Sir Robert Peel's Act of 1845, the object of which was to amend the evils of Scotch banking by the introduction of restrictions on the issue of bank-notes. With that exception, to which we shall devote a separate chapter, the following, we believe, is the whole Black-Book of Scotch Banking from the middle of last century to the present time:—

I.—*Banks sometime existing in Scotland which failed or stopped payment, but afterwards paid their creditors in full.*

Banks.			Year in which Established.	Failed or Stopped Payment.
Ayr Bank—Douglas, Heron, & Co.			1769	1772
Liabilities at Stoppage, June, 1772—				
Deposits, ...		£300,000 0 0		
Note circulation, ...		220,000 0 0		
Drafts on London correspondents outstanding, ...		600,000 0 0		
		£1,120,000 0 0		
Capital called up,	£130,000 0 0			
Arrears of calls,	25,587 0 0	104,413 0 0		
Assets—				
Cash (no record found)				
Debts at Edinburgh, Dumfries, and Ayr, ...		694,175 0 0		
Of which by partners themselves, .	£400,000 0 0			
Debts at several agencies, . . .		133,788 0 0		
Bills of Exchange, .		409,079 0 0		
Of which became dishonoured, .	180,000 0 0			
		£1,237,042 0 0		
Sum raised after Stoppage upon Redeemable Annuities, . . .		£457,570 0 0		
Number of partners, 225.				
At 31st March, 1804, there had been called up from partners and paid into "Stock Account," .		£248,141 1 7		
And received from them as "Contribution,"		419,867 2 7		
		£668,008 4 2		
The Assets then recoverable were estimated at .	£8,940 6 3			
Debts still due by Bank, . . .	4,329 0 7	4,611 5 8		
Leaving a loss to the partners of		£663,396 18 6		

Banks.	Year in which Established.	Failed or Stopped Payment.
Glasgow Merchant Bank, ...		1772
Glasgow Arms (sequestrated; 5 or 6 partners). Claims ranked, ... £183,000 0 0 Assets of Bank realized about . 113,000 0 0 Compounded for 20s. per £ without interest.	1753	1790
Stirling Banking Company (afterwards sequestrated; 8 partners). Liabilities, ... £251,061 0 0 Assets of Bank at Stoppage, . 218,553 0 0 Private estates valued at . . 90,504 0 0	1777	1826
Andrew George and Andrew Thomson, Glasgow (sequestrated; 3 partners). Debts, ... £64,564 0 0 Assets, ... 69,232 0 0	1785	1794
East Lothian Bank (sequestrated), ... Liabilities, ... £129,191 16 7 Assets, ... 63,185 7 11	1810	1822

II.—*Banks sometime existing in Scotland which failed or stopped payment, and did not pay their creditors in full:—*

* Marked thus were not Banks of Issue.

† Marked thus not known if Banks of Issue.

Banks.	Year in which Established.	Failed or Stopped Payment.
*Thomas Kinnear & Son; retired in 1831, and were joined by David Smith & Co.; new firm, . .	1748	
*Kinnears, Smiths, & Co., ... Liabilities about . . . £320,000, of which Liquidated about . . . 175,000 Short, ... £145,000 [Immediate composition of 11s. per £ to creditors from Company and private estates.]—Mr. James Brown, Trustee.	1831	1834

BANKS.	Year in which Established.	Failed or Stopped Payment.
* Bertram, Gardner, & Co., Edinburgh, existing in .	1778	1793
Liabilities about . . . . £145,000, of which		
Liquidated, say 127,000		
Short, ... £18,000		
[Sequestrated dividend about 17s. 6d. per £.]—Mr. Richard Hotchkis, Trustee.		
Johnston, Smith, & Co., Do.,		1772
† Fordyce, Grant, & Co., Do.,		1772
[Paid about 6s. 6d. per £.]		
Allan & Stewart, ...	1781	
Robert Allan, ...	1791	
* Robert Allan & Son (sequestrated), ...	1800	1834
Liabilities, ... £108,800, of which		
Liquidated about 22,000		
Short, ... £86,800		
[4s. per £ paid to creditors to this date.]—Mr. Robert Christie, Trustee.		
* William Scott, ... existing in	1781	1795
Scott, Smith, Stein, & Co., ...	1795	1812
[Sequestrated; paid 12 per cent.]		
Merchant Bank of Stirling (sequestrated), ...	1784	1804
Funds, £59,000,		
Liabilities, ... 50,140, of which		
Liquidated, ... 34,500		
Short, ... £15,640		
Law expenses great; number of partners originally 6, at stoppage 2.		
[14s. 9d. per £ paid to creditors.]		
Leith Bank—Number of partners originally 18, at stoppage 9.	1792	1842
Total debts about . . . £130,000, of which		
Liquidated, ... 84,000		
Short, ... £46,000		
[12s. 11d. per £ paid to creditors up to 1847;		

Banks.	Year in which Established.	Failed or Stopped Payment.
other 4d. per £ expected from Company and private estates. 5½d. a final dividend paid May, 1849.]—Mr. James Brown, Trustee.		
Renfrewshire Banking Co., Greenock, ... Total debts at failure, . . £226,545, of which Liquidated about . . . 87,500 Short, ... £139,045 Originally 9 partners, at close 3. [From 7s. 6d. to 9s. 2d. per £ paid to creditors.]	1802	1842
Union Bank of Falkirk (sequestrated), ... Liabilities at stoppage, . . £60,000 Ranked, ... £51,998 15 Of which liquidated, . . 24,700 Short, ... £27,298 15 14 partners at commencement, 8 at close. [9s. 6d. per £ paid to creditors.]—Mr. James Russell, Trustee.	1802	1816
Dumfries Commercial Bank, ... 3 partners—James Grace, his son, and another. Liabilities uncertain—believed to be under £20,000. Assets of Bank small. Creditors paid, about 10s. per £.	1804	1808
* David Paterson, of Costerton, . . existing in Liabilities, ... £118,047 6 2 Assets about . . . . 90,000 0 0 [Sequestrated; paid about 14s. per £.]	1804	1813
Inglis, Borthwick, Gilchrist, & Co., ... retired in 1816, and succeeded by	1807	
James Inglis, & Co., ... Liabilities, ... £23,006 18 4 Assets about . . . . 3,000 0 0 [£18,827, 10s. 10d. is included in the £23,006, 18s. 4d. for which other parties were primarily liable. 10s. per £ was paid on the proper debts of the Company.]	1816	1834
Exchange and Deposit Bank, ... John Maberley & Co., Aberdeen (under English fiat of bankruptcy). Debts proved March, 1835,	1819	1832

BANKS.	Year in which Established.	Failed or Stopped Payment
£149,082. Assets realized, £76,669. Both items include the Linen business as well as the Bank. [4s. 2d. per £ paid to creditors. 3d. per £ additional paid November, 1850.]—A. A. Stanfield, 76 Basinghall Street, London, official assignee.		
Shetland Bank—Hay & Ogilvie, Lerwick, . . . The debts amounted to £140,000, of which liquidated £35,000. They issued their own notes till 1827. [Sequestrated. Dividend of 5s. per £ paid. A further small dividend expected.]—Mr. Archibald Forme, Accountant, Trustee.	1821	1842
* James & Robert Watson, Glasgow, ... Liabilities, ... £79,500, of which Liquidated about . . . 19,000 Short, ... £60,500 [Sequestrated. About 4s. 9d. per £ paid.]		1832

In submitting these Tables we freely draw a darker picture of Scotch Banking than M. Wolowski was enabled to pourtray if he had been willing; but the information, having not before been published, is the more valuable, and is welcome to all who wish to study, with whatever view, the history of banking in Scotland.

In the hundred years from 1745 to 1845, when Sir Robert Peel's innovation occurred, and during which hundred years "the constitution of the Scotch Banks," as M. Wolowski observes, "allowed the issue of notes without any limit," 23 banking houses failed in Scotland. Of these, six, involving a greater amount of aggregate liabilities than all the other 17, paid their debts in full. The rest paid compositions varying from 12 per cent. to 17*s.* 6*d.* per pound. With the exception of Douglas, Heron, & Co., at Ayr, the number of partners in these failed banks was small, and was smaller at the period of their failure than they had once been. Thirteen of the 23 were simply private bankers; and several, such as the Merchant Bank of Stirling, the Renfrewshire Banking Company, and the Dumfries Commercial Bank were private bankers in reality, though not in name. The competition betwixt the large Joint-Stock Banks and the private banking firms could not but be trying to the latter, and the weaker and worst managed had, as usual, to go to the wall. But the point most important to be observed, in connection with M. Wolowski's remarks, is, that the issue of notes has no discoverable part in these banking misfortunes. Many of the failed banks were not banks of issue at all; and in the payments ultimately made to the creditors the issuing banks compare most favourably with the non-issuing banks. It has been long the fashion to associate bank failures with the issue of notes; but we have never found, except perhaps in the case of some of the American Banks—which traded on notes alone, committed fraud as regards the contribution of capital, and were probably intended to be a fraud from the beginning—that this accusation is founded on fact. The paper which destroys banks is not their own promissory notes payable on demand, but the paper on which extravagant or unfortunate advances are made to others. The former is limited by a law which no mismanagement can trespass; but the latter, equally whether the discount or advance be in notes or in gold, may increase far beyond not only the cash, but the whole available assets of the Bank. A banker having 300,000 gold pieces to lend may shortly acquire on that basis a portfolio in bills and other securities of a million of gold pieces, because the same money which he lends to-day returns to him as deposits to-morrow, and is useful or profitable only in so far as it can be immediately put out again at interest. It is remarkable that M. Wolowski, when insisting so strongly on the "solid basis of deposits," fails to perceive that not only does the obligation which a bank contracts by deposits differ in no respect from that contracted by its notes in circulation, but that it is the former alone which really affords it that broad margin on which serious danger to its solvency may arise. The issue of notes has thus had to bear a responsibility for bank failures which nowise belongs to it.

Were a list of banking failures in England and Ireland, over the same period as our list of similar failures in Scotland, to be produced, the superiority of the Scotch banking system would be at once apparent.

During the great commercial distress in 1793, when twenty-two commissions in bankruptcy were issued against country bankers in England,* and nearly a hundred were obliged to stop payment†, not a single Bank of any mark in Scotland appears to have given way.

In 1797 an order in Council authorized the Bank of England to suspend the cash payment of its notes, and the Scotch Banks, of course, had in self-defence to follow the same course.‡ The years of the great wars, and the reaction which followed on a return to peace, and the resumption of cash payments, passed without any serious mishap among the Scotch Banks.§ The subsequent history of banking in the three kingdoms till 1845 is told us upon very high official authority. Lord Liverpool, in a letter to the Governor of the Bank of England, in 1826, reviewed the banking question as it appeared to British statesmen in the severe crisis of that time; and Sir Robert Peel, in 1844, resumed the tale, and in his speeches in Parliament filled up

* *History and Principles of Banking.* By James William Gilbart.

† Lord Liverpool's Letter to the Bank of England, Jan. 13, 1826. *Parl. Paper.*

‡ *Memoirs of a Banking House.* By Sir William Forbes, Bart. Pp. 82, 83.

§ The number of commissions in bankruptcy issued against country bankers in England from 1809 to 1830, not to speak of the Banks which temporarily stopped payment, was 311. See *Appendix to Report on Bank Charter*, p. 116.

the catalogue of banking disasters which had marked the crisis of 1837 and subsequent years.

The letter of Lord Liverpool, then Prime Minister, is very remarkable, because it gives the most direct and emphatic testimony of the superior solidity of the Scotch banking system, and frankly acknowledges that the cause of the crisis and of the banking failures that had occurred was to be sought elsewhere than in the issue of notes. Lord Liverpool and his Chancellor of the Exchequer, Mr. Robinson, were of opinion that the principal source of the recent distress was to be found "in the rash spirit of speculation which had pervaded the country for some time, supported, fostered, and encouraged by the country banks." The remedy, therefore, which suggested itself to them, for the future, was "an *improvement* in the circulation of country paper." By "country paper" they evidently meant the bank-note issues, and were so far inattentive to the other and more dangerous paper of unsound bills and advances that would equally have grown up whether there had been an issue of notes by country banks or not. But it will be observed that it was "an improvement," not an extinction of the country issues, which Lord Liverpool and Mr. Robinson recommended. An outcry had been raised for a repeal of the Act that permitted country banks in England to issue one and two pound notes, and for a recurrence to a gold circulation. While thinking that such a measure would be productive of good, Lord Liverpool and Mr. Robinson asserted that "it would by no means go to the root of the evil;" and in support of this assertion they adduced two considerations, which in their opinion were conclusive. *First*, they pointed out that in 1793 the convulsion in the money market, the Bank stoppages, and the commercial distress, had been as extreme as they could well be; and yet at that period there were no one or two pound notes in circulation in England, either by country banks or by the Bank of England. And *secondly*, they adduced "the experience of Scotland, *which*"—and it is well to mark their words—"*has escaped all the convulsions which have occurred in the money market of England for the last thirty-five years*, though Scotland during the whole of that time has had a circulation of one-pound notes, and the small pecuniary transactions of that part of the United Kingdom have been carried on exclusively by means of such notes."

It must be admitted to be extremely difficult to reconcile these facts with the opinion that monetary crises and bank failures have their origin or even an aggravation in the issue of bank-notes payable on demand. The object of the Government in 1826 was to lay its hand on what was undoubtedly a grave and lamentable error of the banking law of England at that period—namely, the most impolitic restriction of banks of issue out of London to not more than six partners. Lord Liverpool and Mr. Robinson saw clearly that this was a law to make country banks of issue weak and unsolid in favour of the Bank of England, that "the improvement in the circulation of country paper" which they sought could only be realized by an improvement in the constitution of country banks; and accordingly the greater part of their communication was employed in persuading the Bank of England Directors to give up their exclusive privilege as to the number of partners engaged in banking beyond a certain distance from the metropolis. The effort of the Government was successful; and in the same year (1826) the Act was passed which permitted banks having more than six partners to carry on business in England at a greater distance than 65 miles from London, *provided that they had no establishment as bankers in London*. But it must be observed that while this was an important reform, it stopped much short of the due line of justice and equality. It still kept up the divorce in banking of the metropolis and the provinces. The town was left under one banking rule and the country under another. The law still condemned all banks of issue in England, other than the Bank of England, to a narrow provincial existence, and, of course, prevented that free and grand movement under which the Banks of Scotland have for the most part become national Banks, and have bound up together the great towns and the rural provinces in the same banking co-operation and solidity. It is not a little amusing, though also somewhat tantalizing, to hear the opponents of the formation of banks on an equal basis, as regards issue and other rights and privileges, exclaiming loudly against the erratic action of the country banks, such as extending their issues and discounts when all monitions at the centre of affairs commend an opposite course, and other irregular and unruly proceedings that entail disaster not only on themselves but on the Bank of England itself, while all the time the exclaimers are forgetful of the fact that this erratic action is largely to be ascribed to the exclusive privileges on the one hand, and the legal disabilities on the other, in which the constitution of banks is involved by their own favourite legislation.

Sir Robert Peel, in bringing forward his banking measures in 1844, had the same dismal report to give of failure among the country banks of England; but he had no similar report to give from Scotland. He held in his hand a return of English Banks which had failed in the years 1839, 1840 1841, 1842, and 1843. They were 82 in number, but though his great argument bore against the issue of notes, which he proposed to place under restraint, only 29 of these broken banks were banks of issue. Well might Mr. Charles Buller, following him in the debate, say that "the argument of the right hon. gentleman appeared to tend more against the system of banking than the issue of notes." *

It will probably be argued that these various crises and disasters arose under a system in which banks were permitted to issue notes, and that if they do not raise a presumption of the evil consequences of such a system, they at least say nothing in its favour. But, in the first place, the

* *Hansard*, Vol. LXXIV., May 20, 1844.

system of issue thus permitted in England is not a system that can be recognized as equivalent to, or based on the same principles as, that of Scotland. It cannot be held to be an example of the operation either of free banking or free issue. Till 1826 banks of six or fewer partners only were allowed to issue. The issue was rendered weak and unsound through the enforced weakness and unsoundness of the mediums of issue. After 1826 banks of issue were still debarred from the metropolis, and from 65 miles round it. They were shut out from the great centre of money and exchange; they had not only to contend against the enormous *prestige* of the Bank of England, but they could not affiliate or combine with metropolitan banking companies; and banks of issue in England have consequently been prevented by law from acquiring the breadth, expansion, and solidity that are necessary to the regular and enlightened exercise of their functions. Such a system cannot be taken as a basis of reasoning on the operation of freedom and plurality of issue. In the second place, when it is considered that the numerous and recurring bank failures in England have not been traced to the issue of notes as their cause, that on the contrary the failures of banks of non-issue have always greatly exceeded the failures of banks of issue, and that in Scotland, where banking and issue were alike free, there has been comparatively the most striking success and prosperity, there are surely in these facts the elements of a conclusive argument in favour of the Scotch system. It is impossible not to be impressed with the repeated proofs of strength and stability displayed by the Scotch Banks in crises when the banking system of England was tottering on the brink of ruin. The merit of this result in our opinion must consist largely in the system, and in nothing else. The English, indeed, are a more speculative people than the Scotch, and speculation may be expected to run to greater riot and excess in the one kingdom than the other. But the fact remains that, as regards those speculative manias which are common to all commercial nations, which no banking system can prevent, and which all banking systems probably and almost unavoidably encourage, nothing has yet been found that keeps them so well in hand, and that passes through them with less injury and disaster, than the system of banking and issue which had been developed on free, liberal, and equal principles in Scotland.*

The difficulty of accounting for a stability so marked as that of the Scotch Banks, under a constitution so much at variance with cherished theories, has led to various attempts to explain it away, and to show that Scotland is a country existing under altogether exceptional conditions. The weightiest of these, and the only one which the Scotch can venture without excessive self-flattery to notice, is, that Scotland is isolated from the great maelstrom of exchange, and that a system of banking which may operate safely enough among the Scotch must not be thought of in the great commercial thoroughfare of England, in London, the capital of the monetary world, where the foreign exchanges act so powerfully, and where all commercial transactions must be balanced. M. Wolowski has caught the infection of this idea, where he speaks of the

* Mr. Gilbart, in his *History and Principles of Banking*, has some excellent remarks on the supposed connexion of the issue of bank-notes and speculation, which he thus concludes:—"All speculation, by increasing the number and amount of commercial transactions, puts into motion a greater quantity of money. This money is supplied by the bankers either in the way of repayment of deposits, or of discounting of bills, or by loans. Now, as increased issues on the part of the Banks are almost simultaneous with a spirit of speculation, it has been inferred that the issue of notes have excited the spirit of speculation, whereas it has been the spirit of speculation that has called out the notes. In the years 1824 and 1825, as the speculation increased, the issues of notes increased; and when the speculations were over, the notes returned. This was the case, not merely in England, but in Scotland, though none of the Scotch Banks sustained the least diminution of public confidence." The cause in this matter, we suspect, has too frequently been mistaken for the effect, and the effect for the cause.

evil of the one-pound note issues as having been deadened "by the isolation of Scotland, and by the continuance of the support that country always meets with in London when she requires to rectify the circulation." Scotland, the contributor to England in so many ways, and the seat of a commercial and manufacturing activity which is certainly not exceeded in any part of the United Kingdom, less exposed to the action of monetary exchange than England herself! Is this a proposition to be seriously advanced? Look at the facts. A large proportion of the land rental of Scotland has to be remitted yearly to the account of the great landowners resident in England. Not only do the Scotch Banks keep from £12,000,000 to £15,000,000 of their funds constantly in London, but the deposits of the National Security and Post Office Savings Banks, amounting to upwards of £4,000,000 sterling, are transmitted to the metropolis, and invested by the Government, like so much free revenue. The Imperial revenue from Scotland, which, in the year ended the 31st March, 1866, amounted to £8,441,677, has annually to go the same road.* There is reason to believe that less than one million of this sum is expended in Scotland, including the costs of collection. The customs' duties collected in Scotland, with a population only one-tenth of that of the United Kingdom, amounted in 1871 to £2,502,127, being one-eighth of the total Customs revenue of the United Kingdom. While Scotland thus bears her full share in imports and in the Customs revenue, her exports to foreign countries are no less active. The iron of Lanarkshire and Ayrshire, and the manufactures of Glasgow and Dundee, must be of some account in the foreign exchanges of the kingdom. Not an ounce of gold comes into London in which Scotland may not be said, indeed, to have a part, because there is not a market in the world to which the goods and manufactures of Scotland do not penetrate.

* *Parliamentary Paper*—Revenue and Taxation—ordered to be printed March 11, 1867.

We scarce know what meaning M. Wolowski may attach to "support." But when a country, a bank, or an individual takes up his own, it is not usually held that he has thereby claimed or received "support." The Scotch Banks only "rectify their circulation" by taking up in London what they have already placed there. So far from Scotland being favourably placed as regards the action of monetary exchange, she labours under obvious disadvantages. Besides having to provide for adverse balances in her foreign trade, she has to remit land rental and Imperial revenue annually to large amounts, from which latter exchanges England is not only exempt, but favoured, by circumstances. In short, Scotland is exposed to a constant, not a merely periodical, drain of the precious metals, and in this respect, indeed, lies under the disadvantage to which all parts of a country distant from the seat of government, of revenue, of expenditure and of monetary settlement, are more or less subject. For, when one thinks of the conditions of the case, the balance of exchange must always be against the provinces and in favour of the metropolis—a fact which only goes to establish the wise policy of an issue of notes by banking companies, which have monetary power and resource not only in the districts, but in the capital and great towns, and are thus able to obviate any undue pressure that may arise from deficiencies of gold and silver in the provinces.

The question whether £5 or £1 notes should be the limit of denomination is immaterial to the main principle. This is a question of custom, of education, of manners—of personal jewellery, so to speak. There are some people who delight to adorn themselves with gold chains and rings, while others are more plain in their attire, and reserve their precious stones and metals for other purposes. Where one-pound notes are issued, the Banks must hold a larger reserve in small coins. It would be vain to lay down a peremptory rule on such a point as this. The English loving a gold sovereign, and disliking a one-pound note, it would be a sheer impertinence to enact that they must take the paper money for which they recognised no use, and feel no predilection. The opinion of Adam Smith in favour of £5 as the lowest bank-note, was most probably, in all the then circumstances, a sound opinion. Were banks of issue to be introduced in France, it might be expedient to adopt the higher limit until at least the popular mind were familiarized with the new system, and public confidence in the issuing banks had been fairly earned and fully established. At the same time it would seem a work of legislative supererogation to prohibit the issue of notes of a lower denomination than £5, since the public custom and liking will infallibly rule the currency of notes.

The Bank of England, in 1826, found it extremely advantageous to discover a box of undestroyed one-pound notes, and to issue them. Jeremiah Harmer, one of the Bank of England magnates, when the question was put to him by a committee of Parliament, "Do you think that the issuing of the one-pound notes did avert a complete drain?" replied, "As far as my judgment goes, it saved the credit of the country."

The value of a paper circulation, when free and plural, does not consist in the saving only of the gold and silver which would otherwise be required, but in the convenience and elasticity it imparts at all times to banking operations, and the calamities which it may be instrumental in averting in particular crises.

CHAPTER V.

SUSPENSION AND LIQUIDATION OF THE WESTERN BANK.

It is not unworthy of remark, that the most signal and disastrous of Bank failures that have befallen Scotland since her first essay in banking, should have occurred thirteen years after the Acts of 1844–5. Though it would be irrational to contend or imply that "the Currency principle," enshrined in these statutes, had any direct part in the troubles of the Western Bank of Scotland, yet the fact that this great banking company did fall, and fall after thirteen years' experience and plenipotence of the new theory, with a crash the like of which had not before been heard in Scotland, must be held in reason to dispose of the high pretensions of the legislation referred to, and to show what a feeble hold it had established, or was capable of establishing, over the evils of which it was contended to be a sure and admirable corrective. The experience of the Western Bank practically negatived the assumed conditions of the "Currency theory" of 1844; while at the same time, as the sequel showed, it proved the inherent and adamantine strength of the banking structure that had been reared in Scotland before this legislative tinkering in currency began, and how impossible it was under such a structure for depositors or note-holders, or any bank creditors, to lose their due.

The fall of the Western Bank of Scotland occurred in one of the decennial crises, which have swept like tempests over the commercial world with such coincidence during the present century, as to be almost as certainly to be looked for as the equinoctial gales; and of whose usual time of appearance the banking companies, both of the present and the past generation, have been sufficiently admonished. The crisis of 1847, brought to a culminating point by railway speculations at home, which the great statesman who had persuaded the Legislature to pass the Currency Law of 1844, did much to impel and nothing to control, had followed in due succession the crisis of 1837, which was largely of American origin; and in 1857, when other ten years had passed away, it was followed in turn by another great crisis, precipitated by American embarrassments and suspensions again. It is probably not of much importance from what point of the compass the storm first breaks on these occasions. The general atmosphere of credit is so explosive, that a spark no sooner flashes from a distant cloud than it encircles, disturbs, and darkens the whole commercial heavens. Sometimes the failure of a single house, as of Overend, Gurney & Co., in 1866, is enough to break up violently a whole course of confidence and transaction which, but for some significant event of this kind, might have proceeded a year or two longer without rupture or collapse. But the course of commercial and financial affairs in the United States, in 1857, bulked largely in the crisis of that year; and to the Western Bank of Scotland—although the prime source of its disaster lay in long-growing evils within—dealt more than one heavy blow in the last critical struggles, which determined the question of the preservation or fall of that great company.

It may be well to describe in a few outlines, the general situation in which the Western Bank met its doom.

On Monday, 12th October, the Bank of England's minimum rate of discount, which had been as high as 6 per cent. during the summer, and at 5½ throughout the month of September, was advanced to 7 per cent.—an unusual figure, betokening circumstances of gravity, if not of immediate danger. The stock of bullion had fallen in the previous week from £10,078,315 to £9,539,510. The private deposits of the Bank had *decreased* by £335,159, while the advances of the Bank on private securities had *increased* from £21,835,843 to £22,398,879. The reserve of unemployed notes, though the notes in circulation remained substantially the same in amount, had decreased from £4,606,040 to £4,024,000.* There had been for some time before, and there still was at this date, a severe and increasing pressure for money in New York; the banks in that city were so strenuously contracting their lines of discount as to produce alarm and panic among the mercantile classes; and gold, through the action of British firms engaged in the American trade, was going from England to the United States. Within ten days the Bank of England again advanced the minimum rate of discount from 7 to 8 per cent. In the Bank return of 24th October, the stock of bullion in the issue department was further reduced to £8,771,105: the effect, however, of the action of the Bank in its own proper department of banking was disclosed in a decrease of advances on private securities of no less than £1,994,282, and a counter increase of no less than £1,596,863 in private deposits; but the Bank had parted with £3,640,585 of its public deposits in payment of the public dividends, reduced its "rest" from £3,959,288 to £3,239,499, and sold of its Government securities £306,066; the result, under all these vast banking changes, of the action of the issue department being that the reserve of unemployed notes in the Bank, following, though in a slightly smaller proportion, the diminished issue deposit of gold, was less by £538,160 than it had been a fortnight before, and stood, 24th October, at £3,485,840. The notes in circulation, though slightly reduced, showed no material change. During this fortnight the advices from the United States were simply lists of the suspension of leading firms, lengthening through all the great cities of the Union, till it seemed to have been resolved, by the mercantile community of the United States, as a general rule of safety to themselves and their creditors, that they should stop, and wait the best or worst that might then arise. The power of the banks over the

* Bank return for the week ending 10th October.

commercial community is great at all times, greater still when they proceed in self-defence to contract the limit of discount usually afforded; but the power of the mercantile community over the banks, when put to the last extremity, is greatest; and in the progress of this movement of mercantile suspension in the United States, it was announced that the Banks of New York and Boston had themselves universally suspended specie payments, and that, in point of fact, suspension was general throughout the American Union. The *Times* of London, and all our leading organs of opinion, welcomed this act of the American Banks on the reasonable ground that it would allay the stricture among the mercantile firms, and give a basis on which all the complications might be most effectually re-solved. In the meantime, mercantile failures of mark were of more and more frequent occurrence in the United Kingdom. The Borough Bank of Liverpool, with a million of paid-up capital, but with a business of deposit and discount little extended beyond the confines of the great port, was in much difficulty. On 26th October, the directors of the Bank of England consented to give assistance to this Bank; but in a few days afterwards, though the other local Banks of Liverpool offered a joint liability, the Bank of England withdrew from its offer of assistance, and the Borough Bank of Liverpool suspended, and passed into liquidation and extinction. On 5th November, the Bank of England raised its minimum rate of discount to 9 per cent. The Bank return of 4th November exhibited, as compared with that of the preceding week, an increase of advances on private securities amounting to no less than £2,223,654, with an increase in private deposits of only £646,684, so that all the advantages gained under these heads by the payment of the dividends had in one week been lost; the issue stock of bullion showed a decrease of £872,014; and the reserve of unemployed notes, from this cause and from an increase of half a million of notes in circulation, was cut down by the large amount of £1,330,525, and stood at only £2,155,315. The state of the Bank of England was reduced to a much lower point than this before the crisis was surmounted; but as the subsequent changes were largely the result of the fall of the Western Bank, they will be recorded with most effect in connection with that event.

The Western Bank of Scotland had all the elements of stability and prosperity that any banking company, apart from management, could possess. Its paid-up capital was a million and a half, the largest banking capital in Scotland but one; and among its leading shareholders were some of the very wealthiest men in the United Kingdom. One advantage of the Bank was not only the undoubted substance of its shareholders, but the fact that its shareholders consisted largely of persons who, in addition to great personal wealth, had extensive industrial and commercial relations, and were capable of securing to the Bank a large and profitable business both of deposit and discount in the richest, most populous, and most productive districts of Scotland. During a long period of years the Western Bank satisfactorily sustained the *prestige* of this position; and in the summer of 1857, so soon to be followed by an autumn of overwhelming catastrophe, there was scarce a ripple on the surface of affairs to indicate the crippled and dangerous position of the Bank. On 24th June, the company held its annual meeting, and declared from the profits of the year a dividend of 9 per cent., with a sum over, to be carried to profit and loss account, now showing a profit balance of £227,000.

The following was the balance-sheet of the Bank for the year ending 27th May, 1857:—

BALANCE SHEET OF THE BOOKS OF THE WESTERN BANK OF SCOTLAND, FOR YEAR ENDING 27th MAY, 1857.*

ASSETS.

	£	s.	d.
Credit Accounts,	£1,932,024	3	1
Bills Discounted,	1,464,492	14	7
Bills for Agencies,	402,005	5	6
Bills of Exchange,	1,006,795	19	0
Bills in the hands of Country Agents,	266,272	19	1
Bills Lodged,	152,803	6	0
Bills Protested,	108,840	16	11
Sundry Debtors,	283,661	16	3
Bank Note Paper,	17,000	0	0
Stamps on hand,	856	4	11
Law Expenses,	3,000	0	0
Property in Miller Street,	49,608	13	9
Government and other Securities,	232,542	7	6
Adjusting Account of Interest,	14,307	7	7
Balances due by sundry Bankers,	108,085	7	2
Do. do. Branches,	594,283	12	1
Balance of Cash on hand,	685,391	10	0
	£7,321,972	3	5

LIABILITIES.

	£	s.	d.	£	s.	d.
Capital of the Bank, paid up,				£1,500,000	0	0
Notes Issued,				1,627,176	10	0
Deposit Money:—						
Deposit Accounts,	£453,381	12	7			
Interest Receipts,	287,737	19	10			
				741,119	12	5
Bills for Collection,				309,157	18	3
Guarantee Fund,	£20,106	13	10			
Rest,	226,777	3	3			
				246,883	17	1
Dividends, Payable 1857,				131,062	10	0
Unclaimed Dividends,				2,418	2	0
Balances due to Sundry Bankers,				49,129	4	3
Do. do. Branches,				2,715,024	9	5
				£7,321,972	3	5

* This form of Balance Sheet differs from that now generally adopted by the Scotch Banks. Instead of presenting the whole state of the Bank, both Head Office and Branches, in a consolidated form, it appears to present only the state of the Head Office, and treating the Branches as separate concerns, sums up its relations with them in "balances due by," and "balances due to Branches." The consequence is, that the total amount of deposits held, and the total amount of the various forms of advances made by the Bank are not brought out as in the Balance Sheets of the Scotch Banks now annually published.

The £50 shares of the Bank, when rarely brought into the market, were selling, about the date of the annual meeting in June, at £84, 5s. But it had been known for some time to a few, and was becoming known to an ever-widening circle, that the Bank had accounts with four or five private firms, sustained from year to year in a wondrous magnitude of business by the resources mainly of the Bank, though having little or no share either in its capital or directorship, and that the accumulating losses on these few accounts, through a lax and inconceivably blind, partial, and shrinking administration, were threatening to absorb the whole paid-up capital and profit reserve of this solid and apparently prosperous company.* It was also known

* It is hard to understand how, under any amount of mismanagement within bounds of explanation, funds equal nearly to the whole Bank capital could be lavished on four or five private firms, having no control over the direction of the Bank, as they were undoubtedly lavished in the case of the Western Bank of Scotland. Mr. Taylor, manager of the Bank, in its downward period, has been made the scapegoat of this monstrous error. But the responsibility is one that cannot be lifted wholly from the body of Directors, however changeable in its constitution, by whom Mr. Taylor was appointed, and under whose eye he was daily acting. There are two facts, in this Western Bank case, worthy of general observation. One of the firms in question, D. and J. Macdonald & Co., as was afterwards proved in the Police Courts of London, in order to conceal the fictitious character of its bills from the management of the Bank, organized an agency in the metropolis to obtain the signatures of sham acceptors of its bills at half-a-crown a piece! The other fact is that the Western Bank, in providing for the discount of the bills of this and similar firms, was in the practice of re-discounting in the London market other bills, for which purpose, of course, the best in its portfolio had to be selected. The amount of re-discounted bills of the Bank, at the date of its suspension, was £1,073,771. There are two obvious rules, therefore, to be observed in the governance of this matter of discount, in comparison with which all restriction of issue and legislation thereupon sink into comparative insignificance, viz., (1) That Bank managers and directorates should take pains to know something of the genuineness of the acceptors as well as the drawers of the bills which they discount, and (2) That they should never part with superior bills in order to pro-

that the Western Bank had established in New York an agency under James Lee & Co., to give the Bank's acceptance to bills of exchange and collateral securities, and had thus, in order to benefit by the higher rates of discount in the American city, wandered a long way out of its proper sphere. This American account loomed the more largely in imagination as the financial disorder in the United States went on. The first visible result of these grounds of distrust was a more frequent offer of Western Bank shares for sale in the Glasgow Stock Exchange, and to this was added a quiet but sapping withdrawal of deposits, felt by the Bank, though not seen by the public. Whatever the losses sustained by a banking company may be, the distrust thereby engendered, in so far as it leads to a withdrawal of deposits, the chief part of its funds, intensely magnifies the difficulty of all effective measures of recovery. This fact was painfully experienced by the Western Bank of Scotland, as the shareholders, however wealthy and potent, were made gradually conscious of the danger of the Bank, and sought in vain a remedy amidst the difficulties, real and imaginary, thickening daily around it. The critical speculation outside, even before it had extended beyond a limited circle, was in this instance a too exact image of the anxious and stormy deliberations in the Bank parlour. On 16th October, it was announced that Mr. John Taylor, manager of the Bank, had resigned his office; that his resignation had been accepted by the directors; and that Mr. J. S. Fleming, who, as law secretary of the Bank for some time, was the first to discover the impending dangers, and in the subsequent proceedings brought a degree of skill and assiduity to the affairs of the Bank only too late of being called into exercise to be crowned with success, had been appointed sole manager *pro tempore*. This announcement simply verified and ex-

vide means of discounting inferior ones. It is only, indeed, from some habitual and systematic inattention to plain and obvious rules of this kind that such a disastrous situation as that of the Western Bank can arise.

tended the adverse presentiment existing in mercantile circles as to the difficulties of the Bank. On 19th October, Western Bank shares were sold in the Glasgow Stock Exchange at £59, a fall of £25 per share on the price at the period of the annual meeting of the Bank in June. On 28th October, when the suspension of the American Banks, the failure of the Borough Bank of Liverpool, and many bankruptcies in Glasgow and other parts of the country, had emerged, the "business done" in Western Bank shares on the Stock Exchange of Glasgow, was "£56, £52, £51;" the closing price being a fall of £8 per share on the value of 19th October. The Directors, upon this disclosure of deepening distrust, closed the transfer books in order that the public might have assurance of the ample means of the advertised and original shareholders.

It will easily be seen, in such circumstances, how little the notes of the Western Bank in circulation, and the right of the Bank to issue, were a source either of danger to the public, or a means to the Bank of the most temporary recovery from its deeply-seated difficulties. The "authorized circulation" of the Bank, by the Act of 1845, was £337,938; and in the *Gazette* return, at the period of the annual meeting of the Bank in 1857—for the four weeks, that is to say, ending 6th June—the "actual circulation" of Western Bank notes was shown to be £458,568, and the average gold and silver held by the Bank during the four weeks, in terms of the Act, to be £174,435, being £53,805 more than the Act required. The question of issue, however important and incalculably valuable in its own relation, is of little account one way or other in presence of the difficulties of banking companies, arising either from some general financial disorder or from special errors of administration within their own spheres of action. The function of issue and circulation proceeds under such difficulties, as it did proceed in the case of the Western Bank amid all the closing agonies of its dissolution, harmlessly to any interest involved in the situation, and yet with all the efficacy that belongs to it as regards the interest of the public. A banking company that has contracted an enormous amount of loss may, by renewal of the bills on which the loss has accrued, and rediscounting the best commercial securities in its possession, conceal for a period its actual condition; but its notes payable at sight are incapable of any manipulation of this kind. On the contrary, the issue of the Western Bank, so far from having had any part from first to last in complicating or embarrassing the affairs of the Bank, was in reality, as must always be the case under such a system of interaction and note-exchanges betwixt banks of issue as obtains in Scotland, the very point of the whole mechanism where the serious impending danger of the Bank was first strongly disclosed to the Bank officials themselves, became positively known to the other banking companies, and so induced the first active measures of relief. In proportion as the Bank, through the successive failure of the five large but unsound firms it had long fostered, was unable by renewal and rediscount of bills to recover even temporarily its lost funds, and in proportion chiefly as depositors, in the growing distrust, withdrew their deposits in Western Bank notes to be lodged a few hours afterwards in the other Banks, the semi-weekly note exchanges in Glasgow became continuously more deeply adverse to the Western Bank, and the balances at every exchange had to be met by Consols or Exchequer Bills. The labouring condition of the Bank was thus primarily and most palpably revealed within the Banking circle itself. Early in October it was resolved by the Edinburgh and Glasgow Banks to place £510,000 in Consols at the credit of the Western Bank, to be repaid within a given period in Consols of the same amount. The transaction was a safe enough one. Consols, in periods of great commercial dissolution and banking difficulty, when capitalists are driven from pillar to post, and do not well know where most safely to place their funds, have a tendency to rise rather than fall, and the Western Bank, in its subsequent liquidation, lost £43,000 by this loan transaction, substantially creditable in its origin to the fraternal spirit of the Scotch Banks.* But this large sum of half a million was not large enough to sustain the Bank. The actual losses it had incurred could be estimated with tolerable approximation; but under the withdrawal of its deposits from day to day, the deficit necessary to be covered in order to maintain it as an active and solvent company became more unfathomable; and when the Western Bank had to appeal to its sister Banks in Scotland for further aid, the question presented itself under less hopeful aspects. It is true that in proportion as the Western Bank was suffering, they were profiting by the transference of deposits; but this was too vague an element of strength, however flattering at the moment, on which to base any *impromptu* rule of common and generous action, and it is hardly to be wondered, in the gloomy excitement and circumstance of the time, that all further appeals of the Western Bank for help to the Scotch Banks were met with refusal. The directors of the Bank applied to other sources of relief, and chiefly to the Bank of England. But the Bank of England, having already in the case of the Borough Bank of Liverpool, the great seaport of England, resiled suddenly from its engagement to extend support even under a guarantee of the leading banking companies of the district, could not be reasonably supposed to have any help to spare for a bank in Scotland—a part of the kingdom which, from the differing character of its banking institutions, is held to be outside the active sympathy and co-operation of the Bank of England.

The idea that the existing system admits of any common centre of banking confidence and resource from which support may be obtained in periods of difficulty, is a simple delusion. Whatever healing influence the Bank of England, with its

* Report of Liquidators of the Western Bank of Scotland, 4th October, 1858.

great and stable resources, might exert in the free and sound judgment of the Court of Directors at such times, is destroyed by the fetter imposed upon it by the Act of 1844; and any one who looks at the circumstances of the Bank of England in October, 1857, must perceive that, reduced to the necessity of resorting to the most extreme measures, not only in high and weekly increased rates of discount, but in forced sales of its Government Securities, and in large drafts from its "rest," in order to maintain a meagre balance of unemployed notes with which to commence the business of each day, the Bank of England was in no position to give help to the Borough Bank of Liverpool, or any other banking company in the kingdom. Before the end of October, it was manifest that there was no hope of relief to the Western Bank of Scotland from without, and that the only means of recovery could come from some great act of power and vigour within.

On Saturday, 7th November, the bills of Messrs. Dennistoun, Cross & Co. of London (A. & J. Dennistoun of Glasgow), were returned unpaid. This firm had no direct connexion whatever with the Western Bank, but, being large dealers in American exchange, the all but universal suspension of payments in the United States had placed them with a free surplus of £900,000 at their last balance, in this painful but temporary dilemma. The whole debts of the firm were paid within a short period with interest. Yet being one of the oldest and wealthiest houses in Glasgow, its failure at this juncture could only have an unfavourable influence on the waning fortunes of the Western Bank; for the public were not slow to conclude, that if the failures in America had compelled Messrs. A. and J. Dennistoun to suspend, all the previously conceived difficulties of the Western Bank, with its American account, and the certain embarrassment of its clients engaged in the American trade, must be greatly aggravated. Monday, 9th November, when this event had become fully known, opened, therefore, with a degree of gloom exceeding all that had gone before. The offices of the Western Bank resumed business as usual, and at the counters there was not more than the ordinary bustle; but the traffickers consisted in larger proportion; first, of some who wanted change for notes; and, second, of others who demanded their deposits. At two o'clock, p.m., the doors of the Bank were closed, and the Directors, after briefly announcing "suspension of payments," immediately issued a circular to the shareholders, which said that they had appealed to all quarters for support, that the principal Scotch Banks, "after conceding assistance to a limited extent, had seen it right to withhold all further aid;" and, as regarded the future, evinced that their views were oscillating betwixt measures for carrying on the business of the Bank, either separately, as it had been, or by amalgamation with some other banking company, or, in the last resort, for liquidation under the Joint-Stock Companies Act. The evening of the 9th was spent in the gravest anxiety by the managers and directors of the Scotch Banks. It was seen that an event so unexampled in the history of Scotland, and in the case of a Bank of such magnitude and repute as the Western Bank, could not fail to produce a great public commotion; and the common resolution adopted in self-preservation, was to draw freely on their funds in London in the purchase of gold coin. One of the Glasgow Banks brought down 300,000 sovereigns, which were conveyed on the 10th, in several waggons, guarded by policemen, from the railway depôt to the head office of the Bank. The whole amount of gold withdrawn from London at the instance of the Scotch Banks, in this emergency, was said to be £1,500,000; but other parts of the kingdom may have caused some proportion of the loss of metallic treasure which the Bank of England sustained, on the fall of the Western Bank, with the suddenness of a thunder-clap from the interior situation alone. The Bank return of 11th November showed the bullion in the issue department to have been reduced during the week by £1,280,995. The total issue of notes, which had been so superfluously high under the Act as thirty-eight millions in 1852, was now only £21,141,065. The private securities had been increased in the week by no less than £3,485,202, while the private deposits had increased by only £1,024,674; and the result, as regarded the true position of the Bank under its Charter of 1844, was that, though the notes in circulation had actually decreased by £83,390, the whole amount of notes in the banking department had fallen from £2,155,315 on 4th November to £957,710 on 11th November. The minimum Bank rate of discount was at once put up, of course, to 10 per cent., whatever good that might do. But the state of the Bank was rendered much worse by the obvious figures showing it could not have had even this small margin of £957,710 of notes, on which to conduct its ordinary banking operations, but for forced sales of its Government Securities to the amount of £675,276. The excitement of the Stock Exchange on 10th, 11th, and 12th November—the broker of the Bank appearing day after day as a more peremptory seller of Consols—was extreme, and a sensible relief was felt when he whispered to the crowd that his transactions were about an end, and that the Bank Act was presently to be set aside. On 13th November the usual Treasury letter, suspending the Bank Charter Act, was published; and the country was allowed to recover some degree of reason and reflection from the nullification of a law incapable of being executed with safety to the Bank of England itself.

The apprehensions of panic entertained by the Scotch Banks, as an immediate consequence of the suspension of the Western, were fully realized. On Tuesday, 10th November, the doors of the Banks were no sooner opened than they were entered by eager and excited depositors demanding payment of their accounts, and in most cases the sums to their credit had to be paid in gold. This movement extended from Glasgow to Edinburgh and other towns, but the main strength of it was directed on the Bank offices in Glasgow. There were some city people who caught the prevailing infection, and carried their whole cash balances about with them in their pockets, or otherwise acted as their own bankers, for several days; but farmers and other country people, brought into the town with engine speed by the trains, were conspicuous among the applicants for gold in payment of their deposits. The Banks resorted to no art of any kind to hold this frenzy in some check, or to allow it time to work itself down. On the contrary, the tellers, becoming excited by the clamours around them, toiled with an energy and rapidity of movement much exceeding their utmost despatch in the liveliest hours of more regular business. On the following day the "run" seemed for some hours to be little abated; but in the course of the afternoon it began to show signs of exhaustion, and on Thursday it entirely subsided; the Banks having fulfilled all demands upon them, only one of their number having been driven into temporary suspension, and that one the one of all others whose circulation, under the Act of 1845, was conducted on a strictly metallic base. The notes of the Banks, indeed, having been the cause of none of the trouble, gave them little or no trouble in the hour of supreme peril. The notes of the Western Bank itself never lost their vitality. There was just a moment, on the announcement of suspension, when some of the tellers in the other Banks were said to have refused the notes of the Western; but this, if it occurred, must have been an act of mere bewilderment and inadvertence. The managers of all the Banks at once met, and resolved to accept the notes of the Western Bank presented to them in payment. The Lord Provost and Magistrates of the city issued a proclamation, in which they declared that not only every note-holder, but every depositor of the Western Bank of Scotland would be paid in full. The Earl of Eglinton, whose eminent public spirit, no less than his extensive possessions in the adjoining county of Ayr, rendered his word a source of confidence in such calamitous circumstances, announced that he would take payment of his rents and other dues as usual in the notes of the Western or any other Scotch Bank. Hundreds of leading firms in Glasgow subscribed and published a document to the same effect; and many of the Glasgow shopkeepers, in the height of the panic, put cards in their windows, "Western Bank notes accepted here." There cannot be said to have been a day or an hour, therefore, through all the alarm and distrust, before or after the suspension, at which the notes of the Western Bank of Scotland did not maintain, in the market and in every form of exchange, their full written value in gold or silver.

The Western Bank, now suspended and drifting betwixt vague and changeful notions of reinstatement and amalgation, swiftly lapsed into voluntary liquidation at the cost, whatever it might prove, of the unlimited liability of the shareholders. A Committee of Investigation was appointed, and at a meeting of the shareholders on 17th December this Committee presented the following vidimus of its affairs at 9th November, the date of the suspension:—

LIABILITIES.

I.	Notes Issued, ...	£720,083	0	0
II.	Deposits—			
	1. Due to General Public, . .	5,043,124	0	0
	2. Due to Shareholders, . .	263,445	0	0
III.	Acceptances and Obligations to Accept, .	920,654	0	0
IV.	Debts to Other Banks on Notes Payable May, 1858, and Balances of Exchange, .	780,640	0	0
V.	Bills Lodged for Collection by Customers, .	61,888	0	0
VI.	Balances due to Banking Correspondents, .	48,327	0	0
VII.	Bills Re-Discounted, . . .	1,073,771	0	0
	Total Liabilities, . .	£8,911,932	0	0

ASSETS.

				ESTIMATED LOSS.		
I. Credit and Overdrawn Accounts, including American Debts and Securities, . .	£3,652,433	0	0	£885,857	0	0
II. Past Due Bills, or Debts in Suspense, . .	970,640	0	0	685,597	0	0
III. Bills Current, . .	4,343,039	0	0	437,945	0	0
IV. Property and Furniture, .	148,987	0	0			
V. Securities Held Against Bank's Acceptances for Customers, . .	919,573	0	0	60,000	0	0
VI. Government and Other Securities, . .	93,471	0	0	22,347	0	0
VII. Life Policies, Valued at .	70,000	0	0			
VIII. Balances Due by Sundry Banking Correspondents, . . .	295,100	0	0			
IX. Cash with Bankers, and on Hand, and Bill Stamps, . .	205,823	0	0			
Gross Assets, .	£10,699,066	0	0			
Estimated Loss, . . .				£2,091,746	0	0
Deduct Estimated Loss in Realizing Assets, . . .	2,091,746	0	0			
Estimated Value of Assets, .	£8,607,320	0	0			
Estimated Deficiency to be Provided for by the Shareholders,	304,612	0	0			
	£8,911,932	0	0			

It will be observed that, while the estimated deficiency in this account of the Committee of Investigation was £304,612, the paid-up capital of the Bank £1,500,000, and the Bank reserve £227,000, had disappeared from the "liabilities," where they had been properly and duly stated in the annual balance-sheet of the Bank in June. So that the Bank had lost its whole capital and reserve, and this £304,692 besides. It was therefore clear that in any effort to resume the business of the Bank the shareholders should have to subscribe a new capital, and resume, after all, with a deficit which, however moderate in amount, was only an estimated deficit, and might turn out to be larger in reality. It was certain, indeed, that the ultimate loss would be much greater under liquidation than under any adequate process of reinstatement, and that the shareholders, being not only unlimitedly liable to refund the whole loss, whatever it might be in any case, but having abundant means by which this liability could be fulfilled, had the strongest possible motive to adopt the course that gave assurance of the least aggravated amount of loss, not to speak of the promise, under a resumption of business, of profit in the future. Various efforts were made among the shareholders to reinstate the Bank and carry on its business. But to any great and resolute operation of this kind, under such discouraging circumstances, the ready consent and vigorous action of the largest and wealthiest shareholders is indispensable; and this was precisely what could not be obtained. The new subscription of capital to the Western Bank by shareholders never rose above £400,000; and on the first of February, 1858, the winding-up of its affairs passed into the hands of four voluntarily appointed Liquidators.*

One of the first duties of the Liquidators was to issue a call on the shareholders sufficient to cover the amount of deficit shown in the report of the Committee of Investigation. The call was £25 per share, payable in two equal instalments of £12, 10*s.* on the 1st of March and 1st of June, and fully realized the object of the Liquidators, having produced by the end of July £439,995. In other words, a

* Robert Lumsden, Charles Gairdner, Samuel Raleigh, and J. S. Fleming. The last-named acted only one year.

call which, supposing the shares to be all equally lively and responsive to a demand of this kind, should have yielded £750,000, yielded promptly nearly two-thirds of the amount. When the Liquidators came in October to present a *vidimus* of the affairs of the Bank at 31st July, it was seen what surprising progress the produce of this call and the accruing assets of the company had enabled them to make in discharging the liabilities, and also, it must be added, how progressively in the same period the losses of the Bank had increased. Nearly two-thirds of the whole claims against the Bank had been paid by the 10th of May; but the estimated deficiency was three times greater than it was conceived to be by the Committee of Investigation. The following was the state of the affairs of the Bank, at 31st July, rendered by the Liquidators:—

LIABILITIES.

		£	s.	d.
I.	Notes Issued, ...	£10,698	10	0
II.	Deposits—			
	1. Due to the Scotch Banks, . .	1,944,472	5	9
	2. Due to General Public, . .	833,863	10	2
	3. Due to Shareholders, . . .	238,182	17	6
	4. Re-deposited since 10th May last, .	95,336	10	10
III.	Acceptances and Obligations to Accept, .	0	0	0
IV.	Debts to other Banks on notes payable May, 1858, and Balances of Exchange, .	0	0	0
V.	Bills lodged for Collection by Customers, .	3,478	14	0
VI.	Balances due to Banking Correspondents, .	5,075	1	7
VII.	Bills Re-discounted, ...	0	0	0
VIII.	Outstanding Letters of Credit and Drafts, .	3,397	7	10
IX.	Interest, subsequent to Nov. 9, Estimated at	300,000	0	0
X.	Loss on Consols, ...	43,000	0	0
	Total Liabilities, . .	£3,477,504	17	8

Assets.

	£	s.	d.	Estimated Loss. £	s.	d.
I. Credit and Overdrawn Accounts, including American Debts and Securities, . .	£2,508,959	10	7	£1,247,064	4	10
II. Past Due Bills, or Debts in Suspense, . .	1,888,475	15	11	1,450,149	10	8
III. Bills Current, . .	405,233	12	7	38,941	7	0
IV. Property and Furniture,	145,209	9	10	35,000	0	0
V. Securities held against Bank's Acceptances for Customers, . .	0	0	0	0	0	0
VI. Government and Other Securities, . .	22,202	5	1	22,202	5	1
VII. Life Policies, valued at .	68,000	0	0	0	0	0
VIII. Arrears of Call of £25 per Share, estimated as likely to produce .	65,088	7	3			
IX. Balances Due by Sundry Banking Correspondents, . . .	16,412	7	3			
X. Cash with Bankers, and on hand, and Bill Stamps, . .	234,416	10	1			
Gross Assets, .	£5,353,997	18	7	£2,793,357	7	7
Deduct Estimated Loss in realizing Assets, . .	2,793,357	7	7			
Estimated value of Assets, .	£2,560,640	11	0			
Estimated Deficiency Falling to be Provided for by the Shareholders, .	916,864	6	8			
	£3,477,504	17	8			

The Liquidators added to their Report the following Schedule, showing, in brief, the amount of Loss as estimated by themselves at 31st July, 1858, and by the Committee of Investigation at 9th November, 1857, respectively:—

	Committee.			Liquidators.		
John Monteith & Co, . .	£276,841	3	5	£339,968	15	10
D. & J. Macdonald & Co., .	147,727	8	2	246,739	17	0
J. & W. Wallace,. . .	140,813	17	2	159,577	19	0
Henry Watson & Co., Watson & M'William, and J. G. Kinnear & Co., ...	99,851	14	10	130,548	5	0
Godfrey, Pattison, & Co., .	42,821	2	6	86,876	16	5
William Smith & Co., . . .	26,484	11	1	34,861	3	10
William Brown & Co., . .	27,600	0	0	31,458	12	1
John Macvicar, . . .	5,671	8	1	27,671	8	1
American Account, . .	60,000	0	0	100,000	0	0
Loss at Branches, . . .	505,333	19	3	585,026	13	1
Government and Other Securities,	22,347	0	0	22,202	5	1
Property and Furniture, . .	0	0	0	35,000	0	0
Sundry Accounts embraced in Branches 1, 2, 3 of the Assets, .	736,253	15	6	993,426	0	3
	£2,091,746	0	0	£2,793,357	15	8
				2,091,746	0	0
Difference, ...				£701,611	15	8

All the minor items of ascertained loss that had occurred in the interval are not embraced in the above schedule; and the Committee of Investigation had not included the interest due on deposits and other liabilities of the Bank on 9th November, whereas the Liquidators had not only taken that liability into account, but had debited their statement of affairs with an estimated sum of £300,000 for interest due subsequent to 9th November. These facts not only explain the disparity betwixt the estimated loss of £701,611 in the above schedule and the estimated deficiency of £916,864 shown in the "vidimus of affairs," to which it was an appendix, but the much more astounding result, when it is roundly stated, that even after exhausting the proceeds of the call of £25 per share, the Liquidators, in their first report, had to present a deficiency three times greater in amount than the deficiency estimated by the Committee of Investigation as necessary to be provided for by the shareholders. It was certain that, under the total suspension and liquidation of the Bank, the losses would increase at every step,—that many even of its otherwise solvent debtors would be driven into bankruptcy or composition,—that the estates of many insolvent debtors would be rendered less productive; and that even the heritable property and securities of the Bank, brought to immediate and necessary sale, could not fail, in all the adverse circumstances, to realize less than their fairest previously estimated value. "As the liquidation proceeded, it became evident," said the Report of the Liquidators, "that the valuations put upon the outstanding assets by the Committee, although at the time apparently just and reasonable, would not be realized. Debtors for large amounts, taken as good, became insolvent; and in almost every instance the dividends realizable from the estates of bankrupts were found to fall short of the Committee's estimates. Besides these, new sources of loss and deficiency were discovered in the process of realization, many of which it was impossible to foresee at the commencement of the liquidation; and although the call was being paid by the shareholders to an extent greater than had been expected, it became impossible to doubt that a second call would be required."

The progress made, however, during the first six months of the liquidation was remarkable in its magnitude, and presented some features which are well worthy of observation. The whole of the Bank's notes payable at sight had been paid and retired, with the exception of £10,698 not presented for payment—a residue that gradually dropped down to £7,028 in 1870, and that, in its absolute diminutiveness, reduces to nothing the popular notion of the gain accruing to banks of issue from the accidental destruction or loss of notes in the hands of the public. The deposits due to the general public were reduced from £5,043,124 to £833,863. This immense relief was largely owing to an arrangement which sprung up betwixt the depositors and the other Scotch Banks, whereby the latter undertook to give credit to depositors of the Western Bank to the amount of their free deposits, upon the latter being transferred as a debt due by the Western to them. Of the more than four millions of deposits due to the public discharged, £1,944,472 appear in the report of 31st July as having thus become due to the Scotch Banks. The large debt contracted to the other Banks, immediately before the suspension, was at the same time extinguished. The acceptances of the Bank, and its obligations to accept, and the bills re-discounted by the Bank, were all run off. The balances due to banking correspondents, and the bills lodged with the Bank for collection, were also paid, with only a trivial exception. In short, the total liabilities of the Bank were reduced from £8,911,932 to £3,477,504 in a few months. The creditors of the Bank, of every kind and degree, were paid principal and interest, with surprising rapidity. The only loss or difficulty experienced fell upon the shareholders, and that now exceeded in aggravation all that had been feared.

The Liquidators, having an estimated deficiency of nearly a million to provide for, after the exhaustion of the first call of £25 per share, resolved to issue a second call for £100 per share, to be paid in one sum, on 1st November, 1858. It was a bold and gigantic measure; but the result proved with what consummate judgment it had been conceived as regarded all the interests of the shareholders, and with what care how such a sacrifice could be borne had been studied. They had estimated the produce of the call of £25 at £505,084; it had already produced £439,995, and it finally did produce, before the liquidation practically closed, £529,408. They now estimated that the call of £100 per share would produce £1,000,000 sterling or more; it had produced by 1st February, 1859, £1,117,627; and it did finally produce, as at 1st February, 1865, £1,477,626, with a further estimated produce of £14,060. The result of this prompt response of the shareholders was, that the Liquidators obtained complete mastery over all the embarrassments of the situation; were enabled to save large sums in accruing interest; and proceeded to devote their chief attention to the realization of the assets of the Bank, and the vindication, in every practicable way, of the available claims and interests of the shareholders. On the 1st February, 1859, the liabilities had been reduced to £1,800,452, with £520,734 of cash on hand; on same date of 1860, the liabilities had been reduced to £550,666, with £204,307 of cash on hand, and estimated valid assets £991,027; in the following year all the liabilities had disappeared, save a few items of notes unpresented for payment, unclaimed letters of credit, deposits, and dividends on shares, amounting in all to £133,506. The estimated loss on assets, on the other hand, had been gradually, though not largely increasing, during all this period. On 1st February, 1860, the estimated loss on assets was £3,007,058; and on same date of 1865, the last report of the official Liquidators, it was £2,926,326. Yet it was obvious, the first year after the call of £100, that the suffering shareholders would have the satisfaction of receiving some considerable return of the vast sums of money they had contributed to the honourable liquidation of the Bank.

The American agency account, that had been a source of much anxiety, and the subject of repeated visits to New York, presented from time to time an increasing estimated deficiency, and was finally wound up in 1869 at a loss of £185,250. Many of the assets, though of smaller amount separately, had a similarly unfavourable result; and actions at law, which the Bank had to defend against protesting shareholders, or to sue against debtors and directors, tended to protract and to increase the expenses of the liquidation.

But the Liquidators, in their report of 1861, were enabled to announce an interim return of £25 per share to the shareholders, and felt warranted in stating that an equal sum in addition would be ultimately restored to all who had paid the calls. The actual returns made to the shareholders were as follows:—

1861.	First return of £25 per share, . .	£282,483	11	2
1862.	Second return of £10 ,, . .	120,155	5	4
,,	Third return of £5 ,, . .	61,802	18	6
1863.	Fourth return of £5 ,, . .	62,362	13	10
,,	Fifth return of £5 ,, . .	63,160	13	4
1865.	Sixth return of £7 10/ ,, . .	96,337	10	0
1867.	Seventh return of £7 10/ ,, . .	98,767	10	0
1868.	Eighth return of £3 ,, . .	39,507	0	0
	Total return of £68 per share,	£824,577	2	2

The capital of the Western Bank was £1,500,000, divided into 30,000 shares of £50 each. But of these there were held directly by the Bank, or indirectly in names of parties for behoof of the Bank, 2,719 shares,—leaving 27,281 shares in the hands of the shareholders. These were held by 1,332 contributories, or partners of the Bank. The 27,281 shares, representing, at the date of the suspension of the Bank, a clear and free paid-up capital of £1,364,050, formed the only basis, therefore, on which the calls could operate. The response to the calls made by these 27,281 shares is shown in the following Abstract from the report of 22d March, 1872:—

On 13,169 shares, the first and second calls were paid in full, and the holders participated in the eighth return.

,, 13,815 shares assigned to the Bank, calls were compromised, including 842 assigned by Directors.

,, 109 shares were in name of parties who proved bankrupt, and whose trustees declined to grant assignation.

,, 40 shares in process of being assigned.

,, 148 shares in arrears of calls to a greater extent than £32 per share of the second call, of which 90 stood in name of trustees either dead or without valid resource.

,, 2,719 shares held by the Bank at the commencement of the Liquidation.

30,000 shares.

The aggregate loss sustained by the shareholders, including charges of interest, expenses of liquidation, and law costs, £88,958, £109,237, and £50,201 respectively (*Liquidator's Report of* 1872), may, in its most rigorous form, be stated thus—

Actual Capital of the Bank, . . .	£1,364,050
Reserve at Credit of Shareholders, . .	227,000
Total Calls paid (1872), £2,049,881, *minus* the Eight Returns, £824,577, ...	1,225,304
	£2,816,354

The law suits of chief importance which the Liquidators either instituted or had to defend, consisted—(1.) Of cases involving the personal liability of Trustees of shareholders for calls; (2.) Of claims of shareholders, who had bought shares under alleged circumstances of misrepresentation, or after the Annual Report of the Bank in June, 1857, which was contended to be a misrepresentation, to be redeemed; and (3.) the claim of the Company itself for redress against Directors on the ground of their responsibility for the mismanagement of its affairs. On the first of these questions, the Supreme Court in Scotland decided by a majority that, where there are no trust funds, Trustees are not personally liable for calls. But the Liquidators appealed from this decision to the House of Lords, and in 1865 the Court of last resort reversed the judgment of the Scotch Court of Session against trustees and in favour of the Bank. Under the second head, a number of shareholders, who deemed themselves specially aggrieved, associated and brought into Court two actions, one at the instance of John Inglis and the other of David Landale, who claimed not only against the Bank, but against individual Directors of the Bank named in their summonses. At the same period the Liquidators had felt bound to institute actions against the Directors in the interest of the Company. It was discovered in this antagonism of claims and counter claims that no progress could be made in disposing of the special case of the associated shareholders till the general question of the liability of Directors was determined; and in this dilemma all the parties—representatives of associated Shareholders, of Directors, and the Liquidators—came together, and agreed to an arrangement by which the Bank was to allow £100 per share to Inglis and Landale, in respect to prior diligence used by them on Directors, and £20 per share to the associated Shareholders and all other Shareholders after June 1857, on the one hand; and that the Directors, parties to the arrangement, on the other hand, were to pay to the Bank the sum of £162,000, and surrender their shares therein, 842 in number, with all their fulfilled burdens of call, to the funds of the liquidation.* This agreement was ratified and carried out. The sum which the Bank thus became bound to pay to Shareholders was £25,500, while it received in payment from Directors £162,000; so that its assets were considerably improved by this settlement. The only Shareholders on substantially the same basis as Inglis and Landale, with whom the Liquidators were now in litigation, were Mr. Addie and Colonel Graham, who allowed their suits to take the full course of law, and after obtaining verdicts of juries in their favour under the direction of the Court of Session, only to be set aside and new trials granted, were finally defeated in 1867 by a judgment of the House of Lords. Under the third head—viz., the responsibility of Directors, the sole remaining case was that of William and James Baird, of Gartsherrie, who had resolutely declined to be parties to the foregoing negotiation, and against whom the Liquidators, after much counsel, determined in January 1863 to issue summonses for £299,736 against William Baird, and

* The Directors, on surrendering their shares, were cut off from participation in the "eight returns" made to the other call-paying Shareholders. So that their total contribution to the liquidation of the Bank consisted of £125 per share on 842 shares, or £105,250, and £160,000 which they became bound to pay under this agreement—in all £265,250.

£863,618 against James Baird. These important actions are "dragging their slow length" very tardily in Court; and though it would be valuable to know what the law of the country is as regards the responsibility of Bank Directors, yet, the only case of this kind emerging from the suspension of the Western Bank having been settled by a voluntary arrangement and sacrifice on the part of Directors themselves, this is not a question on which any substantial or profitable remark can meantime be made.

A question of another kind, involving a suit, not to the Courts of Law, but to the Government, for some time occupied the attention of the Liquidators and the Shareholders, which it would be improper to omit. The Western Bank enjoyed, under the Act of 1845, an "authorized issue" of notes to the amount of £337,938. This authorized issue, founded not on privilege, but on the free attainment of the Bank in circulation prior to 1845, was an asset of the Bank; and had an amalgamation with any other Scotch Bank been effected in 1857 when the difficulties were first manifested, it would have been treated as an asset, and have had a value in the balance-sheet. It occurred to the Liquidators, and to the Shareholders who had successfully paid every debt of the Bank, that this asset remained as valid as it had been; and, whether for the purpose of sale to one or more of the banks of issue in Scotland, or for the purpose of resuming the business of the Bank under the abundantly established solvency of its proprietary, it could be operated upon as rightly and justly as at any former period. But successive Governments, and the Imperial Parliament itself, before which a Bill to this end was brought in the Session of 1864, gave an emphatic negative to this simple and reasonable proposition. The answer given by "My Lords" that "they could not separate the general body of the shareholders from the directors under whose management the troubles of the Bank had occurred," was singularly narrow, mal-appropriate, and inconclusive; because the right of issue in question was claimed in behoof of shareholders who, at their own cost, had retrieved the Bank from all errors and consequences of management, whatever they had been, and was also a part indeed, under the Act of 1845, of the national right of Scotland. But the absoluteness of "the currency theory" of 1844, even after this lapse of time, continued to possess both Government and Legislature with a bigotry impervious alike to considerations of justice or mercy; and the Shareholders of the Western Bank, who had to sustain so many disappointments in their assets, had also to endure, on the same side of their affairs, a petty and profitless theft on the part of the State.

In 1865, the remaining affairs of the Bank passed from the original Liquidators, into the hands of Messrs. M'Clelland and Mackinnon, Accountants; and the last incident to be mentioned is an arrangement in 1870, whereby the whole outstanding liabilities of the Company, amounting to £22,344 were transferred to, and assumed by, the National Bank of Scotland, on a payment to that Bank of £7,448, and a further sum of £1,000 in respect of the estimated interest on their liabilities, £2,267.* The last dregs of Western Bank obligation were thus placed under secure responsibility, and the Company ceased to be a debtor for a farthing, with £51,375 of cash on hand, with the prospect of such driblets as might still accrue from its mass of dishonoured banking assets, viz.,—Credit and Overdrawn Accounts, £1,367,117, and Past-due Bills and Unadjusted Claims, £1,434,596—and such contingency of loss in law expenses or gain in redress

* The liabilities at the date of this arrangement consisted as follows:—

			£	s.	d.
1.	Unpresented Notes,		£7,028	0	0
2.	Unclaimed Letters of Credit,		1,022	10	10
3.	,,	Dividends on the Bank's Stock,	459	11	0
4.	,,	Bills for Collection,	426	0	1
5.	,,	Deposits,	13,408	2	3
			£22,344	4	2

as may be found in its weighty actions against James and William Baird.

Such is the history of the fall of the Western Bank. Though it forms a long chapter, yet an event of such magnitude, and so unprecedented in Scotland, could scarce be treated satisfactorily, in a work of this kind, with less completeness of detail. Not only unprecedented as a banking disaster in Scotland, the liquidation of the Western Bank, whether as regards the colossal amount of obligations, or the promptitude and regularity with which they were discharged, in principal and interest, is perhaps unique in the annals of commerce. That it brought great loss and calamity on the partners of the Bank is manifest. It is no less certain that the creditors of the Bank lost nothing; the noteholders, among all the creditors, if such a degree of comparison may be allowed, less than nothing; and that the partners of the Bank lost all that was really lost. It made some superfluously rich men in the copartnery less rich than they were before, and some moderately rich men comparatively poor; it drove one or two into utter distraction of mind, probably more into a premature grave; and it plunged a larger number into a degree of ruin for the moment which they could have little hope in their after-life to retrieve. It is impossible for any one versant with the circumstances, to recall individual calamities of shareholders of the Western Bank of Scotland without anguish of feeling. But the general result, in a politic sense, attained through all these trials of partners or shareholders, on whom the management of the Bank rested in varying degrees of moral and commercial responsibility, was to prove, in the first place, the perfect security which the Scotch Banks, as they are constituted, afford, even under gross exceptional mismanagement, to the public; and, in the second place, how possible it is, through inattention to mismanagement, growing and widening over a long period of years, that the Bank shareholders, however numerous and wealthy, may find themselves suddenly reduced, in one of the periodical crises of the country, to this extremity. The last conclusion which, with any show of reason, could be drawn from the fate of the Western Bank is, that the note-issue of the Bank had either any part whatever in producing or aggravating the losses of the Bank, or that it failed, whether before or after the suspension, in discharging with altogether wholesome effect its modest but invaluable function in the monetary and banking economy of Scotland.

CHAPTER VI.

RATIONALE OF THE RELATION OF BANKING ISSUE TO THE DEVELOPMENT OF BANK DEPOSITS, AND THE EXTENSION AND WORKABILITY OF BANKING PROCESSES.

It is only grateful to acknowledge the accuracy of M. Wolowski's delineation of many practical features of the Scotch banking system, and the pains he has taken to supply information from authentic sources as to the form in which the Scotch Banks advance money to the public, the terms on which they take deposits, the rate of discount, the semi-weekly exchange of notes betwixt the Banks by which the total issue is effectually controlled, and the liability of shareholders. These are details highly worthy of exposition, and M. Wolowski expounds them with a degree of care and intelligence which leaves little room for animadversion.

But the ground is now sufficiently clear for us to approach the chief error or misconception which runs through the whole of M. Wolowski's treatise, and is prominently advanced in his Chapters IV. and V.

The one object M. Wolowski never loses sight of is to disparage the value to the Scotch Banks of the issue o notes; but he is most unfortunate in his mode of illustration when he places in relief to the note-issues the amount of deposits held by the Banks, since nothing is capable of more certain and irrefragable proof than that it is the right of issue which enables the Banks, in the first place, to offer such advantages as they afford to depositors; in the second place, to establish so many branch banks, which are offices for the collection of deposits; and that, consequently, without the right of issue the Scotch Banks could not have hoped to develop the munificent array of deposits so highly and justly praised by M. Wolowski.

The prominent features in the position of the Scotch Banks are these:—They have 600 branches, and £66,000,000 sterling of deposits in a population of only 3,360,000; and, as M. Wolowski himself informs us, "at a time when the Banks in England afforded to depositors no other advantage beyond that of collecting the scattered sums, while promising for them a security too often deceptive, and facilitating transactions with them, the Scotch Banks soon created the true mechanism of a *Bank office*, as understood in a wide acceptance of the term. They organized, under an ingenious form, the system of deposits and open credits, and combined the increase of disposable resources with the most profitable and the safest employment of the accumulated reserves." Well, these are the strengths, the peculiar and unexampled characteristics, of the Scotch banking system; but M. Wolowski should have inquired more carefully what it is that has enabled the Scotch Banks so greatly to exceed in these respects the banking institutions of other countries. To have looked into all this banking mechanism, counting its treasures, examining all its wheels and springs, and perceiving not without wonder and admiration all its resources and advantages, and yet have failed to discover the key of the whole—nay, to discover it only to despise and throw it away as worthless—is a singular and regrettable act both of omission and commission.

The Queen of Sheba went away from the Court of Solomon with a sinking heart, but her sorrow was the result of the extent of her observations and the accuracy of her conclusions. She had found an unwelcome truth. M. Wolowski retires from the study of the Scotch Banks elated and triumphant, because he has found nothing that jars in the least with his preconceptions.

He contrasts the notes in circulation with the amount of deposits, and sees that relatively they are quite inconsiderable. To make them look still more so, he properly deducts from the notes in circulation the specie which the Banks hold as a guarantee for their conversion on demand, or as a satisfaction to the law of 1845. The £4,500,000 of notes thus dwindle down to £2,000,000 as the measure of the credit which the Banks receive from the public by their notes. "It is easily seen," he says, "how very narrow the margin is." He then applies to the problem the arithmetical rule of fractions. The profit gained by the Banks on these notes does not reach on the average $\frac{3}{4}$ per cent. per annum on their combined capital—taking the actual value of the stock, it scarcely reaches $\frac{3}{8}$ per cent! M. Wolowski thus shaves, and shaves again, till the value of the right of issue becomes under his scalpel truly small. This way of looking at the benefit of bank-notes is original; but it proceeds upon a total misunderstanding of the service which notes render to the Banks, and the inestimable facilities they afford in the collection and economizing of the funds from which the banking profits are derived. The value of the right of issue to the Banks does not consist in the positive profit accruing from their notes in circulation, though this may not be contemptible,* but negatively in relieving them from an

* The direct profit of the Scotch Banks from the issue of notes was thus stated by Mr. Primrose Kennedy, manager of the Ayrshire Bank, before the Parliamentary Committee on Banks of Issue in 1841:—"A banker's profits are derived from two sources—the brokerage upon the deposit money, and the return that he gets from his circulation. We have tried to estimate the amount of deposits in Scotch Banks, and we calculate it at about £30,000,000; that at the brokerage of 1½ per cent. yields £450,000 annually. The currency we will take at £3,000,000, and that at 5 per cent. is £150,000, making a gross sum of £600,000, which is the whole profit derived from banking in Scotland. Out of that are to be deducted the whole of the charges. From those figures it will be perceived that the gross profit of the currency is a fourth part of the gross profits of banking; but the expense that falls upon the currency is not so large as the expense that falls upon the other portions of the banking business, so that I should be inclined to say that upon the average, the profit derived from the circulation bore the proportion of a

absorption of funds that, without the right of issue, would be unavoidable at their branch offices, and from the dislocation and impediment that would be thrown into the whole system of deposit as organized in Scotland.

In the early history of banks, while their deposits are yet small in amount, the notes which their transactions enable them to put into circulation may form comparatively a considerable element of their total profits; but as the amount of deposits increase, the note-circulation, while continuing to perform a most important and invaluable function, necessarily withdraws, as far as figures are concerned, into the background, and becomes a small fraction of the credit which the banks receive from the public. Notes are then seen, from the bank accounts, in their true light as mere instruments for the conveyance of the immense funds which pass under the care and management of the banks. While the Scotch Banks have £66,000,000 sterling of deposits, their note circulation has not been known to rise above four-and-a-half millions. But this great disproportion, which is the test and proof of the soundness of the system, should not blind us to the actual relation which the right of issue bears to the accumulation of deposits, and the arrest which would instantly be placed on the latter were the former withdrawn.

The question is very simple, and turns upon such obvious matters of fact and expediency, that it may be made plain and evident to every understanding.

The Scotch Banks have become the receptacles of such an enormous mass of deposits, because they have held out every motive of profit, economy, and convenience to de-

third to the aggregate profit of banking."—*Minutes of Evidence*, p. 200. The larger reserve of gold and silver required by the Act of 1845 has no doubt increased the charge on the note circulation since Mr. Kennedy gave this evidence; and it will be observed that as the deposits increase the proportion of the profit from notes to the aggregate profit of banking diminishes. The deposits have doubled since 1845, but the circulation of notes has increased in a much smaller degree.

positors. They not only pay interest on all sums lodged with them, but afford the utmost freedom and facility to depositors in drawing and lodging, in paying from and repaying back into their account with the Bank, the sums at their disposal. A bank depositor in Scotland feels that his money is still in his possession while he has parted with it to the Bank, and while he is obtaining interest on the sums at his credit with the Bank. Those who have large or moderate amounts of money, which they can lodge on deposit receipt, have the benefit of a special arrangement whereby they are allowed a larger interest than is given for deposits on open account. But this class alone could not have filled the coffers of the Banks, which have consequently always sought to get into relations with the people of business who have daily cash transactions, and whose custom is a source of profit to the Banks in more than one form. Hence the liberal terms conceded to open deposit accounts, hence the interest on monthly or daily balances as may suit the depositor, and hence the cash credits in which the transactions, though beginning with a debt to the Bank upon adequate security, ripen, under the industry and frugality of the creditor, into a balance on the other side, and become the source of increased deposits and extending business to the Banks. By these means the Scotch Banks have attracted deposits from every source; they have not only gathered depositors, but have created them; and, while offering a secure lodgment to the realized savings of the country, they have not been inattentive to the new industries and the new men rising up, whose labour and aptitude only required the aid of capital to render them productive, and to increase in due time the aggregate amount of deposits.

Yet all these advantages and inducements to depositors would not have sufficed unless the Banks had taken a still further step, and gone down into the country, opening branches, and extending on every hand their agency and organization. An office in one or two of the larger towns could never have brought them into contact with the mass of depositors even on deposit receipts, while it would have been physically impossible to open the multitude of deposit accounts which have brought the Banks into relation with the money and traffic of nearly the whole population. It must be observed that, as regards the large capitalists in Scotland, the Scotch Banks suffer a formidable diversion of the funds which would otherwise be deposited in their coffers from the competition of the London money-market, and the identity of Scotch and English commerce and means of investment. The Scotch deposits in England amount to many millions; but English deposits in Scotland are scarcely known. The great bulk of the deposits of the Scotch Banks are contributed by people of moderate means. They consist largely of the savings and surplus funds of classes of society just above those who carry their small sums to the National Savings Banks. To place themselves in relation with, and secure the confidence of the popular masses, it was necessary that the Scotch Banks should popularize their business—in other words, that they should open branches in all parts of the country at which the same facilities and advantages should be offered, and the same relations be established and fostered as at their head offices.

The question, therefore, which we have to ask M. Wolowski to consider is, how all these relations could be formed, all these engagements met, all these obligations fulfilled, and how all this mechanism could stand, but for the facility and resource afforded by the issue of notes? Let him take in the various conditions of the problem, and give us the solution. In the first place, every pound of the £66,000,000 sterling of deposits held by the Scotch Banks bears interest. Yet the Banks cannot, without loss, pay interest on funds which they are not at liberty to put to a profitable use, and if to be utilized, the funds cannot be left idle in the cash-boxes of 600 branch offices. The difference betwixt the rate of interest paid by the Banks on deposits and the rate of discount charged by the Banks on bills and credits is never more, sometimes less, than from 1½ to 2 per cent.; so that, if any profit is to accrue to the Banks, even the reserve which the Banks hold against the demands of depositors must be invested as far as possible in profit-bearing securities. In the second place, the great bulk of the deposits held by the Scotch Banks is at call. The depositor may walk into the Bank office at any moment and demand his money in whole or in part. There are various rates of interest as the deposit happens to be lodged on a receipt or in open account, but there is no deviation from the rule in Scotland that deposits of every class and amount shall be paid on demand. The notes of the Scotch Banks, while in practice paid at the branches, are legally payable only at the head offices; but deposits are payable on call at the offices where they are lodged. It would shake confidence utterly were a depositor in a country town to be told, when he called for his money, that he must wait till a remittance be brought down from Edinburgh, Glasgow, or London. These two conditions, of interest on the money lodged and repayment on demand, may fairly be pronounced essential to the introduction and extension of a system of deposit among the great body of the people. The rich capitalist or merchant may be induced to reason differently, and to conform to other arrangements; but the commonalty will not readily part with their surplus money on less stringent conditions. Then, in the third place, this liability to depositors has to be sustained at all the offices of the Banks. The 600 branches are like 600 points of attack, at each of which the Banks must be equally fortified, and equally ready to fulfil their engagements. There is in all this what seems an inextricable difficulty. Can the funds lodged by depositors be employed and turned into a source of profit by the Banks, and yet be always drawable by the depositors at the same time? Can they by any possible means be in two places at once? The truth is, that the great difficulty thus presented, and otherwise insurmountable, is surmounted in Scotland, and has never been a difficulty at all, because the Banks pay their depositors in their own notes. The right of issue solves the whole question, and solves it in the most simple and satisfactory way. The notes do not relieve the Banks from payment, since they pass immediately in the course of the circulation into the note exchanges at Edinburgh and Glasgow, where they are either paid by counter claims of the head office, by Exchequer Bills, or a draft on London. On the other hand, the notes perfectly satisfy the depositor. If he has a debt to pay, or a purchase to make, or a deposit to lodge in another bank, they are as available for his purpose as gold. The Banks are thus delivered from the necessity of keeping a large and indefinite reserve of cash at each of their branches, and enabled, by concentrating their banking reserve, to place the funds on which they rely to meet the demands of depositors in a productive, while at the same time immediately accessible form. The notes given out at the branches are issued against, and act upon a reserve which may be lying at the head office hundreds of miles distant, in the form of Exchequer Bills or Consols yielding interest, or on money deposited at interest in London. No safe source of profit in this arrangement is lost; and it is because the Banks are at liberty to make much out of the funds at their disposal that they are enabled to give such liberal terms to depositors.

Without the right of issue how great would be the difference, and how completely would the whole problem be changed! The Banks in that case would be thrown back on the money of the kingdom, whatever it might be, gold coins or Bank of England or State legal tender, for which an equivalent value should have to be given. Of this money a large stock would have to be kept at all the branches, the amount thus kept on hand having to be increased beyond what might even be a sufficient proportion—first, on account of the uncertainty of the demands to be provided against; and, secondly, on account of the impossibility, owing to the distance of the banking offices from the source of issue, of quickly obtaining a further supply when necessary. The absorption of the funds of the Banks would thus be enormous. The 600 offices of the Scotch Banks would in all probability require to keep idle in their tills not less than one-third of the whole deposits; and if one-third or any nearly as large a proportion of the deposits had thus to be kept in the form of unused money, it is clear that the Banks could not pay interest to depositors—could not afford those facilities of drawing on accounts which have hitherto been enjoyed, and could not defray the expenses of the branches. They would not only lose the profit that accrues to them when their notes go into circulation, but they would suffer the greater loss of having £15,000,000 or £20,000,000 of their deposits sterilized. Take away the right of issue, and the Scotch Banks would either have to withdraw most of their branches in the rural districts, or to propose a lower interest and less promptitude of repayment to depositors; but in either case the shock given to the deposit system and the diminution of deposits would be inevitable.

People may say many things against the system of banking thus supported and developed in Scotland by virtue of bank-notes. They may say that this intense gathering together of deposits is carrying penuriousness too far, that it is scraping up the dregs of public wealth, and that the trade and industry of the country should not depend for loans and discounts on funds that are collected by such elaborate means from so many small sources. It may be said that capital should not be made too abundant, and that an excess even of capital is not desirable. Or, adopting another line of objection, it may be complained that the branches of the Banks are a costly agency, and that the merchant has to pay in the discount and other charges of the Banks for this elaborate organization of banking offices, each occupying a somewhat stately building, and employing a manager and accountant in small towns to do very little work. Some may no doubt think that they lose on both hands, and that while the immense loanable funds developed by the Banks in Scotland are not cheap to those who borrow them, they call into the field against the larger mercantile establishments a host of competitors. We have heard from the lips of Glasgow merchants something which conveyed to our ears that they would both have easier terms from the Banks and more complete possession and control of their own departments of business, if the Bank deposits in Scotland were of smaller amount, and if one-half of the branch offices were abolished. But, whatever may be said against the Scotch banking system, there is one argument that cannot be used. It cannot be permitted to point to the magnificent aggregation of deposits, and to admire the virtues of character which have called them into existence, and which in return they have strengthened and fostered in the Scotch population, and at the same time to depreciate or condemn the right of issue; for the two things are inseparable. And this is the inconsistency into which M. Wolowski has fallen.

The value of the right of issue by banks, constituted on a free and equal basis, consist principally in the facility it affords for concentrating and economizing the banking funds of the country. Its action on time and space in the conduct of banking business may be likened to that of the telegraph in the general affairs of the world. By these little pieces of paper the Bank practically pays at its most distant branches the funds which are reserved and utilized in the centres of monetary business. The effect of this on the general economy and administration of banking is talismanic. It enables to be done through all the various departments of banking business, from the first act of deposit upwards, what is otherwise simply impossible.

If there be any ground, therefore, on which the issue of notes payable at sight by banking companies may be condemned, let it be understood in what the function and advantages of such issue consist, and what must be lost by its rejection or suppression.

CHAPTER VII.

THE ACT OF 1845—HOW THE OPPOSITION TO IT IN SCOTLAND WAS OVERCOME—AND ITS EFFECTS ON THE SCOTCH BANKING SYSTEM.

It is unnecessary to track an obvious misconception, as to the true place and merit of issue in the Scotch banking system, too doggedly through all its windings. That the issue of bank-notes has caused disasters in Scotland, that the profit of issue is insignificant, and that the withdrawal of issue would make no material difference in the position or profits of the Scotch Banks, are statements which, however frequently they recur, need not occupy us more.

But M. Wolowski hazards the further assertion that "the Act of 1845 in no way modified the essential features of the constitution of the Scotch Banks." This assertion, though justifiable in the main, must be received *cum grano salis.*

The Act of 1845 cannot be well understood without reverting to the principles of the Bank of England Charter Act of 1844, and the extra-Parliamentary transactions which led Sir Robert Peel to compromise, as regards Scotland, the application of these principles.

Under Sir Robert Peel the banking legislation of England took a great stride forward in the direction of a new theory, that had been slowly forming from the period of the Bullion Committee, with respect to "paper-money" and its relation to the foreign exchanges. The issue of notes especially was placed on an entirely new footing. It had hitherto been a monopoly, free and unrestrained as regards the law, in the hands of the Bank of England, within certain local bounds. It was now to become a State issue conducted through the agency only of the Bank of England. The Bank was to be deprived of all power, though not of all profit, in the matter. It was conceived, in short, that the issue of bank-notes is a prerogative of the State, that the strong and direct action of the State can alone keep the issue under proper control, and that the State, moreover, is entitled to any profit accruing from the circulation of notes. The State had up to this time been content, in consideration of certain loans and debts which it could not or would not repay, to give the Bank a monopoly of issue, and to guard this monopoly by the most invidious and impolitic legislation as regarded all other banking companies. It now conceived the idea of converting the issue of notes into a source of annual revenue.

Sir Robert Peel's opinions, indeed, went wider and deeper than this. He had a notion that the issue of notes, when left in the hands of banking companies, have an irrepressible tendency to over-issue, even though payable on demand;* that from such over-issue an inflation of prices ensues; that imports of foreign commodities are thereby factitiously encouraged, while exports are discouraged, and that this leads to adverse exchanges and a drain of bullion which threaten periodically the security of the bank-note, as well as the whole superstructure of credit.

We are careful to state these grounds of the law of 1844, because, though we do not mean to examine them just now, we may advert to them before we conclude.

What we wish to bring into the foreground at present is the fact, not always recognized, that the design and effect of the Act of 1844 was to introduce a State issue of notes. This was the fundamental idea of the new system.

But it was soon found impossible to travel far in the line of this idea, without encountering insuperable obstacles, not only in existing customs and institutions, but in the working

* This was a very different opinion from that reported and demonstrated by the Bullion Committee, which had reference solely to the action of *inconvertible* bank-notes during the operation of the Bank Restriction Act,—an Act authorizing the Suspension of Cash Payments.

of the theory itself. When gold sovereigns or other coins are issued from the Royal Mint, they go forth and do their work without further care or obligation on the part of the State, and only require to be gradually withdrawn at certain periods when they have become too much worn or defaced. But notes convertible on demand are constantly coming in for payment, and a large reserve of cash has to be kept and replenished in order to pay them. The average currency of a bank-note in Scotland is ten or eleven days. Every fortnight at least the Scotch Banks have to retire an amount of their notes fully equal to their average circulation. While it may be convenient enough for the State to issue notes, it is not so convenient to undertake the responsibility of paying them, and, in periods of adverse foreign exchanges, of paying them in bullion. It is no part, indeed, of the functions of a well-regulated Government to enter upon a traffic of this nature. No State, that has a proper regard to its financial integrity, will readily assume the obligation of paying the convertible paper currency circulating throughout its dominions; nor will any intelligent public, considering the ready power with which a State can always suspend postpone, or evade its obligations, be desirous to place its paper currency on such a basis. Suspension of cash payments would probably be much more frequent, the reign of legal tender more absolute, and the inconvertibility of notes more the rule than the exception under the assumption by the State of the issue and payment of notes than under any other system. The commercial liability of banking companies to convert their notes on demand, to which the State stands simply in the relation of executor of legal obligations, seems to offer a more sure and more powerful lever for maintaining the convertibility of the bank-note, than any other contrivance consistent with any moderate freedom and flexibility of issue. Since there is a constant danger of the metallic reserves diminishing and disappearing under the operation of a commercial activity, fostered and stimulated by bank-credits and discounts, it appears but good policy, in the first place, that the responsibility of maintaining the metallic reserves should be laid on the shoulders of some practical and potential interests directly concerned—that it should not be left to chance, or even to quasi-natural law filtrated through the individual action of everybody, which is but too apt to result in its being the serious care of nobody, but that it should rest on such distinct agencies as have at once a lively sense of the responsibility, an immediate interest in studying it, and the means to fulfil it; and, in the second place, that this responsibility should, above all, devolve upon those who, by their administration of credit, have so much influence whether in accumulating or dispersing the reserves of bullion. In a word, that note-issues and banking, in their interdepending relations, are clearly fitted, not to say destined, to go together, and to be conjoined in the same corporate responsibilities.

The old Scotch system of freedom and plurality of issue is thus more firmly knit, and presents a stronger side to all points of the monetary difficulty, than the school to which M. Wolowski belongs have hitherto recognized.

The difficulty of devising any mechanism which responds so well and so fully to all the requirements of a sound paper currency and a sound administration of credit, is at once felt when it is attempted to carry out other theories. The obstacles to a State issue of notes, to be converted by the State into gold and silver on demand, are apparent and incontestable. The State may issue, but it cannot undertake to pay, without imminent danger of introducing confusion at once into the public and commercial finances.

In this dilemma Sir Robert Peel, with his usual adroit statesmanship, made use of existing circumstances while advancing on the line of his own theory. He resolved to abolish the power of issue hitherto exercised by the Bank of England, but to make the Bank of England the medium of a State issue of notes, from the circulation of which the

State should derive a certain share of profit. The monopoly of issue hitherto accorded to the Bank of England by Act of Parliament, and extended and buttressed by various legal provisions, made the transition to the new system easy and simple. The Bank had the whole circulation of the metropolis, and besides, competed in the provinces against banks of issue that were directly hampered and disabled by statute; it had already all the *prestige* of a great national and State Bank. To introduce the new system required only a mechanical separation of the issue and banking departments, and a change in the form of stating the weekly Bank of England account. As for the liability to pay the notes, Sir Robert Peel adopted what cannot but be regarded as an ingenious *per saltum* solution of a grave difficulty. The State could not undertake to pay the notes, but the next best artifice was to lay down a fixed rule by which, in all probability and under all supposable circumstances, the notes would be able to pay themselves. For the *data* of this hasty solution, Sir Robert Peel only inquired what was the lowest point below which the notes in circulation had not at any time been known to recede, and, having ascertained this, he fixed it arbitrarily as the measure of "the authorized issue"—*i.e.*, of the amount of notes which should be issued without any further guarantee than an equivalent deposit, in the issue department, of Government securities. Beyond this limit notes were only to be issued on a deposit of bullion.

Such was the Act of 1844. It was a law not only to substitute a sole and central issue for a plural issue, but to establish a State issue from which the State would derive some modicum of profit without entailing upon itself any inconvenient obligation—an issue that would regulate itself, and impose no care or responsibility on any one, beyond the caution, the alarm, or panic that might be produced in certain crises through high advances of the rate of discount, and a constantly diminishing amount of paper currency.

The application of this system in England encountered little difficulty. The provincial banks of issue were allowed to continue to send out notes to the amount of their attained circulation in previous years, but not beyond this amount, even on the basis of bullion, or on any condition; while various provisions were made to facilitate the gradual lapse and extinction of all country issues even on the narrow and restricted basis which was thus tolerated for a period. The time was looked upon as not remote when the system would be wholly perfected in England, and when a State issue of notes, on this self-acting principle, would prevail solely and universally in that part of the United Kingdom.

But Scotland presented a more difficult field for monetary innovation and experiment. Not only could no abuse be alleged against the Scotch banking system, but Scotland had no such framework of monopoly as that on which it was so easy to engraft a State issue in England.

The Act of 1844 having acquainted the whole country with the general principles on which Sir Robert Peel deemed it necessary to legislate, much interest and ferment, and among the bankers not a little anxiety, arose north the Tweed as to the mode in which the great statesman would seek to apply these principles in Scotland. The right of banking companies to issue, and, in particular, the one-pound notes, which were thought to be in peculiar danger, were again defended through the columns of the press with all the vigour of Sir Walter Scott, in his letters of "Malachi Malagrowther," at a former period.* Sir Robert Peel, however, kept his own counsel. No one was allowed to know what his precise propositions with respect to Scotland would be. He called upon the Banks for returns of their notes in circulation; and the Banks, fearing that their notes were going

* Among others, Hugh Miller, who had been in early life a bank clerk, published a series of articles in the *Witness*, marked by all his usual beauty and lucidity of style, in defence of the Scotch banking system in its more simple and practical features.

to be taxed for the profit of the State, returned the *minimum* circulation, when, as the result showed, the *maximum* would have suited their interest better. It was not, however, until a deputation from nearly all the banking companies of Scotland went up to London that the Act of 1845 took final shape in the hands of the Prime Minister. It should moderate the weight which M. Wolowski seems to attach to the opinions given in 1856 by the five Edinburgh Banks in favour of the Act of 1845, to know that the representatives of the same great companies had not only given the strongest evidence to the Committee on Banks of Issue in 1841 in favour of the Scotch system in all its integrity, but that they heartily concurred, up to a certain point in their negotiations with Sir Robert Peel, in the opposition given from Scotland to the legislation pending in 1845.

The Minister, in point of fact, had two grand concessions in the matter of issue, by which he hoped to secure the assent, or at least quiescence, of the Scotch Banks. In the first place, he proposed to distinguish betwixt them and the provincial banks of issue in England in so far as to allow them to increase their issue above the "authorized" or antecedent amount, on condition that they should hold an equivalent reserve in specie. The plurality of Scotch Banks gave him no opportunity of forming a common issue department as in England, but he might have forced on the Scotch Banks, and on the circulation of Scotland, the "legal tender" paper of the Bank of England as the only provision for future expansion. On the other hand, he said to the Scotch Banks, "I not only allow you to issue as many notes as you have hitherto circulated, but as many more as you can on the basis of a reserve of specie which you shall each hold for yourselves." When it is considered that the Scotch Banks were already in the practice of holding reserves of specie, and that the whole amount of these would reckon under the new law as a basis for increasing the circulation, which neither much nor rapidly increases under any circumstances, it must be admitted that this was putting the very finest point on innovation. But the master-stroke of Peel, in his interviews with the Scotch Banks, was yet to come. He said to them, "While I propose to lay very slight fetters, if fetters they can be called, on you, I will bind with iron rods all who might in the future venture to compete with you. I will prohibit the issue of notes in Scotland on any conditions now and henceforth, by any others than yourselves." A monopoly of issue, which was more than likely to result, and which, as the event proves, has resulted in a monopoly of the whole banking business of Scotland, was not a small concession. It was one of those good things that cause the teeth even of patriots to water; and so the representatives of the Scotch Banks, who had gone to London in the spirit of the heroes of Bannockburn, smiled upon the good Sir Robert, bowed, withdrew, and sent round among the Scotch M.P.'s the pleasing announcement that they yielded a coy though reluctant assent to the propositions of the Minister. The Act of 1845, as all the world knows, was then passed.

M. Wolowski is right, in a temporary sense, when he says that the Act of 1845 left "the essential features of the constitution of the Scotch Banks" as they were. All went on as before. The Banks had some little change to introduce in their internal provisions, and some few official returns to make, but their powers as regards the service of the public remained substantially intact. The adopted rule of returning the issues after the final weekly note-exchanges of the Banks have been effected, and when the circulation of each Bank is at the *minimum*, removes the difficulty and the annoyance that would have been experienced in a finical attempt to observe the puerile principle of the Act that the specie reserve must be conformed at every moment to the notes issued.

But while making these admissions in favour of M. Wolowski's statement, let us not be forgetful of the adverse effects of the Act of 1845. We will mention three respects in which that Act has had only a damaging effect on the ancient and unimpeached constitution of the Scotch banking system.

In the first place, it has imposed unequal conditions of issue on the Scotch Banks respectively. M. Wolowski will observe from his own Tables that the metallic reserves of the several Banks are in the inverse ratio of their circulation. The Banks which have the largest issue have the smallest reserves of gold and silver. This arises, of course, from "the authorized issue" being much greater in some cases than in others, the Banks of older date having greater privilege by the Act of 1845 than Banks of more recent origin. Some of the latter can scarcely be said to have any "authorized issue" at all. We read in M. Wolowski's Table, for example:—British Linen Company, total of notes £509,399, reserve of gold and silver £230,970—City of Glasgow Bank, total of notes £367,804, reserve of gold and silver £345,928.

But in a Table, which will be found in the appendix, we have placed in juxtaposition the paid-up capital, the authorized issue, and the actual circulation of each of the Scotch Banks, and have shown (1) the proportion of authorized issue to paid up capital, and (2) the proportion of gold held to the actual circulation in each case. From these figures will be seen the inequality and injustice, as betwixt one banking company and another, imposed by the settlement of issue under the Act of 1845. It is incomprehensible on what principle, unless it be from a mere love of doing injustice, one banking company should be allowed only £1 of authorized issue for £11, 18s. 7d. of capital, while another is allowed £1 of authorized issue for £2, 5s. 8d. of capital; or why one banking company should be required to hold 20s. in specie for every pound note in circulation, while others are required to hold only 5s. 10d. in specie for every pound-note in circulation. For, supposing some fixed legal proportion betwixt the metallic reserves of the Banks and the note circulation in Scotland to be necessary, this object might be attained by a more fair and uniform arrangement. The practical effect of the law as it stands is to swell the dividends of the favoured Banks 1 or 2 per cent. above, and to depress those of the unfavoured Banks 1 or 2 per cent. below what they would otherwise be, and, of course, to give a corresponding elevation and depression to the value of the respective stocks—to do either of which things by Act of Parliament, betwixt companies operating alike honourably and competently in the same department of business, is about as nefarious a purpose as legislation could well be applied to.*

In the second place, the reserves of specie in the Scotch Banks, which formerly were available for all banking purposes and emergencies, are practically sequestrated under the Act of 1845, and rendered of no utility except as general assets in the event of bankruptcy and liquidation. Under any casual demand for gold and silver, or any periodical expansion of the circulation, such as occurs in Scotland at the Whitsunday and Martinmas terms, or any temporary distrust, such as was strongly excited in the crisis of 1857 when the Western Bank stopped payment, the Scotch Banks, though their strong rooms may be filled with gold and silver, have no recourse but to draw new supplies of coin from

* The inequality of the arrangement of issue made by the legislation of 1844-45 extends beyond Scotland. The "authorized issue" of the Scotch Banks is in every case much below the paid-up capital. What will be said of Banks under the same law whose "authorized issue" greatly exceeds their capital? Take two examples. The Provincial Bank of Ireland, with a capital of £500,000, has an authorized issue of £927,667, while the Royal Bank of Scotland, with a capital of £2,000,000, has an authorized issue of only £183,000! The National Bank of Ireland, on a capital of only £450,000, is allowed to issue £761,000, while the City Bank of Glasgow, on a capital of £870,000, is allowed to issue only £72,000! One must have great faith in the wisdom of legislation even to conjecture that there may possibly be some science or principle of issue in a system marked by such anomalies.

London, and, of course, to add to evils which may be already extreme in the metropolis. The Act of 1845 has not only rendered the Scotch Banks less regular in remitting their superfluous specie to London, but has put them under conditions which compel them, in various circumstances, instead of using the abundant gold and silver in hand, to employ their funds at London in bringing down additional supplies of specie. They have been upbraided for doing this, even in Parliament; but it is the law of Parliament that is responsible. The Act of 1845, so far from strengthening, has thus tended to weaken the general money-market of the kingdom.

In the third place, a phenomenon has been introduced, under this legislation of Sir Robert Peel, which was certainly unknown and unheard of under the ancient constitution of Scotch Banking, and the simple mention of which carries its own condemnation. No new banking company can, under the Act of 1845, be formed, or contrive to exist in Scotland. The monopoly of issue operates in this part of the kingdom practically as a monopoly of banking. It is so difficult to recognize as possible a result so contrary to every principle of modern commercial legislation, and a result, indeed, which may neither have been foreseen nor intended by Sir Robert Peel himself, that it may be worth while to enter into some explanation how this consequence of the Act of 1845 arises.

If banking companies without any power of issue can be formed and successfully conducted in England, why not also in Scotland? This is what is usually said. And the force of this instance might reasonably be increased by another, viz.,—If the City of Glasgow Bank, whose actual note-circulation is now one of the largest in Scotland cannot only live, but prosper so well with an "authorized issue" of only £72,000, why may not another banking company succeed without an "authorized issue" of any amount?

The Act of 1845, as we have seen, not only restricts the "authorized issue" of the Scotch Banks to the *minimum* amount of their note-circulation at the date of enactment, but it also prohibits issue under any condition—under the condition even of holding in reserve a sovereign for every pound-note issued to any Bank not existing in 1845. So that, even the City of Glasgow Bank, in the little foothold it has acquired under the Act of 1845, possesses a power the want of which would be severely felt by any new banking company in Scotland.

A bank must deal in the currency of the country in which it transacts, and, if not to be placed under serious disability, must have the same means of supplying itself with this currency as other banks.

One of two courses, or rather both together, would be open to any new banking company in Scotland under the Act of 1845. It might endeavour to introduce the notes of the Bank of England, and of these it could obtain any amount by lodging equivalent value in gold for them in the Issue Department. But notes of the Bank of England, besides being confined to the higher denominations of £5 and upwards, would have an irresistible tendency to return to their source of issue, and consequently the lodgments of gold by the new Bank in the Issue Department, in order to keep itself in supply of this currency, would have to be constantly renewed. Still, the new Bank, even with abundance of Bank of England notes, could not dispense with the use of the notes of the Scotch Banks, the popular currency of the country. The great bulk of the payments made to it would be in Scotch notes, and the payments made by it to the public, in order to be convenient and acceptable, would have largely to be made in the same currency. So that the new Bank, in addition to its onerous dealings with the Issue Department of the Bank of England, would find it to be one of its first necessities to open an account by some adequate deposit with one or more of the Scotch Banks, and at once place itself in an inferiority to establishments with which it claimed an equality and professed to be a competitor. It is not probable that the Scotch Banks of issue would consent to open an account with a banking company on the same terms as with a mercantile firm, and pay interest on deposits, the calls on which would be so constant and so uncertainly large in amount, as the calls of a banking company might be expected to be. An ordinary mercantile firm brings various sources of profit to a Bank, which are a compensation for the interest and facilities allowed on its cash account; but the cash account of a banking company would have no set-off of this kind, and would simply imply that the Bank of issue, with which the account was opened, was to supply its new customer with its own notes against other notes placed in deposit, and that any expansion which its circulation thus received would have, under the Act of 1845, to be accompanied with an equivalent increase of its specie reserve. The account necessarily to be opened by any new banking company in Scotland with one or more of the existing Scotch Banks would differ in little or nothing from its equally optional, if not as necessary, account with the Issue Department of the Bank of England. Whatever amount of Bank of England or Scotch notes, therefore, the new company should have to keep in its till, would be a deduction from its funds and a charge upon its capital, from which the existing Banks are entirely exempt. If it opened branches, this charge, and worse even than the financial charge, this practical difficulty would be repeated *in cumulo* at each branch, till it would be immediately discovered that the absorption of the funds of the company, and the mechanical inconvenience arising in the primary act of supplying itself at all points with the customary currency, were so great, that to carry on the business of banking, to pay interest on deposits at call, and open cash and cash-credit accounts on the same terms as the Scotch Banks, exempted from all this absorption of funds and inconvenience by the right of issue alone, were simply impossible.

This is the practical course in which the Act of 1845 operates as regards the creation of any new banking company in Scotland.

An attempt has been made more than once under the most respectable auspices to establish a new banking company in Scotland, that should conform in all respects to the conditions of the Act of 1845; but as soon as the parties proceeded to the consideration of actual business, the attempt was seen to be surrounded with too much difficulty to be made with any hope of success. No new company has, in point of fact, ventured to brave the disabilities of the Act of 1845, and all idea of conducting bank business in Scotland, save through the existing companies, has long been abandoned as impracticable. At the same time, there are discount agencies outside the Banks in Scotland; the bill brokerage of London has offshoots in Glasgow as well as in Manchester or any other English centre of trade; and Scotch bills of exchange payable in London, and accepted or indorsed by Scotch firms of national repute, are placed under no disadvantage as compared with any other bills of exchange of a similar class.

It is only because a strong tendency, arising out of the freedom of banking in Scotland, had been in progress for many years before the Act of 1845, not towards the formation of new banking companies, but towards the amalgamation of those already existing, that this seed of monopoly attracted so little observation at the passing of the Act; and though the free movement of union is now exhausted, yet with eleven great banking companies in Scotland, eight of which may be said to be national in their amount of capital, in the number of their branches, and in the magnitude and distribution of their resources, it may be some years to come before the hardship of this monopoly be sensibly felt. But the *virus* of a bad principle remains vital and operative in the Act. In the rapid growth of the country eleven banking companies will at some point or other not be deemed enough; it will be considered that banking dividends from 10 to 15 per cent., and bank stock worth three times its original par value, with both dividends and value of stock constantly increasing, should not be in any sense the law-bestowed perquisite of any given bodies of shareholders; and an Act, which thus lays a permanent arrest on the free development and equalization of public interests, will not only be more and more condemned as a grave exception to our whole economical system, but be ultimately resented as an intolerable grievance.

CHAPTER VIII.

REVIEW OF THE ARGUMENT ON WHICH THE LEGISLATION OF 1844-45 WAS BASED—THE EXACT DIFFERENCE BETWIXT "THE CURRENCY PRINCIPLE" AND "THE BANKING PRINCIPLE" OF ISSUE—AND THEIR RESPECTIVE BEARINGS ON THE ADMINISTRATION OF CREDIT AND THE MAINTENANCE OF SPECIE PAYMENTS.

THE views, whether of monetary science or banking policy, which led to the great change made in the Charter of the Bank of England in 1844, and the consequent attack on the Scotch system of banking and issue in the following year, open various matters of inquiry and examination that are somewhat beyond the scope of these remarks; the main object of which is to place in relief the true nature and action of the issue of bank-notes as long practised and developed in Scotland, whereof it may be justly complained that the advocates of antagonist theories have been strangely ignorant or willingly oblivious.

The necessity of a strongly concentrated regulation of the rate of discount, based on the deposit of bullion in a National Department of Issue; the assumed infallible action of rapid cumulative advances of the rate of discount in attracting, not only home and foreign capital to the money-market, but metallic deposits to the Issue Department; and the virtue of the same specific in increasing or diminishing the imports and exports of goods and produce so as to secure "a favourable state of the exchanges," or a state in which foreign nations should have to remit us more or less gold; are among the questionable propositions which have been prominently advanced in this connexion.

When loanable capital is abundant, a low rate of discount, the necessary consequence, tends to promote production, and to encourage export, so far as consumption and the demand for goods allow; but it would insult the understanding of producers and manufacturers to tell them that they can always safely increase their production and exports when the rate of discount is low. This increase is governed by the existing relations of demand and supply, and the rate of discount has only a modified and subordinate action within the circle of a superior law. So also when loanable capital is less abundant, a higher rate of discount, then an equally sure and unavoidable incident of the loan market, neither enlarges directly the volume of exports nor diminishes the volume of imports, both of which are still regulated supremely by the actual need of the one description of merchandise abroad and of the other at home. This result finds illustration in all our periodical crises, wherein it has been seen, however high the rate of discount, or great the panic, or general the collapse of trade and confidence produced by the action of the Bank, some imports increase, while some exports diminish in obedience to a law above all this monetary concussion. It was signally exhibited in 1855-56, when various abnormal specie movements, arising from the war in the Crimea, a continued drain of silver from Europe to meet the demands of a rapidly expanding trade with India and China, and a consequent increased coinage of gold, more especially in France, where silver, under the double standard of that country, was relatively abundant, reduced the issue of the Bank of England to a low point, and put commerce unawares to the test of rapidly advancing rates of discount and a degree of panic. Commerce, so far from changing its current in obedience to the Bank, sprang forward vigorously in the opposite direction; and the importation of foreign produce, which had been unusually moderate during the twelve months before the Bank began to act, increased rapidly and largely during the twelve months after; while in Manchester, and all our great seats of production, there were only manifestations of gloom and stagnation. The Board of Trade returns for these years abundantly show that the rate of discount has not such control over imports and exports as has been presumed in the argument of the supporters of the Bank Charter Act of 1844.

The effect of increasing the rate of discount in attracting foreign capital and bullion, while proceeding on the same natural law as the effect of higher price in attracting commodities, presents in practice quite as much counteraction, together with as uncertain and indeterminate results, as the supposed effect of the rate of discount on imports and exports. The sense of security, the uniform maintenance of the standard of value, and the fidelity with which the monetary system of a country is customarily conducted, outweigh the force of the rate of discount in attracting bullion and foreign capital to a money-market. The product of the mines at any given period, the amount of our exports to the countries where the mines are situated, and the extent to which the capital of a country has been invested abroad, rendering other nations tributary to its wealth, are further elements that enter into this problem, and modify the effect of a high rate of discount in attracting supplies of capital or bullion in any given circumstances from abroad. The consequence is, that capital and bullion do not flow, as a rule, in greatest abundance where the rate of discount is highest. The gold and silver of California and the Western Territories of the United States do not stay at New York because the rate of discount may be 3 or 4 per cent. more in New York than in London, nor do they pass to Paris and not to London because the rate of discount may be 1 or 2 per cent. higher in the French than the English metropolis. A comparatively high rate of discount is not, indeed, to be cast out of the question; it is an influence among other influences; but not even where it is permanent, and still less where it is most temporary and fleeting, has it the force of a supreme law. The periods at which the Bank of England, under the system of 1844, has startled the money-markets of Europe by overtopping them all in advances of the rate of discount, have been uniformly followed, within two or three months, by long reigns of a much lower rate than is known anywhere else than in this country.

The theory of controlling imports and exports, and attracting supplies of foreign capital and bullion by the rate of discount, receives an awkward counteraction in the fact that advances of the rate of discount in London—so close is now the sympathy of the money-markets of the world—are usually followed by corresponding advances in all the great centres of money and commerce. So that when it is hoped by this form of Bank action to force sales of British goods, and to diminish British purchases abroad, and to attract from other nations some portion of their specie, they, on the other hand, must be quite as strongly induced to buy as little and sell as much as possible, and to keep their bullion at home, as far as similar causes and means can induce them. It is easy to perceive how a deep stagnation of trade and general depreciation of prices may be brought about by such means; but the relative state of the exchanges must remain unaltered by a rise of interest which is general and uniform in its operation.

These are matters of economic inquiry which, however ingeniously and dogmatically dragged into the argument in favour of the legislation of 1844, cannot be said to have received a final solution in that sense; and which are here simply noticed, without any formal discussion, in order that our remarks may be the more rigorously confined to what is their main subject—viz., the issue of bank-notes.

The rate of discount, with all its incidents of rise and fall, and of necessary and wholesome action, is not an exclusive attribute of the Act of 1844.

It cannot be pretended that the rate of discount did not rise and fall in sympathy with the market before 1844, just as it cannot be asserted that periods of commercial and financial crisis and disaster have not been quite as frequent and severe since that year as they were before. All experience points to a permanent tendency of the banking system and of commercial enterprise which the Act of 1844 has neither removed nor even mitigated.

The exact respect in which the English system of 1844 differs from such a system of plural issue as has been exemplified in Scotland is, that whereas the former devolves the regulation of the rate of discount on a central issue of notes, based in all its movement of increase or decrease on equivalent deposits of bullion, the latter, without excluding the element of bullion with which the convertibility of notes on demand connects the whole banking administration by an indissoluble tie, embraces as proper elements of consideration the demand and supply of loanable funds, and the general conditions of the market.

The Bank of England, while endeavouring with much intelligence and propriety to execute strictly the principle of the Act of 1844 as to the rate of discount, has not been able wholly to dominate in this respect. It is constantly kept in check by the outside market; sometimes advances and sometimes does not advance the rate, when advocates of the theory of 1844 contend that the action of the Bank should have been the reverse; and it is only, indeed, when the Bank's reserve of unemployed notes is nearly exhausted—when the special currency, which under the Act of 1844 is all but the only medium of Bank circulation in England, has reached an impassable legal limit, and merchants and bankers are brought to a pause—that the Bank of England attains complete supremacy in the execution of the law of 1844. But at this point the Bank at once produces a degree of public alarm and discontent, and an imminence of overwhelming disasters, that have only hitherto been subdued by a summary suspension of the Act, and a relegation of the Bank Directors to the exercise of a reasonable discretion.

A plural issue of notes after the Scotch model has not had trial in England, or in any other country than Scotland, we are aware of. There is need, therefore, of some reserve in criticising a type of banking institutions which has been so rarely exemplified. But if any experience of a free and plural issue of convertible bank-notes tends to show that it leans too broadly and vaguely on the actual demand and supply of loanable funds for its rule of action, it cannot be denied that all experience of the English system of 1844 proves that, in taking a central issue of notes on bullion as its only guide, it is much too narrow in its induction, too precise and finical for operation in ordinary times, and too violently impracticable for observance in periods of difficulty or crisis.

The question, under all its phases and on all the converging lines of debate through which it has been pursued, is thus essentially a question of the mode and principle of issue.

That the attention of Sir Robert Peel and the promoters of the measures of 1844–45 was wholly directed to issue is apparent from the measures themselves. They were measures for the regulation of issue; and they changed the system of issue, and nothing else. The sole object which they sought to attain, and which, though they did not fully and perfectly reach, yet did largely accomplish, was to centralize and unify the issue of bank-notes on bullion deposited in a National Issue Department; and it was argued that under this arrangement the country would be protected from many irregularities, much evil, and frequently recurring disasters. It was contended that the inherent tendency of bank-notes to be over-issued, to depreciate in value, to inflate the nominal rate of wages and prices of goods, to hinder export and stimulate import, to encourage a reckless extension of credit, and, finally, to exhaust the specie and coinage of the realm, would be effectually stopped; and that the whole monetary and commercial system would be kept in tolerable equilibrium, harmony, and order. These were the arguments used to commend the great change contemplated by the Act of 1844. They were arguments applicable to an inconvertible paper currency, but they had no strictly logical relation to bank-notes payable at sight, and subjected to constant, daily and hourly, exchanges and retirement as in Scotland.

Let us examine a little these arguments in detail.

First, as to *over-issue*. Notes payable at sight have such an irresistible tendency to present themselves for payment, that to speak of their over-issue may be perceivėd at once to be of the nature of a *non sequitur*. Over-issue, in the only sense in which it is intelligible, does not, and cannot follow in notes payable at sight. If people keep bunches of bank-notes in their pockets or their safes, there may be said in such a case to be more notes issued than are necessary; but this is a case of bank-notes in a state of complete dormancy and innocence, and can be attended, therefore, with no evil beyond a loss of interest to the holders by their own choice, which comes out in gain to the issuers. On the other hand, if bank-notes are only held by the public for the purpose of discharging debts, and buying what they need, the bank-notes thus held discharge an essential function of the circulation; and the more actively bank-notes are thus employed, the more certain it is that they will go immediately into the hands of some who will take them to the bank of issue for payment, or lodge them in bank to their credit—in either of which events they cease as issue. Yet in all this circle the notes do nothing that would not be done by the coin which they "promise to pay," while doing all they do more perfectly than the coin itself could do.

Secondly, as to *depreciation* (from which the idea of over-issue can hardly be disjoined), it is plainly a contradiction in terms to say that bank-notes are changeable into a fixed quantity of gold, and yet may be of less value than such fixed quantity of gold. Bank or State notes, the payment of which has been suspended by law under some State or commercial necessity, may be over-issued; because by the act of suspension they are cast outside the source of issue, have no place of return, and are retained and kept afloat in the circulation by the fluctuating value attached to them in the market. They are simply false coins sustained in circulation by force of law, and the issuers being under no immediate obligation to retire them, all their holders have an interest in keeping them in currency as long as possible. Since inconvertible notes may thus clearly be over-issued, it is equally manifest that they are depreciable. They not only depreciate at the first moment of the suspension of their payableness at sight, but their depreciation is doomed to follow all the vicissitude of the public fortunes, and of daily speculations as to the credit of the issuers, as long as the suspension lasts. To apply the legitimate inferences from such notes to bank-notes payable at sight is, to say the least, irrational. A bank of issue, as in Scotland, is not only bound to meet its notes with full specie value as soon as presented, but failure to do this in any instance, or any attempt to temporize or compound, would, in the nature of the case, involve the instant stoppage and withdrawal of its entire circulation—a penalty more fatal to a banking company than has been imposed by statute on any commercial or financial default. It may, therefore, be assumed that to fulfil the promise of its notes when presented, and keep its circulation unimpeached, will always be a cardinal object in the policy of every bank of issue; and since in case of default in this respect by any banking company, its notes would be immediately obliterated from the circulation, it follows, further, that over-issue and depreciation are alike impossible. As long as the legal obligation to pay a given weight of gold stands, it is inconceivable in what sense, however indirect, or in what degree, however small, depreciation can arise; for what holder of a pound-note will take

17s. or 19s. 6d. for it, when by returning it to the bank he can get 20s.? As matter of fact, there is no example in Scotland, from one end of the country to the other, of the one-pound note of the Banks exchanging, in transactions wholesale or retail, for less than a gold sovereign.

Sir Robert Peel was not unaware of this attribute of bank-notes payable on demand, and could even employ it as an argument when it suited his purpose. In the course of the debate on the Bank Charter Bill on 20th May, 1844, in reply to a member who inquired what limitation the measure would impose on prices, he said, "Don't you suppose that if the great dealer in exchanges in London, Mr. Rothschild, found that by presenting £500,000 of paper at the Bank of England he could get 500,000 sovereigns, and that they were more valuable than paper, he would avail himself of the power the law gave him, and demand the gold? And don't you suppose that every other man whose transactions were less extensive, but who had a right to receive five sovereigns for his £5 note, would immediately demand it?" Sir Robert answered one question by asking two other questions. But the suggestion apparently intended to be conveyed was that the new measure would entail no greater limitation on prices than the accustomed obligation of bankers to pay their notes on demand; and this suggestion, however imperfect as an explanation, was at least an honest testimony to the virtue of convertible bank-notes in guarding against any inflation of prices attributable to an over-issued and depreciated paper currency. Yet Sir Robert Peel, in the same discussions, could assert and reassert that the "convertibility of the paper into gold was not sufficient of itself to prevent over-issues and depreciation." The *data*, however, of this conclusion have never been produced.

The principle of convertibility, wherever stedfastly observed, seems not only adequate to secure the issue of bank-notes alike from excess of issue and depreciation of value, but this result becomes all the more certain, and more strictly guarded, in proportion as banking processes, whether of issue or deposit, are developed on a free and plural basis. The effect of issue from more sources than one, on this principle, is simply to bring to book the total issue, through the note-exchanges of the banks, more sharply and rigorously than could be possible under one source of issue. The practice of deposit at interest has the same effect of withdrawing notes from the circulation, and returning them to their place of payment, with the swiftest expedition. The so-called wild-horse of bank-note issue is thus, at every bound forward, held more closely by the head, and kept under more effectual rein, by its own proper obligations and conditions. There is no result of natural economic law more certain, under a system of banking and issue like that of Scotland, than that the notes of the Banks present in their amount a constantly diminishing proportion to the funds which they are the means of circulating, and to the burden of transactions which they easily and harmlessly sustain.

This fact, so well-established and so manifest, is probably the reason why the Scotch Banks betray of late years a perceptible tone of indifference with respect to the right of issue, whether as a source of profit to themselves or of any imaginable evil to the public interest. The notes do not figure largely in their balance sheets, nor do they give any trace of trouble to the country. Issue in Scotland has attained that wholesomeness, characteristic of all natural functions, in which the immense service performed is scarcely perceived. But when Scotch bankers come seriously to consider the advantages of the right of issue, or what would ensue were it withdrawn, it is seen at once that the little instrument of the bank-note is as indispensable to the banking structure of the country now as it was at any former stage of its progress.

Thirdly, as to *inflation of prices.* Bank-notes payable at

sight being, in their nature, incapable of over-issue or depreciation, their alleged tendency to inflate prices falls to the ground. It is the effect indeed of capital, of the demand for labour and services which capital collected and organized for purposes of profit so largely stimulates, and of the consequent extension of the means of consumption and enjoyment, to impart a buoyancy to prices, which is only checked by the increased powers of production brought into operation by the same means. Since the effect of bank issue, as we have shown, and as may be proved of every banking process as well, is to develope and organize capital for purposes of profit, it would be idle to deny to bank-notes some influence in this general movement. But this cannot be held to be a fault, unless it is to be assumed that want of capital, poverty of industrial means, absence of all commercial impulse, and general dullness and stagnation of business, are the proper conditions of prosperity. The inflation of prices, really charged against the issue of bank-notes with any show of reason, must be that inflation which arises from a paper currency issued in excess because its payment has been suspended, and because it is not immediately referable to the common standard of value, below which it necessarily falls more and more in proportion as it is increased, leading to higher nominal wages of labour and higher nominal prices of all materials of labour, in comparison with other countries, till it becomes always more difficult to sell abroad the products of native industry, and more profitable to buy abroad than to produce at home what is necessary to the national existence. The situation of any country under an inconvertible paper currency, as regards foreign commerce, cannot be better expressed than by saying that it is doomed to produce in the dearest, and to sell what it produces in the cheapest market. But bank-notes payable at sight do not belong to this category, and can have no effect of this kind on prices or on foreign trade as long as their plain legal obligation and their natural place in the circulation are maintained.

The hypothesis of Sir Robert Peel as to the tendency of bank-notes payable at sight to be over-issued, to depreciate from the metallic standard in value, to inflate prices, to derange the foreign exchanges and induce a drain of bullion, are thus capable of refutation at every point; and this, indeed, has been fully and unanswerably shown by Mr. Tooke, Mr. Fullarton, Mr. Gilbart, Mr. Mill, M. Chevalier, and other writers.* Mr. Gilbart remarks, that even increased issues, in so far as they stimulate production, have the effect of lowering prices, or at least of keeping them at a moderate level; and this is an opinion of much significance in the question of a plural system of issue, the effect of which, as we have seen in Scotland, is greatly to promote the extension of banking processes over all parts of a country, and consequently among the productive classes in particular. The cultivators of the soil, the inland traders, the manufacturers, the artizans, and the miners are not the dangerous classes of commerce—the speculators—whose buying and selling, and transferences of capital on a large scale from one market to another, have the most direct and powerful effect on the exchanges and on the influx and efflux of bullion. They are, on the contrary, in an emphatic sense, the producers of every country. The speculators are found in the great cities among the capitalists, the dealers in foreign loans, and the adventurers of the Stock Exchange, to whom the system of central or State issue affords every facility they care for. But a system which gives free and full play to the speculative elements of money and commerce, and leaves the productive elements under comparative restriction and difficulty, cannot be eminently adapted to the public well-being; and a free development of banks of issue, with their peculiar powers of ramification, seems all the more necessary, in order that the whole field of national production, from agriculture up through all the various branches of manufactur-

* See *History of Prices and State of the Circulation*, by Thomas Tooke, F.R.S., and William Newmarch.

ing industry, may have a due share of wholesome stimulation and activity.

Fourthly, as to *unsafe and excessive extensions of credit.* The attempts made in the debates of 1844 to show that unsound augmentations of advances and discounts were the offspring of a too great freedom of issue on the part of banking companies, imposed largely on public opinion at the time; but experience since that period must have revealed the superficiality of such a conclusion, and demonstrated, indeed, to all who have given attention to the subject, that the extension of credits and discounts is not a consequence of issue or circulation at all, but a matter solely of banking administration, whatever the principle or system of issue may be.

There can be no doubt that Sir Robert Peel was under a strong impression that, by cutting off the issue of the Banks, and providing that the circulation of notes should not increase save on the basis of an equivalent increase of bullion in the Issue Department, an effective restraint would be laid on the discount of commercial bills and other forms of bank credit. Yet there could not be a more palpable fallacy, or a conclusion betraying less insight into the nature, origin, and renewal of the fund on which bank discounts and credits are based. The Act of 1844 had not been three years in operation till all trade and industry were involved in one of the vastest whirlpools of speculation and credit which this country has ever experienced; and in the extra-session of Parliament, at the end of that year (1847), Sir Francis Baring was able to ask how it could possibly be reconciled with the views of the framers of the Act that the bullion in the Bank of England had *decreased* £7,024,000, while the Bank of England notes in circulation had in the same period *increased* £346,000. Lord Russell, in the same debate, confessed himself non-plussed between the theory and practice of the Act, and thought that more light was necessary.

It was, in point of fact, the depositors of the Bank, whose deposits as a general rule increase with the increase of the Bank's advances and discounts on "private securities," that ran off these seven millions of bullion; while the holders of the Bank's notes, who, according to the theory of the Act, should have forthwith diminished their holding by seven millions, took their own way and increased it by £346,000. A singular want of perception of the intimate relation betwixt the "private securities" and the "private deposits" of the Bank, of the non-relation of the circulation to either the one or the other, and of the supreme power of the owners of "private deposits" over the stock of bullion in the Issue Department, though legally and theoretically a matter of circulation alone, is apparent in all this legislation of 1844. It may be added, as a striking proof of the huge peril of the Act of 1844 in periodically recurring circumstances, that the same power of depositors which withdrew seven millions of gold from the Issue Department in 1847, while the notes in circulation increased instead of being diminished, could have gone on, when the notes in circulation were, as in 1847, no more than covered by the Government securities and bullion in the Issue Department, to demand seven millions more of gold, and to reduce not only the Bank to impossible conditions, but the whole monetary and banking integrity of the country to a state of chaos and dissolution.*

* The theory of the Act of 1844 keeps itself in countenance by a peculiar nomenclature. The notes produced in the department of issue, and carried to or withdrawn from the banking department, are an exact reflex in their increase and decrease of the bullion deposited in the office of issue. The whole amount of notes thus issued at any period are called "circulation," though they may be lying, nine or ten millions deep, for years in succession unused and uncirculated, and of no account in any active or economic sense. It would be much simpler and better to let the bullion speak for itself as an ordinary banking resource. As a basis of *issue* it has no significance whatever. The only "issue" and the only "circulation" of any avail or any consequence in practice or discussion are the "bank-notes" in the hands of the public. The force of this

There is nothing more certainly established by facts and experience than that the amount of bank-notes payable at sight in circulation, and the amount of bank-credits and discounts, do not follow the same rule of proportion, and have no relation to each other by which it could be inferred that the expansion or contraction of the one implied the expansion or contraction of the other. This truth is written plainly in all our banking returns; and the only difficulty is to select with sufficient comprehension from the statistics by which it is conclusively established.

statement is seen at once when a man, who discounts a bill and lodges the proceeds with the Bank, acquires the same power over the bullion in the Issue Department as the holder of notes in circulation. It is very singular—now at least—that the framers of the Act of 1844 did not see this inevitable power, not only of depositors in the Bank of England, but of owners of circulable capital in any part of the kingdom, over the bullion in the Issue Department, and that their whole theory of a circulation responding in its movement of increase or decrease with the amount of bullion in the Issue Department was a purely fanciful structure. The largest hoards of treasure accumulated in the Issue Department since 1844 have been withdrawn and dispersed periodically without any material change of the amount of "notes in circulation;" and it is when this process has reached the point when the Bank of England, however high and indisputable its credit, has no banking means left to meet the demands of its "private deposits" account, that all the impracticability of the system is revealed. The general position of the Bank in such crises is this: while there may be five or six millions of gold left in the Issue Department, the unemployed notes at the disposal of the banking department may be less than one million, and its obligations to depositors 20 or 25 millions! In this situation, to discount commercial bills is out of the question. The Bank, while curtailing its discount business, can only attempt by forced sales of securities to draw back day by day notes in circulation, which the circulation has held in nearly equal quantity under all vicissitudes of bullion in the Issue Department. But this produces a friction so violent that, were it prolonged a few days, it would grind the whole financial system of the kingdom to powder. Hence the letters of the Executive to the Governors of the Bank suspending the Act, which, though too late to avert all the mischief already done, have hitherto saved the country from the overwhelming catastrophe an observance of the Act would involve.

All the leading monetary phenomena may be reasonably held to be comprised within the ten years which usually elapse from one of our great periodical crises to another. The following is the Bank of England account, as regards "notes in circulation" and "other securities" (or discounts and advances of the Bank on private securities), in the last decennial period of this kind, at the end (18th December) of each year given:—

	Circulation, including Bank post bills	Other Securities.
1857,	£20,133,558	£28,088,186
1864,	19,669,007	18,754,485
1865,	20,784,065	21,627,653
1866,	22,591,312	19,825,202
1867,	23,439,574	17,218,755

So, the year 1857, in which all but one the amount of notes in circulation was smallest (£20,133,558); the amount advanced to the public on securities was the largest (£28,088,186), while the year 1867, in which the amount of notes in circulation was the largest (£23,439,574), the amount advanced to the public on securities was the smallest (£17,218,755)! Though this result would have much perplexed Sir Robert Peel in 1844, yet it contains really nothing to astonish any one when adequate information is brought to bear upon it. One explanation is, that in sluggish times notes of the Bank of England denomination, £5 and upwards, are most apt to loll in the purses, drawers, and strong boxes of the merchants and others. When people are slow in buying and selling they pass their bank-notes slowly. On the contrary, in more active times, the same bank-notes may affect half a dozen transactions in the course of a day, and very probably be returned to the Bank before the close of business. In the case of one-pound notes, we should anticipate a different result, since such notes being used largely in the payment of wages, the greater the amount of labour employed the greater will be their absorption in the circulation. But it is the big wheel, the large sums and the large operations, which set the smaller in motion, and the increased circulation of one-pound notes in a period of the greatest commercial and industrial activity would probably not be found, by reference to the actual statistics, to make up for the diminution of the larger notes in circulation. The whole circulation thus bears no common ratio to the amount of credit or discount, but rather to be in the inverse ratio of these—reduced in amount when credit and discount are expanded, and expanded when credit and discount are reduced. The reason of this is that it is not upon note-issues that bills are discounted and credits extended, but on deposits, and on the daily conversions of goods and produce into money by which fresh funds are returned to the banks, and the capital available for loans is constantly renewed. The fund of the banks is not determined in any sense or degree by a given amount of currency or circulation, but is a flux and reflux of means, constantly supplied and modified by the transactions of the community, and superior in its laws and conditions of amount, of increase or decrease, to the control of a merely mechanical and book-keeping separation of the issue and banking departments.

The immediate action and reaction (one on the other) of the "private securities" and "private deposits" of the Bank of England, the coincidence of a decline of the stock of bullion with the withdrawal of deposits, and the immaterial fluctuation of the notes in the hands of the public under every vicissitude, are strongly marked in all our monetary and commercial crises; and these phenomena are as conspicuous in the crises since the passing of the Act of 1844 as in those preceding the Act. For example, the memorable years 1825, 1837, and 1847, are precisely alike in all the broad movements of the Bank of England account.

In February, 1824, the deposits had increased from £7,827,350, at which they stood in the previous autumn, to £10,097,850; in February, 1825, they were £10,168,780, and by the end of August the same year, they had fallen to £6,410,560. The private securities held by the Bank had increased, in 1825, to £24,951,330, greatly above the highest amount in the preceding years; in 1822, they were £15,973,080. In the same interval the stock of bullion had fallen from £11,057,150, to £3,634,320, two-thirds of this decrease having occurred in 1825. The highest circulation of Bank of England notes in 1825 was £20,753,760; in February, 1822, a period of great depression, the Bank of England circulation was £18,665,350.

In the crisis of 1837 there was the same series of results. In February, 1836, the deposits had increased from £10,823,010 in February of the previous year, to £14,322,530, and in February, 1837, they had fallen to £10,593,800—in February, 1838, to £8,627,700. In February, 1837, the private securities had increased to £27,699,210, while the note-circulation was only £18,232,680, less even than it was in 1822, when the private securities were only £15,973,080; but coincident with this expansion of discounts on the one hand, and withdrawal of deposits on the other, the stock of bullion had again been reduced to £4,089,600.

In 1847, under the law of 1844, which was to have corrected all previous disorder, there is no difference in the character, if in the degree, of the phenomena. In 1846, the private deposits of the Bank had increased from £8,350,465, to £18,912,445; at the beginning of 1847, they were only £7,903,959, and in the course of that year as low as £6,791,373. The highest point of the note-circulation of the Bank of England was £21,764,085, only £1,000,000 more than it had been in the crisis of 22 years before; the "private securities," however, were £31,023,504, and the stock of bullion, following the withdrawal of deposits, had diminished from £14,951,372 in January to £8,438,874 in October.

If these facts, found to appear in the same order in the

crises of 1857-58 and 1868, albeit under modifications of the whole monetary and commercial circumstances almost too vast for comprehension, can be held to convey any thoroughly true conclusions, they must be at least these three: first, that it is not in bank-note circulation payable at sight that any danger lies, but in the advances of the Banks on securities; secondly, that the amount of such advances does not depend upon, and bears no relation to the amount of bank-notes payable at sight in circulation; and thirdly, that the same phenomena prevail in these respects under the Acts of 1844-45 as before their enactment.

Since 1844 the Bank of England notes have not only had a more undivided possession of the note-circulation of England than they had before, and might consequently be expected to show, under an enormous increase of traffic and transactions of which every one is perfectly cognizant, a greatly increased amount in circulation which they do not in reality show. But since 1844 there has also been a great development of joint-stock banking companies in London, some of them wielding each a power over capital and over all its incidents of administration scarce inferior to that of the Bank of England itself, without any right of issue or any part in the note-circulation. Were the transactions of these banks in "deposits" and "securities" published and combined, it would be shown with infinitely greater force than from the Bank of England returns alone, how completely the banking elements predominate in the foreign exchanges, in the stock of bullion, and in all else that is deemed most essential to the integrity of the monetary system, over the simple element of issue; and how the issue of bank-notes, without losing its importance as a banking function, becomes, in this enlarged sphere of consideration, unworthy and unneedful of any theoretic or experimental legislation.

There is a remark of M. Wolowski in his First Chapter which is here worthy of notice. The equilibrium between the metallic reserve and the notes issued, he says, was destroyed the moment that an attempt was made to benefit by the deposits in making use of them. This remark occurs in a reference to the Bank of Hamburg. The citizens of Hamburg, engaged in foreign trade, found it necessary at an early period, from the conglomerate and often worn and degraded coinage circulating in the free German town, to establish a bank which should pay the foreign bills of exchange drawn upon them in coin or bullion of an assured weight and fineness. By this means they protected themselves against heavy and uncertain rates of exchange against Hamburg in foreign markets. The process was very simple: the merchants lodged the true coin and bullion in the Bank, and paid their foreign bills with it either by withdrawing the sums or portions of the sums thus lodged, when export of bullion was necessary, or by mere transfers in the books of the Bank when in the state of the foreign exchanges export of bullion was unnecessary. The equilibrium under such a system betwixt the notes or warrants issued to the merchants for their gold was exact and perfect; but an institution of this kind has no relation or suggestiveness to a system of banking in which the practices of deposit and discount are combined. There was current money and coinage of various value in Hamburg as well as bank-money, and deposit and lending of money of all the various kinds went on there as elsewhere, under an agio or premium greatly in favour of the bank-money. M. Wolowski, however, is quite right in his remark, that this equilibrium between the metallic reserve and the notes issued was lost when bank-deposits began to be made profitable by being used. It was doubly lost in this country, because it cannot be said to have ever existed before the Act of 1844; and it is equally certain that it has been as greatly lost since that revolution in the legal and formal principle of issue. If M. Wolowski, therefore, thinks that there is essential virtue in the maintenance of an exact equality betwixt the metallic reserves and the notes issued to the public, and that the banking practice of deposit and using the deposits is the element of disturbance to this theory of equality betwixt circulation and the metallic reserves, as it no doubt is, there would seem to be no alternative but that this banking practice of taking deposits and giving them out on discount must be extinguished, as far as law can extinguish it! Conclusions of this kind, of course, are simply preposterous. The only equilibrium, and the only practical test and rule of equilibrium betwixt the metallic reserve and the bank-notes in circulation is the instant convertibility, and equivalence in value, of the notes to the gold standard; and since this is a result which cannot be endangered, under the small and constantly receding proportion of the circulation to the enormously augmenting resources of the Banks, save by some extreme and inconceivably universal abuse of these resources, there would seem to be no such sure and perfect place of rest and obligation for the maintenance of this equilibrium than in the banking companies themselves, and in such arrangements and relations as they are not only competent, but most competent to establish.

The plan, tried in England since 1844, of a metallic reserve formed by a deposit of gold for every note issued formally, though not circulated actually, and yet a reserve as accessible to the bank depositors and to the daily discounters of bills of exchange as to the holders of notes, has at all events not answered its purpose, but, on the contrary, has failed.

It would be extremely desirable if, by some little device of law or form of issue, all monetary and commercial difficulty could be averted from this and other countries. But it is obvious that this is a result which, subject to the action of the public itself, depends mainly on the care, accuracy, and prudence of banking administration; and that such banking qualities must be relaxed rather than strengthened by an assumedly infallible, but not really infallible, Act of Parliament. There is nothing gained, however much may be lost, by fixing the attention of banking companies on the mimic operation that proceeds in the Issue Department of the Bank of England as the sole rule of guidance, instead of requiring them to study closely the phenomena within their own circle of action and obligation, together with a more perfect reference to the general banking conditions of the kingdom, than is possible under the present system. On this more real and enlarged induction, the rate of discount—the only operative agency professed to be brought into more successful play by the Act of 1844—would probably never fall so low, under "the banking principle" of issue, as it falls under the present rapid artificial creation and multiplication of notes in periods of great abundance of bullion; while, on the other hand, it would certainly rise more promptly and regularly when the commercial and banking phenomena betokened a growing pressure of demand on supply of loanable funds, or an approach of danger to the specie reserves from adverse foreign exchanges, which the state of the existing Issue Department is by no means the first, but rather the last to exhibit, since any index it gives is only the effect after the cause. And when a crisis of real difficulty came, it would be surmounted with less panic, and less of shock, violence, and disaster to public and private interests than occur under the present law, when the reserve of notes in the Bank of England is seen to be exhausted—when every banking company, however ample and solid its resources, is consequently struck with alarm and contracts as much as possible its most ordinary operations, and when it becomes certain that every further step taken by the Bank of England to force back from the banks and the public the notes which they have customarily held in circulation can only intensify and aggravate the crucial difficulty under which it is visibly placed. It is not the mere contraction thus attempted of the ordinary amount of notes in circulation that is the main source of the paralysis that ensues, but the fact that the more the Bank is compelled by the law of the Issue Department to buy up notes daily and hourly from the market, banking companies, commercial firms, and all persons holding notes independently become the more resolute to hold them and to lock them up from the circulation, which is the same rule in such circumstances as that of the Bank itself, though of a directly opposite tendency; and, of course, traverses and defeats the intended effect of the action of the Bank at every point, till the result is a simple *garotte* of all vital circulation, and of all means of recovery.

Whatever view may be taken of the comparative tendency of the two systems as regards the rate of discount, the maintenance of specie reserves sufficient to guard against a suspension of specie payments, and the regulation of the money and other markets, there is at least one conclusion to which these reasonings bring us, and which may be given as a challenge, viz., that it must baffle the most skilful advocate of "the currency theory" of 1844 to name in these respects a single wholesome economic action of that theory, which is not as certain to arise, and to exert as wholesome and necessary an effect, under plurality of issue, on "the banking principle" that has been so signally and successfully illustrated in the experience of Scotland.

CHAPTER IX.

INCREASE OF BULLION RESERVES SINCE 1844 IN PROPORTION TO CIRCULATION OF BANKS OF ISSUE, AND ITS PROPER VALUE.

ONE admission may be freely made. Sir Robert Peel was too great a statesman to be supposed, either not to have had some definite object in view, or not to have well adapted his measures to the attainment of his object. The Acts of 1844-45, it must be owned, have developed larger reserves of coin and bullion in the *Banks of issue*, in proportion to notes in circulation, than were customary prior to these enactments.

Taking the three years immediately preceding the Act of 1844, and the three years immediately after, as the best means of discerning what was intended by the Acts, we find that the Bank of England, in 1841-42-43, held monthly average amounts of bullion ranging from £4,218,000 to £12,996,000, against a circulation ranging in monthly average during the same period from £16,292,000 to £21,108,000; whereas in 1845-46-47, the bullion held by the Bank ranged from £8,478,000 to £16,544,000 against a circulation from £18,918,000 to £23,136,000. There was thus a manifest access, under the Act of 1844, of bullion held by the Bank of England, in proportion to the amount of its promissory notes in circulation. In 1842-43-44, the Scotch Banks held on the last day of the second week in February and November, amounts of coin varying from £324,982 to £481,102, against a note-circulation varying from £2,552,267 to £3,555,789; and at the same dates of 1846 and 1847, they held amounts of coin from £1,100,258 to £1,284,261 against a note-circulation from £3,097,930 to £4,046,526. There was here also a still more manifest access of gold and silver in proportion to notes.* Again, to come to present times, in the four weeks ending 7th September, 1872, the Bank of England held in both departments, £23,126,109 of coin and bullion against a note-circulation of £26,115,484; the English private and Joint-Stock Banks of Issue had £4,941,680 of notes in circulation on the *authorized* basis without any return of specie; the Scotch Banks held £3,324,893 of coin, with a note-circulation of £5,313,560; and the Irish Banks held £2,942,760 of coin, with a circulation of £4,941,680.† In other words, summing up these particulars, with a total bank-note circulation of £43,612,804, there was in the month adduced a total visible reserve of specie in the United Kingdom amounting to £29,393,762, or 13*s.* 5½*d.* in specie for every one pound in paper; whereas, reverting to the figures of the Bank of England and the Scotch Banks in the three years preceding the Acts of 1844-45, the amount of specie held in proportion to notes in circulation, exhibits a wide variation from 2*s.* 8*d.* to 5*s.* 2*d.*, and not rising, even in the Bank of England, when the highest amount of specie held in the three years is compared with the highest amount of notes in circulation, above 12*s.* 3*d.* in specie for one pound in paper. It must thus be acknowledged that as regards banks of issue, the legislation of Sir Robert Peel has compelled a larger reserve of specie in proportion to note-circulation than was formerly customary; and as this is clearly the only object which that legislation had in view, there is but little grace in owning that this object has, in an average and rough nominal way, been realized.

But to arrive at the true value of such a result as this, in any economic or financial sense, various weighty considerations must be taken into account.

For example (1), the inherent tendency of bank-note issues, payable at sight, to diminish in proportion to the

* *Appendix to Reports on Commercial Distress.* 1848.

† The *Gazette* Returns.

aggregate amount of banking and commercial business they accomplish. This tendency, even without any substitutionary media of credit payment, would have been accelerated by the great social and material changes alone that have occurred since 1844; and it has been rendered still more apparent by the extensive use of other notes-of-hand since that date. The cheques of private firms, presented at the clearing-house for this form of paper in London alone, differing from the notes of the banks of issue in nothing but in a somewhat less accredited value, amounted, for the week ended 20th November last, to £128,498,000 sterling, or more than five times the whole note-circulation of the Bank of England. In Scotland, where the use of cheques is not so extensive, though constantly increasing, a similar social necessity may be traced in the great expansion of bank issue on certain days, and certain hours of certain days of the week, as compared with the published returns of circulation, exhibiting only the *minimum* of notes in the hands of the public after the complete exchanges of the Bank offices in Edinburgh and Glasgow have been made.* Were the

* It has always been well understood, and quite in terms of the Act of 1845, that the official return of Bank circulation in Scotland is the *minimum* of notes in the hands of the public when the Banks have effected their mutual exchanges, and that the *maximum* of note circulation in Scotland is consequently much larger. But there has been no information hitherto as to what the *maximum* note-issue in Scotland may be. The liquidation of the Western Bank has put into our hands the annual private balance-sheets of that Banking Company over a series of years. On 27th May, 1857 (the last private balance-sheet of the company), the amount of its notes *out* were £1,627,176; on 28th May, 1856, £1,573,676; on 30th May, 1855, £1,467,676; on 31st May, 1854, £1,455,056; and so on. It is not positive that we have in these figures the *maximum* issue of Western Bank notes, seeing that they express simply the notes due by the Bank on the fixed date of annual balance. But the highest *official* return of Western Bank circulation we have observed during these years in the *Gazette* is £525,852. As there was, and could be, no abnormal action in the circulation of Western Bank notes in the years immediately preceding the suspension of the Company,

Imperial Legislature, following out the narrow and superficial idea of 1844, to prohibit all issue of notes save that of some absolutely central national department, there would be nothing to prevent banks from filling up the void thus created, little less satisfactorily both to themselves and the public, by issuing cheques as other traders do, and cannot be prohibited from doing—an alternative sufficiently conceivable to reduce all legislation on bank-notes, save as to their expedient *minimum* denomination and their peremptory payability in specie at sight, to utter fatuity and abortion. In no sense, therefore, can the higher amount of specie now held by banks of issue in proportion to bank-notes in circulation than they customarily held anterior to the Acts of 1844–45, be regarded as any proof of greater security in our monetary transactions. To argue to the contrary, as was argued in 1844, is to argue on bases which have visibly passed away since that period, and cannot be brought into any arguable form in harmony with existing facts.

It is necessary not only to consider the instant *media* of circulation thus called into existence, both intensively and extensively, but (2), the immense increase and development of banking and discount companies in England, other than banks of issue, since 1844, with the corresponding increase and development, during the same period, of deposits, discount of bills of exchange, and bank credit in all its forms outside the responsible circle of issue. This new and vast access of banking business is directly absolved by the Act of 1844 from all obligation as to specie reserves. The language of the Act to all joint-stock banks or discount companies that might arise and form themselves round its principle, was plainly this: "You have nothing to do with

it may be reasonably inferred that the total emission of bank-notes in Scotland at particular periods of any month—or any week, for the monthly returns are merely abstracts of the weekly, and almost daily, data of the Banks in their exchanges—may be from three to four times more than the *minimum* circulation published in the *Gazette*.

specie reserves. That is not your concern. All you have to do is to deal in Bank of England notes, and the Issue Department will answer for all demands on you of specie." Yet it is from these banking processes, so immensely developed and enlarged since 1844, and not from any issue of notes payable at sight, that the roots of all real action on the specie reserves of the kingdom admittedly spring; and which action this panacea of the Issue Department has been so often proved, in woful characters of commercial and social desolation, to be quite unable to control or to meet.

Were a return made of the number and magnitude of non-issuing banks and discount companies in England, of the relative share of the banking business of the kingdom they have acquired since 1844, and what amount of their banking reserve they hold in specie, such a return would show conclusively how nominal and insignificant the access of coin and bullion held by banks of issue in proportion to their notes in circulation under the laws of 1844–45 becomes, when thus contrasted with the mass of financial and commercial responsibility that has grown up beside it. There is a palpable mistake in supposing that a "free and plural" issue of bank-notes payable at sight implies an inadequacy of specie reserve, and that some form of "central issue" on a metallic base ensures a perfect fullness of this necessary commodity. As far as we have been able to see into the matter, the argument is in the opposite direction, and a plural issue of bank-notes payable at sight, accompanied with its natural and conventional obligations, is sure to develop a greater amount of specie reserve, relative to the commercial action, than any exclusive form of central issue on a metallic base that can be contrived.

It is not the least weakness of "the currency theory" of 1844, that in divorcing issue from banking, it has at the same time divorced banking from all direct specie obligation; and in proportion as the amount of bank-notes in circulation, by a natural and irresistible tendency, increases in a diminishing ratio to the increase of the funds and business of which they are the partial instruments, this weakness is one that must become more marked, and be the source of greater instability in our monetary and commercial affairs, the longer this theory of 1844 has supreme sway.

CHAPTER X.

INCOMPATIBILITY OF ANY FORM OF STATE OR CENTRAL ISSUE WITH THE FREE AND REGULAR EXTENSION AND CONSOLIDATION OF BANKING INSTITUTIONS.

THE issue of bank-notes, unrestrained save by the legal obligation which they bear, and by the natural conditions necessary to their acceptability and circulation, and surrounding their use, in proportion as banking and issue are developed on a plural basis, with ever-increased security, has been the subject of much hostile debate. But it is impossible, in the clear light of experience in Scotland, to resist the impression that this feature of a freely developed banking system has been assailed with unfounded and unwarrantable prejudice.

The issue of bank-notes, indeed, may not always have been advocated with discretion. If, as M. Wolowski so often reminds us, there be those who confound notes with capital, the promise to pay with the means of paying, this is an illusion that need not be disturbing, since it may be safely left to the touchstone of practice. Any banking company that proceeds to issue notes under the impression that every fresh emission is the creation of so much capital, cannot fail to be cured of its mistake in a few days or weeks, and the remedial process will be all the more rapid if there are more sources of issue than one, and no attempt has been made to give the *prestige* of State privilege to what is a simple and commonplace commercial document. But, on the other side of the question, the misconceptions are more marked, and not so easily eradicated. It has pleased many, of great name in the rolls both of statesmanship and science, to visit upon the issue of bank-notes convertible at sight, all the evils of inconvertible paper, of a vitiated standard, of "legal tender," and even of an aberration so distinct from, and so independent of note-issues, as the mal-administration and abuse of credit. Allegations of this wide and irrelevant nature must be brought severely to the test of proof before they can have any logical value. It can be averred, as a general and sufficient answer to all incoherency, that Scotland has found a sure antidote to the supposed poison of bank-note issues in the payability of the notes on demand, and in the practice of periodical note-exchanges, which was the early result of her plural system of banks of issue. That the promissory note of the Banks shall be always what it professes to be; that it shall have no subterfuge or no "optional clause;" that it shall consequently not encroach on the standard of value or supersede the money of the realm, but be always resolvable, in the exchanges of the banks themselves and in the commerce of the public, into the value which it represents; and, finally, that it shall have no element of force in its circulation, but shall be left to pass current, and to make its own way by the confidence it inspires;—these are the simple but very binding and searching provisions in which the Scotch system of issue has found its security in practice, and that are its ample defence in argument or in theory.

It is not a little strange that the opponents of the issue of bank notes, the importance of which to the banking system they reduce to insignificance, should associate with it every form of danger and evil, while deposits, the relative magnitude of which they can scarcely find language sufficiently swelling and emphatic to describe, suggest to them no grounds of apprehension whatever, but, on the contrary, ideas only of safety and solidity. It is the deposits of a bank, and not its notes, which enable it to extend its loans, credits, and discounts. If there is danger of an excess of credit, it is its deposits alone that supply the means of such excess. In a period of pressure, it is the demands of depositors, and not of the note-holders, which a Bank has reason to fear; and, when the situation is so bad that distrust or panic sets in, it is the withdrawal of deposits, and not the cashing of notes, that gives the fatal blow to a tottering establishment. The metallic reserves of the Banks, in the case of a drain of gold, are more sure of being attacked through the action of merchants on their bills of exchange and deposit accounts than by bank-notes collected with difficulty from the circulation, which requires in all circumstances an almost equal quantity of currency, and firmly holds what it requires. Every danger, whether of an undue extension of credit or an exhaustion of the specie reserves, attributed to the issue of bank-notes, may be tenfold more reasonably ascribed to deposits, with respect to which M. Wolowski feels only the most perfect and unruffled security, and which no one on his side of the question has yet ventured directly to attack, albeit the line of argument they pursue against bank issues leads up, by necessary sequence, to that last and desperate encounter. To contend that deposits, as well as the issue of notes, must be restrained, and placed under central repression, that loanable capital must not be too much increased, and that banking must not be free, would be too much for public intelligence. Yet, in truth, it is this startling conclusion which one always finds at the root of the ideas and reasonings of the advocates of "the currency theory" on which the legislation of 1844-45 is founded.

M. Wolowski gives various indications throughout his work of a scheme by which banking may be introduced and extended in the agricultural districts of France. But without presuming to limit the ingenuity of our neighbours, it may be safely said that to have abundant and instant means of payment at all the offices of a Bank, and at the same time to allow interest and keep faith with depositors in the form suited to their convenience and to their current transactions, are results not easily reconciled with a central source of issue; and that difficulties of space alone are such a hindrance to the extension of banking, and of the usages and habits formed and required by banking, over the face of a whole country, as the right of issue on the part of banking companies has alone been able hitherto to surmount. The question betwixt a central and a plural issue is in reality a question whether banking is to be confined to the great capitalists, or to a few of the greatest towns, and to the high commerce of nations, or opened to all classes of people, and made to embrace the industry, savings, and interests of the many. The tendency of a State or central form of issue is to aristocratize banking. The effect of a plural issue is to popularize this powerful lever both of moral and material improvement. The one seems, therefore, as conformable as the other is counter to the social tendencies of the age, and to that ever-advancing impulse to raise, enrich, refine, and brighten the whole body of a people, which is the crowning glory of all civilization.

It is very probable that Sir Robert Peel did not suppose that he was placing any fetters on the formation and extension of banking companies by the system of issue which he propounded to the Legislature, and succeeded in making law. His words signify as much. He said, in bringing in the Bill of 1844, that "the business of banking, as distinguished from issue, is a matter in respect to which there cannot be too *unlimited* and *unrestricted* a competition. The principle of competition ought to govern the business of banking."* Mr. Gladstone has more recently expressed himself in similar terms, while adhering tenaciously to a central and State issue of notes on the existing English model. M. Wolowski quotes these opinions with much satisfaction. But, notwithstanding the very high authority on which they come to us, these opinions cannot be right in their conclusion; because if they do not err in one of the premises on which their conclusion is founded, they err in the other, and the result is all the same as if they erred in

* *Hansard*, 6th May, 1844.

both. For, in the first place, if bank deposit and ordinary bank processes are to be free and unrestricted, it is manifest that the sources of evil and disorder, which the postulate in the matter of issue is intended to close, will remain fully open; and, in the second place, it is as manifest that if issue is not to be free from this postulate, bank deposit and ordinary bank processes cannot possibly be so free, nor so "unlimited and unrestricted," in the most technical sense, as they would be without it.

It cannot now be disputed that in Scotland, whatever may have been the calculation of Sir Robert Peel, no new banking company can be established, or no competition in banking take place beyond the competition of the Banks of authorized issue, under the laws of 1844-45. It is also known that the competition, so far now permitted in Scotland, is not equal, the Banks of older formation having larger, while the Banks of more recent origin have smaller privilege. And it is no less evident that the same causes that have dispelled from banking in Scotland the "unlimited and unrestricted competition," which Sir Robert Peel professed to maintain, and of which he said there could not be too much, must operate with more or less force in all parts of England at any considerable distance from London. This is a kind of monopoly to establish which does not require a direct and specific enactment like the corn, sugar, and other monopolies long happily abolished in this country, because it has its source, under the currency law of 1844, in those natural difficulties of time and space which interpose an obstacle to innumerable human operations.

A banking company, on the principle of the Act of 1844, must have access, and if fair play is to rule, must have access equal to that of other banking companies, to the source of issue. It cannot live without immediate command of supplies of the currency in which payments are customarily made. When the right of issue is free every

Bank has this resource in its own hand, and carries it wherever it may establish itself, at its branches as well as its head office. But when this right of issue is stopped, and notes are only authorized from a central source, the facility a bank may enjoy in supplying itself with currency for the uncertain demands upon it can only be in proportion to its proximity to the Issue Department. Suppose that a State Issue Office be opened in London, as such an office practically has been opened in the Issue Department of the Bank of England, where notes are to be given out on a deposit of bullion, it is manifest that a bank in London would stand in a much more convenient and economical relation to the Issue Office than a bank in any of the provincial towns or districts of England. Not only from being in the centre of the bullion market would it possess facilities of buying and selling bullion not attainable in the provinces, but from its immediate neighbourhood to the Issue Office it would have the power of sending every day, if necessary, for a supply of notes, and for the exact amount of notes it required. With the fountain of issue in the next street, it would be under no apprehension of being caught unawares with too small an amount of notes in its till, and would consequently lodge only so much of its funds in the Issue Office as was rendered necessary by the actual demands of its business. Where deposits on call are largely held, and where a bank cannot estimate the amounts it may be asked at any moment to pay, this is no inconsiderable advantage; but in reality involves both an essential security, and a valuable economy of capital. A bank, on the other hand, in Liverpool, Leeds, or Newcastle would be very differently situated. It would be under the necessity of lodging value in the Issue Office not only for the amount of notes which it might fairly calculate on being ample in the ordinary course of business, but for the further amount necessary to protect it against unusual demands. A provincial bank would consequently have to keep a much larger proportion of its funds in the notes of the Issue Office than a bank in London, and would so far be crippled and deprived of means of profit as compared with a bank in London. The farther a bank was removed from the Issue Department, and the more remote the district in which it operated, this burden would be increased; so that the inconvenience, expense, and loss of profit imposed upon banking by this system of issue would be greatest and most oppressive where the amount of banking business is least, where banking finds most difficulty in making a profit, and where it consequently requires to be conducted with the utmost economy.

Nor does it follow that by increasing the number of State Issue Offices, and opening one here and there in the great towns of the kingdom, this injustice would be obviated. The banks fortunately situated in the towns where the State Issue Offices were opened would have the paper-notes thus brought much nearer to them, but they would have to go to London for the gold required for deposit; so that the difficulty would only present itself in a new and worse form, since there would be the same delay and uncertainty of instantly meeting demands, and since gold would be more difficult to convey from London than paper. For all practical purposes the Issue Department might as well be confined to the metropolis. There is an obvious limit, moreover, to the creation of State Departments for the issue of notes. They require, as a necessary adjunct of the office they have to perform, a stock-exchange and a bullion market wherever they may be established. On the other hand, all the branches of a bank need the aid and vicinity of issue as much as the head office. Wherever an office is opened for deposits an ample fund of currency must be kept in the coffers to repay the depositors on demand, and it is all the difference in the world, if the depositors are to receive interest for their money, whether this currency is the Bank's own paper, or the paper of the State for which the Bank

O

at some distant and central point has previously lodged value.

The most weighty and insuperable reasons are surely necessary to induce any community to throw aside an instrument of banking and circulation, which overcomes all these difficulties so admirably, and is at once so simple and yet so capable of being used with safety, as the bank-note payable at sight.

The cause of the periodical drains of bullion is not to be found in the issue of bank-notes, but in the play of the great free capital of the country, in the speculative spirit which reveals itself under all systems of banking and currency, and in the sudden and often enormous derangements produced by wars, revolutions, and failure of harvests, for which it is necessary to stand well-prepared, but which in all their results cannot be brought under absolute command within the limits of a "theory of currency." The notes at sight of banks of issue, by familiarizing the minds of the great body of the people with representative value, tend not only to conserve and strengthen the specie reserves of the banks, but in periods of difficulty to discourage panics and consequent "runs for gold," which, considering the incalculably greater mass of deposits having the same claim for payment as bank-notes, cannot possibly under any conceivable arrangement be either prepared for, save by the enlightened and well-founded confidence of depositors and note-holders in the integrity of the bank administration, or satisfied by any strength of immediate bank resources when such unusual and boundless demands are made. The promissory notes of the Banks present no weakness either to the commercial drain of bullion, or the drain of bullion arising from abnormal causes, which is not common to deposits in banks, and to State or any other form of paper currency payable at sight. As regards the drain of bullion, and the train of economic causes and effects with which the drain of bullion has been connected in defence of "the currency theory," more has not been pressed for in the course of these remarks than that the argument may be held at least equal, and that the essential superiority of the banking system of issue appears in the adaptation and efficacy with which it ministers to all that is meant and desired to be attained by banking institutions. Yet there is one palpable advantage, even in the drain-of-bullion aspect of the question, peculiar to the Scotch or banking principle of issue which cannot be overlooked, viz., that under its action the obligation of maintaining the specie reserves is laid forcibly on the banks of issue, on the chief administrators of discount and credit, who must be allowed to have the greatest practical knowledge, the largest means, and the most powerful motive to maintain them. It thus raises a strong interior defence against an exhaustion of the specie reserves in the vital corporate interest of the issuers. Whereas the "currency theory" of 1844 has no similar interior defence, but throws all its fortification on the miscellaneous and irresponsible "action of the public," and professes, indeed, to have no defence but the rate of discount, which, besides not being by any means its exclusive property, has been proved, when thus left alone, to be ineffective for this particular purpose.

The right of issue contains, indeed, within its own natural conditions, obligations, and developments, such an affluence, as one may call it, of conservative power, that it is all the more wonder that it should be the object of so much prejudice and debate. The obligation of paying the notes in gold and silver on demand is a sure safeguard not only against excess of issue, depreciation, and confusion of the standard of value, but against not a few errors in banking administration itself. It compels bankers to study more closely the general laws of money and commerce than they would otherwise have occasion to do. It binds by a direct obligation in each banking company the business of discount with the influx and efflux of bullion. It is the system most likely to train provincial bankers in the science of foreign exchange, and to carry the enlarged views and general maxims of banking and finance into the bank parlours of the country. But the payment of notes on demand, not only invaluable as a safeguard in itself, is the source of other safeguards scarcely less important. Each bank of issue operates as a check on the issues of all other banks. The exchange of notes, weekly or semi-weekly or thrice-a-week, is at once introduced, whereby every bank of issue is brought to account, and required to retire its notes. The interest allowed on deposits has the same effect, since no one keeps parcels of bank-notes idle in his hands when by carrying them to the bank he can turn them into a source of profit. The issue of notes is thus kept down to the minimum by the most rigorous and inevitable processes. Then, the effect of issue on the organization and substantiality of the bank of issues is most stringent. Sir Robert Peel debarred by statute the formation of any new bank of issue in Scotland, but he might have left this stroke of policy to the conservative action of the Scotch Banks themselves. In a country where banking issue is organized, every new bank of issue must approve itself to the existing banks, which might otherwise refuse its notes, and keep it out of the circle of the note-exchanges. This exclusion, of course, could not be exerted without plain and strong reasons, but it is easy to perceive the scrutiny with which the constitution and resources of every new banking company would be scanned. The fear, indeed, that under liberty and plurality of issue there would be an excessive multiplication of banks is a mere chimera. Under a right of issue banking companies have the power of extending themselves from leading centres over wide tracts of country. The whole tendency, therefore, is towards consolidation. Small, weak, and localized banks disappear in great and solid companies embracing an immense variety of interests, and superior to local accident or misadventure. The play of freedom brings about what is so much desired by the admirers of a grand solitary State issue, namely, bank-notes having an Imperial currency, and representing in the remotest parts of the commonwealth the same value as at the place of issue. So far from legislation being supremely necessary, the difficulty is to see where the State or the law can touch a system so well-poised in its own conditions without spoiling it.

CHAPTER XI.

APPLICABILITY OF THE SCOTCH SYSTEM TO OTHER COUNTRIES.

THE chief aim of this work has been to give a true and popular exposition of the Scotch system of issue, and of its relation to the remarkable development and prosperity of banking in Scotland. The idea of *propagandism* has been no part of its design. Every nation or community must be the best judge of the proper form of its banking institutions, as well as how far an engraftment of banking issue and other features peculiar to the Scotch system may be suitable to its moral and material circumstances. The concentration of social and national life in Scotland; the intimate relations of the most distant parts of the territory with the leading centres of trade and commerce; the practical knowledge and directing skill of prudent bankers, and the light and science of distinguished economists, brought to bear at an early period on all the operations of the system, and on the principles by which they are governed; as well as the aptitude with which a shrewd and intelligent population comprehended, and endeavoured steadily and perseveringly to realize its advantages, have all contributed to the eminent success of the Scotch mode of banking and issue. There can be no doubt that Scotland found, in the characteristic principle of her banking institutions, what was suitable to her own case; and it may be hoped that a more general knowledge and appreciation of this principle will at least save it from further attacks of the Imperial Legislature, if not also promote a disposition in Parliament and elsewhere to conserve it in all its integrity as regards Scotland, though it should be at the expense of some essential modification of the Act of 1845. But, while thus confining our ambition, it must be said that the mode of issue involved in the Scotch system is a question of fundamental and universal interest. Between this plural and distributed mode of issue and a central and unitarian issue under some form of State mechanism, all civilized nations have more or less to choose.

There are now many great joint-stock banking companies of deposit and discount alone, both in the metropolis and the leading provincial centres of England, of quite national repute, which might reasonably and justly assume the right of issue, with its corresponding obligation of bearing a due part in the maintenance of the specie reserves; while the Bank of England could return at a month's notice to its system of action and account before the Bank Charter Act of 1844 with great advantage to itself, and to the public interest. The Bank of England as a corporation, in point of fact, is most grossly injured by being made the *corpus vile* of State experiments in "the currency theory." It divides a modest five per cent. per annum among its proprietors, while the banking companies of deposit and discount that have grown up around it since 1844, divide from 15 to 30 per cent., and scarcely know what to do with their profits. But the last thing they do with them is to increase their capital, which consequently bears an always diminishing ratio to their deposits and discounts, to the magnitude of their transactions, to the extent of their action in the whole monetary problem, and to their growing superiority to the Bank of England itself, bound as it is to the mechanism of the Issue Department, like Ixion to his wheel, for the end only of supplying currency on an assumed but really fictitious metallic basis to all the banking companies acting and profiting around it. The result is, that the Bank of England loses more and more its proper banking and commercial functions, that it becomes more and more an organ of circulation only, and that the interests of its proprietors are sacrificed. That the great national Bank of the English, peerless in its position among all the Banks of the world, should thus be disprofited and degraded, under the barren pretence of "regulating the note circulation," which, as long as payable at sight, is seen, in the experience of Scotland as well as in the whole reason of the matter, so admirably and perfectly to regulate itself, is one of the practical absurdities with which the legislation of 1844 has deeply infected our whole banking policy and organization. Were England to return to a system of plural issue, under the more enlightened understanding in that country of what plural issue means and involves, the Bank of England, without losing its national *prestige*, would recover its freedom as a banking corporation; it would be the centre of affiliation to all other banks of issue in England; while sharing freely with other banking companies in the commercial action of the country, and in its profits, it would be a model,—and more than a model, a controlling power—both as regards the specie reserves and the general rules of banking administration, to all other English Banks of Issue; and the whole monetary and banking state would thus attain a more strong, ample, and stable national development. On the contrary, in the course we are going, there is an enormously increasing progress of banking outside the stationary range of the Bank of England; a growing anarchy betwixt the closely related elements of deposit, discount, and specie reserve, and a constant lessening of the position and influence of the Bank of England in all save the special function to which it has been set by Act of Parliament—viz., of increasing notes in the issue department when nobody wants them, and diminishing them in the circulation by violent measures, in extremity, when to every one they are of vital service.

The United States have found in the inconvertible "greenbacks" of the Civil War a more uniform and satisfactory paper currency, though under constantly varying rates of discount, than they probably ever possessed under a free bank issue—the result having been, in periods before the War, that apart from radical defects in the constitution of banks of issue, which were numerous and flagrant, the farther, through the vast regions of the Republic, notes were directed or circulated beyond their source of issue the more unknown and suspicious they became. This is an admission to the other side of the question. A degree of national concentration, admitting of a mutual understanding and co-relation of the banks of issue, is necessary to the maintenance of bank-notes at par value within the sphere of their circulation. But it may reasonably be supposed that the United States will return at some period or other to specie payment, and when this return comes or is contemplated all the difficulty of a Federal currency payable at sight will be discovered. Or may not this very difficulty give to the resumption of specie payment in the United States an indefinite postponement? The American Republic, while justly entitled to a place in the front rank of civilization, and while professing, indeed, to be ahead of all other civilized countries, is subject to the barbarism arising from natural and territorial conditions, and contains not a few States and extensive fringes of territory where this question of issue and banking can scarcely be said to have a *locus standi*, and whence it would be inept to draw any conclusions. But in so far as the Scotch system of bank issue tends more than any other to develop banking, to increase bank deposits, and to extend in a joint and public form the enriching effect of individual habits of saving and economy, it must be as suitable and as desirable to all the busy and well-organized States of the American Republic as to any other civilized part of the world, if not even more suitable and desirable in proportion as in the United States the amount of loanable capital bears a smaller ratio to the number and energy of the people, and to the rich but undeveloped resources of production, than in probably any other country.

That the system of Scotch banking and issue is thoroughly applicable to all the Western nations of Europe can require little argument to demonstrate. If there be one of these nations which has a special need, as well as a special aptitude, for the ingenious and fruitful organization of banking agencies and resources that has been displayed in Scotland, one would say that it is France, where this question at various periods has been so keenly discussed. The compact national life of France; the current of national sympathy that runs through the whole land, impressing on the nation, despite of all ancient landmarks and divisions, a more homogeneous character than is exhibited elsewhere, unless it be in the much narrower field of Scotland itself; the frugal and saving spirit of its millions of peasant-proprietors and country people, that has more than once astonished the world by the promptitude with which it has taken up vast national loans by hoards of money brought forth from unseen recesses, and for which in ordinary times there appears to be no better or more productive channel; the rich soil that seldom fails to respond fruitfully to every outlay of capital and labour in its improvement; the skilful artizans of the towns, the indisputable superiority of many branches of manufacture, and all the elements of a great and unique national commerce requiring only impulse and support at home to extend it into wider markets abroad;—these and other characteristics of France combine to form the very conditions under which solid banking companies, enabled by right of issue to ramify into all parts of the country, and affiliated to a great and experienced central institution like the Bank of France, so well qualified to give a wholesome tone and model to the whole system, may be confidently expected to produce their most beneficial results.

APPENDIX.

I.

LATEST ABSTRACT BALANCE-SHEETS OF THE SCOTCH BANKS.

THE BANK OF SCOTLAND.

(*From Annual Report of Directors, as at 29th February*, 1872.)

Liabilities.	£	s.	d.	Assets.	£	s.	d.
Paid-up Capital, ...	£1,000,000	0	0	Gold and Silver Coin, and Notes of other Banks, ...	£509,221	3	7
Reserve Fund, ...	300,000	0	0	Government Securities, Cash with London Bankers, and short Loans in London, ...	2,879,272	7	10
Note Circulation, ...	697,232	0	0	Indian Government and other Stocks and Investments, ...	174,388	19	3
Drafts issued payable within fourteen days, ...	149,183	5	4	Liabilities of Customers for Acceptances by the Bank, as per contra, . .	1,532,232	9	5
Deposits, including accrued Interest, .	8,583,782	14	2	Bank Premises at Edinburgh, and Branches, ...	193,823	7	5
Acceptances to Banking and other Customers, covered by Securities, .	1,532,232	9	5	Bills Discounted, Cash Accounts, and other Advances, ...	7,057,180	17	9
Half-yearly Dividend, payable 9th April, 1872, ...	60,000	0	0				
Balance of Profits carried forward, .	23,688	16	4				
	£12,346,119	5	3		£12,346,119	5	3

THE ROYAL BANK OF SCOTLAND.

(*From Annual Report of Directors, as at 20th September,* 1872.)

LIABILITIES.

	£	s.	d.	£	s.	d.
1. To the Public:—						
Deposits, . .	£9,580,177	10	2			
Drafts payable within 14 days, .	383,827	16	4			
Acceptances, . .	374,774	9	4			
Notes in Circulation,	801,459	0	0			
				£11,140,238	15	10
2. To the Proprietors:—						
Capital, . .	£2,000,000	0	0			
Rest, ...	400,000	0	0			
Reserve for equalization of future Dividends, .	30,000	0	0			
Balance of Profit and Loss, . .	109,481	1	4			
				2,539,481	1	4
				£13,679,719	17	2

ASSETS.

	£	s.	d.	£	s.	d.
Bills Discounted, Cash Accounts, and other Advances, ...				£9,306,537	3	3
Bank Buildings, Edinburgh and Branches,				137,192	9	4
Government Stocks and Cash with London Bankers, . .	£2,537,991	12	10			
Gold and Silver Coin and Notes of other Banks, . . .	870,810	9	10			
Bank of England and other Stocks, and Securities, . .	827,188	1	11			
				4,235,990	4	7
				£13,679,719	17	2

THE BRITISH LINEN COMPANY BANK.

(*From Annual Report of Directors, as at 15th April, 1872.*)

LIABILITIES.

Deposits, ...	£7,451,671	7	1			
Acceptances by the Bank and their London Correspondents, . .	296,229	0	0			
Drafts outstanding on demand, or not exceeding eleven days' date, .	249,367	4	7			
Notes in circulation, .	518,150	0	0			
Total liabilities to the Public,				£8,515,417	11	8
Capital, . . .	£1,000,000	0	0			
Reserved Fund or Rest, .	348,651	13	5			
Net Profit of the Year after providing for rebate of interest on bills current, and bad and doubtful debts, . .	143,540	1	8			
Together,	£1,492,191	15	1			
Less Half-year's Dividend paid to the Proprietors at Christmas last, .	55,000	0	0			
Total liabilities to the Proprietors,				1,437,191	15	1
Total liabilities to Public and Proprietors,				£9,952,609	6	9

ASSETS.

Advanced on Cash and Credit Accounts, .	£2,312,817	1	9			
Bills under Discount, and Securities held against Acceptances by the Bank and their London Correspondents, . .	4,812,568	7	2			
Bank Premises at Head Office and Branches, .	124,283	12	0			
Together,				£7,249,669	0	11
Government and Bank of England Stocks, Short Loans in London, and Cash Balances with London Correspondents, ...	£1,911,645	9	6			
Other Stocks, Bonds, Railway Debentures, etc., ...	445,479	4	8			
Gold and Silver Coin, and Notes of other Banks,	345,815	11	8			
Together,				2,702,940	5	10
Total Assets of the Bank,				£9,952,609	6	9

THE COMMERCIAL BANK OF SCOTLAND.

(*From Annual Report of Directors, as at 31st October, 1872.*)

Liabilities.

		£	s.	d.
Paid-up Capital,		£1,000,000	0	0
Deposits,		8,642,390	13	6
Acceptances by the Bank and its London agents, and drafts outstanding,		650,648	8	2
Notes of the Bank in circulation,		861,591	0	0
Rest or Surplus Fund, at 31st October, after providing for Dividend and Bonus payable in January, and £5,000 in reduction of the cost of Bank Buildings,		383,257	6	6
Set apart to pay Dividend in January, 1873,	£60,000			
Do. to pay extra Dividend or Bonus out of Year's Profits,	20,000			
Do. to be applied in reduction of the cost of Bank Buildings,	5,000	85,000	0	0
		£11,622,887	8	2

Assets.

	£	s.	d.
Bills Discounted and Advances on Accounts,	£8,021,170	6	10
Bank Buildings at Edinburgh and the Branches,	133,865	2	4
Government Stocks, Short Loans, and Cash Balances with London Correspondents,	2,161,376	12	8
Bank of England Stock, the Bank's Stock, Debentures, and other Investments,	535,962	1	4
Gold and Silver Coin and Notes of other Banks,	770,513	5	0
	£11,622,887	8	2

THE NATIONAL BANK OF SCOTLAND.

(*From Annual Report of Directors, as at 1st November*, 1872.)

Liabilities.

		£	s.	d.
I. Capital Stock of the Bank,		£1,000,000	0	0
II. Rest, after deducting Dividend and Extra Dividend or Bonus, payable in equal portions, in January and July, 1873,		342,000	0	0
III. Ordinary Dividend of 13 per cent.,	£130,000 0 0			
Extra Dividend or Bonus for the year of $1\frac{1}{2}$ per cent.,	15,000 0 0			
		145,000	0	0
IV. Circulation,		804,853	17	0
V. Deposits, Current Balances, &c.,		9,621,700	10	7
VI. Letters of Credit, Drafts, and Acceptances outstanding,		1,393,588	19	1
VII. Undivided Profits carried forward,		12,644	19	10
		£13,319,788	6	6

Assets.

	£	s.	d.
I. Bills Discounted, Cash and Current Accounts, &c.,	£9,110,552	13	2
II. Bank of England, the Bank's, and other Stocks, Bonds, &c.,	610,488	16	4
III. Government Stocks, Cash with London Bankers, and other available Funds,	2,735,577	6	6
IV. Gold and Silver Coin, and Notes of other Banks,	735,669	10	6
V. Bank Premises at Head Offices, London Office, and Branches,	127,500	0	0
	£13,319,788	6	6

THE UNION BANK OF SCOTLAND.

(*From Annual Report of Directors, as at 2nd April, 1872.*)

LIABILITIES.

Deposits,			£8,532,425 3 3
Balances due to Banking Correspondents,			187,531 8 4
Current Drafts on London,			114,766 7 5
Acceptances by the Bank and their London Agents,			213,927 7 1
Note Circulation,			884,213 0 0
Total Liabilities to the Public,			£9,932,863 6 1
Capital Paid up,		£1,000,000 0 0	
Rest Account,	£307,000 0 0		
Profit and Loss Account, 1st April, 1871, — balance brought forward,	14,166 5 3		
Profit and Loss Account, 2nd April, 1872,	135,355 11 4		
		456,521 16 7	
Total Liabilities to the Partners,			1,456,521 16 7
			£11,389,385 2 8

ASSETS.

Bills of Exchange, Local and Country Bills, Cash Credits, and other Advances on Security,		£8,198,100 6 1
Bank Offices: Glasgow, Edinburgh, and Branches,		159,711 8 9
Consols, and other Government Securities and Short Loans in London,	£1,875,716 15 2	
Other Securities and Investments,	416,527 19 8	
Gold and Silver Coin, and Notes of other Banks,	739,328 13 0	
		3,031,573 7 10
		£11,389,385 2 8

THE CLYDESDALE BANKING COMPANY.

(*From Annual Report of Directors, as at 31st December*, 1871.)

Liabilities.

		£	s.	d.
Capital of the Bank, .	£1,000,000			
Unissued Stock, . . .	100,000—	£900,000	0	0
Reserved Surplus Fund, ...		290,000	0	0
Circulation, ...		505,858	0	0
Deposits, ...		5,670,516	15	2
Acceptances, ...		254,468	15	7
Letters of Credit in transitu, Drafts payable within 8 days, and Balances due to Bank Correspondents, . . .		250,423	11	7
Surplus Profits, ...		130,420	18	2
		£8,001,688	0	6

Assets.

				£	s.	d.
Bills Discounted, ...				£4,404,966	9	4
Credit Accounts, ...				1,262,893	2	11
Bank Buildings, and Heritable Property connected therewith, and Property acquired for new Bank in St. Vincent Place, ...				141,277	7	8
Investments in Consols and other Securities, and Short Loans on Stock, . . .	£1,384,176	12	5			
Gold and Silver Coin and Notes of other Banks, and Cash Balances with London and Country Bankers, . .	808,374	8	2—	2,192,551	0	7
				£8,001,688	0	6

THE CITY OF GLASGOW BANK.

(From Annual Report of Directors, as at 5th June, 1872.)

Liabilities.

		£	s.	d.
I.	Deposits at Head Office and Branches, including Balances at the Credit of Banking Correspondents, ...	£6,613,342	15	4
II.	Bank Notes in Circulation in Scotland and the Isle of Man, .	681,340	0	0
III.	Drafts Outstanding, due, or with a Currency not exceeding Fourteen Days, ...	118,116	9	5
IV.	Drafts Accepted by the Bank and its London Agents on Account of Home and Foreign Constituents, ...	780,386	14	5
	Liabilities to the Public, .	£8,193,185	19	2
V.	Capital Account, £870,000 0 0			
VI.	Reserve Fund, . 270,000 0 0			
VII.	Profit and Loss, . 119,004 15 4			
	Liabilities to Partners, .	1,259,004	15	4
		£9,452,190	14	6

Assets.

			£	s.	d.
I.	Bills of Exchange, Local and Country Bills, Credit Accounts, and other Advances upon Security. . .		£6,624,271	8	1
II.	Advances on Heritable Property, and Value of Bank Buildings and Furniture, ...		215,237	0	0
III.	Cash on hand,—viz., Gold and Silver Coin and Notes of other Banks at Head Office and Branches, . .	£954,984 11 2			
	Government Stocks, Exchequer Bills, Railway and other Stocks and Debentures, and Balances in hands of Banking Correspondents, . .	1,657,697 15 3			
			2,612,682	6	5
			£9,452,190	14	6

ABERDEEN TOWN AND COUNTY BANKING COMPANY.

(*From Annual Report of Directors, as at 31st January*, 1872.)

LIABILITIES.	£	s.	d.	£	s.	d.
Amount due to the Public—						
Deposit and Current Accounts, &c., including Interest, . . . (No Acceptances)				£1,548,087	17	10
Notes in Circulation, . .				175,337	0	0
Proprietors' Accounts—						
Capital Paid-up, .	£182,000	0	0			
Guarantee Fund, .	27,000	0	0			
Net Profits for the Year, . .	23,343	8	0			
				232,343	8	0
				£1,955,768	5	10

ASSETS.	£	s.	d.
Specie, and Notes of other Banks, on hand; and Balances due by other Banks, ...	£201,510	15	4
Investments in Government Stocks, and other Securities, ...	376,141	13	7
Loans, Cash Credits, Bills Discounted, and other Advances, . . .	1,340,717	18	0
Bank Buildings, at Head Office and Branches, ...	37,397	18	11
	£1,955,768	5	10

THE NORTH OF SCOTLAND BANKING COMPANY.

(From Annual Report of Directors, as at 30th September, 1872.)

LIABILITIES.

	£	s.	d.	£	s.	d.
Paid-up Capital, ...				£320,000	0	0
Reserved Fund—						
Invested, per Contra, ...				60,000	0	0
Notes in Circulation, ...				326,339	0	0
Lodged with the Bank on Accounts Current and Deposit Receipts, with Interest added, ...				2,069,508	7	4
				£2,775,847	7	4
Balance of Profit and Loss Account, . . .	£39,873	8	1			
Less Dividend paid in May, . . .	16,000	0	0			
				23,873	8	1
				£2,799,720	15	5

ASSETS.

	£	s.	d.	£	s.	d.
Gold and Silver Coin; and Notes of, and Balances Due by, other Banks, . .				£337,113	8	5
Government and other Stocks, . .				447,442	10	8
Investment of Reserved Fund— £40,000 Stock in the 3 per Cent. Consols, 11,100 „ of the Bank of England,				60,000	0	0
				£844,555	19	1
Bills of Exchange, Local and Country Bills, Advances on Cash Credits and other Accounts and Securities, . .				1,929,788	6	10
Banking Houses and Ground at Aberdeen, Aboyne, Alford, Auchinblae, Banchory, Banff, Cullen, Elgin, Fraserburgh, Huntly, Invergordon, Inverurie, Keith, Laurencekirk, Lumsden, Macduff, Montrose, Old Deer, Peterhead, Portree, Stonehaven, and Strichen—						
Cost, ...	£57,239	5	8			
Written off, as formerly reported, . .	31,862	16	2			
				25,376	9	6
				£2,799,720	15	5

THE CALEDONIAN BANKING COMPANY.

(From Annual Report of Directors, as at 29th June, 1872.)

LIABILITIES.

Paid-up Capital,			£125,000 0 0
Circulation,			91,997 0 0
Deposit Accounts, Interest Receipts, &c.,			891,724 16 11
Surplus Fund,		£54,000 0 0	
Balance of Profit and Loss Account brought forward from 30th June, 1871,	£3,120 19 10		
Net Profits for year ending 29th June, 1872,	24,499 3 11		
		27,620 3 9	
			81,620 3 9
			£1,190,342 0 8

ASSETS.

Bills Discounted, Credit and other Accounts,	£746,693 17 2
Bank's Houses, and Furniture at Head Office and Branches,	24,927 15 9
Government and other Securities and Investments,	291,855 3 4
Specie, Notes of other Banks, and Balances due by Banking Correspondents,	126,865 4 5
	£1,190,342 0 8

II.

DISCOUNT RATES OF SCOTCH BANKS—1868-1872.

The process by which the average rates of discount on the various classes of bills of exchange—London three, four, and six months, and Local three, four, and six months—are calculated in the subjoined Table, is that of multiplying the number of days during which the rates last by *double* the rates, and dividing the product by ten, which gives the equivalent of days at 5 per cent. When this equivalent is obtained for the whole year, there is then a simple rule of three, and if 365 days, or 366 (leap year), give 5 per cent., the smaller number of days give the average actual rates for the year.]

1868.

Dys.	Lon. 3ms.		Lon. 4ms.		Lon. 6ms.		Local 3ms.		Local 4ms.		Local 6ms.	
323	×6=	193.8	7=	226.1	8=	258.4	7=	226.1	8=	258.4	9=	290.7
14	6	8.4	7	9.8	8	11.2	7	9.8	8	11.2	9	12.6
28	6	16.8	7	19.6	8	22.4	7	19.6	8	22.4	9	25.2
365		219.0		255.5		292.0		255.5		292.0		328.5
Average		£3 %		£3, 10s. %		£4 %		£3, 10s. %		£4 %		£4, 10s. %

Average Bank of England minimum £2, 1/11 %.

1869.

Dys.	Lon. 3ms.		Lon. 4ms.		Lon. 6ms.		Local 3ms.		Local 4ms.		Local 6ms.	
91	×6=	54.6	7=	63.7	8=	72.8	7=	63.7	8=	72.8	9=	81.9
35	8	28.0	9	31.5	10	35.0	9	31.5	10	35.0	11	38.5
36	9	32.4	10	36.0	11	39.6	9	32.4	10	36.0	11	39.6
14	8	11.2	9	12.6	10	14.0	9	12.6	10	14.0	11	15.4
20	7	14.0	8	16.0	9	18.0	8	16.0	9	18.0	10	20.0
35	6	21.0	7	24.5	8	28.0	7	24.5	8	28.0	9	31.5
77	6	46.2	7	53.9	8	61.6	7	53.9	8	61.6	9	69.3
57	6	34.2	7	39.9	8	45.6	7	39.9	8	45.6	9	51.3
365		241.6		278.1		314.6		274.5		311.0		347.5
Average		£3, 6/2		£3, 16/2		£4, 6/2		£3, 15/2		£4, 5/2		£4, 15/2

Average Bank of England minimum £3, 4/1.

1870.

Dys.	Lon. 3ms.		Lon. 4ms.		Lon. 6ms.		Local 3ms.		Local 4ms.		Local 6ms.	
203	×6=	121.8	7=	142.1	8=	162.4	7=	142.1	8=	162.4	9=	182.7
3	7	2.1	8	2.4	9	2.7	8	2.4	9	2.7	10	3.0
1	8	.8	9	.9	10	1.0	9	.9	10	1.0	11	1.1
3	9	2.7	10	3.0	11	3.3	9	2.7	10	3.0	11	3.3
7	10	7.0	11	7.7	12	8.4	11	7.7	11	7.7	12	8.4
7	12	8.4	13	9.1	14	9.8	12	8.4	13	9.1	14	9.8
7	11	7.7	12	8.4	12	8.4	11	7.7	12	8.4	12	8.4
7	9	6.3	10	7.0	10	7.0	9	6.3	10	7.0	11	7.7
7	8	5.6	9	6.3	10	7.0	9	6.3	10	7.0	11	7.7
14	7	9.8	8	11.2	9	12.6	8	11.2	9	12.6	10	14.0
14	6	8.4	7	9.8	8	11.2	7	9.8	8	11.2	9	12.6
92	6	55.2	7	64.4	8	73.6	7	64.4	8	73.6	9	82.8
365		235.8		272.3		307.4		269.9		305.7		341.5
Average		£3, 4/7		£3, 14/1		£4, 4/2		£3, 14/		£4, 3/9		£4, 13/7

Average Bank of England minimum £3, 2/.

1871.

Dys.	Lon. 3ms.		Lon. 4ms.		Lon. 6ms.		Local 3ms.		Local 4ms.		Local 6ms.	
61	×6=	36.6	7=	42.7	8=	48.8	7=	42.7	8=	48.8	9=	54.9
42	6	25.2	7	29.4	8	33.6	7	29.4	8	33.6	9	37.8
63	6	37.8	7	44.1	8	50.4	7	44.1	8	50.4	9	56.7
28	6	16.8	7	19.6	8	22.4	7	19.6	8	22.4	9	25.2
70	6	42.0	7	49.0	8	56.0	7	49.0	8	56.0	9	63.0
7	6	4.2	7	4.9	8	5.6	7	4.9	8	5.6	9	6.3
9	8	7.2	9	8.1	10	9.0	9	8.1	10	9.0	11	9.9
40	10	40.0	11	44.0	12	48.0	11	44.0	11	44.0	12	48.0
14	8	11.2	9	12.6	10	14.0	9	12.6	10	14.0	11	15.4
14	7	9.8	8	11.2	9	12.6	8	11.2	9	12.6	10	14.0
17	6	10.2	7	11.9	8	13.6	7	11.9	8	13.6	9	15.3
365		241.0		277.5		314.0		277.5		310.0		346.5
Average		£3, 6/		£3, 16/		£4, 6/		£3, 16/		£4, 4/11		£4, 14/11

Average Bank of England minimum £2, 18/.

1872.

Dys.	Lon. 3ms.		Lon. 4ms.		Lon. 6ms.		Local 3ms.		Local 4ms.		Local 6ms.	
95	×6=	57.0	7=	66.5	8=	76.0	7=	66.5	8=	76.0	9=	85.5
7	7	4.9	8	5.6	9	6.3	8	5.6	9	6.3	10	7.0
28	8	22.4	9	25.2	10	28.0	9	25.2	10	28.0	11	30.8
21	10	21.0	11	23.1	12	25.2	11	23.1	12	25.2	13	27.3
14	8	11.2	9	12.6	10	14.0	9	12.6	10	14.0	11	15.4
7	7	4.9	8	5.6	9	6.3	8	5.6	9	6.3	10	7.0
28	6	16.8	7	19.6	8	22.4	7	19.6	8	22.4	9	25.2
62	7	43.4	8	49.6	9	73.8	8	49.6	9	55.8	10	62.0
8	8	6.4	9	7.2	10	8.0	9	7.2	10	8.0	11	8.8
7	9	6.3	10	7.0	11	7.7	10	7.0	11	7.7	12	8.4
7	10	7.0	11	7.7	12	8.4	11	7.7	12	8.4	13	9.1
30	12	36.0	12	36.0	12	36.0	12	36.0	13	39.0	13	39.0
19	14	26.6	14	26.6	14	26.6	14	26.6	14	26.6	14	26.6
14	12	16.8	12	16.8	12	16.8	12	16.8	13	18.2	13	18.2
19	10	19.0	11	20.9	12	22.8	11	20.9	12	22.8	12	22.8
366		299.7		330.0		378.3		330.0		364.7		393.1
Average		£4, 2/1		£4, 10/5		£5, 3/7		£4, 10/5		£4, 19/11		£5, 7/8

Average Bank of England minimum £4, 2/1.

NOTE.—The Bank of England minimum rate of discount applies only to prime short-dated paper, and must not be taken as the average rate of discount in the metropolis in the same sense as the average rate of discount of the Scotch Banks is shown in the above Table. In reply to inquiries as to the London rates, a member of a leading banking house in London writes me as follows:—"To make a comparison of the average Scotch rates for three, four, and six months' bills with the Bank of England minimum is, of course, unfair. You are also quite right in supposing that the bulk of the "trade" paper passing here is superior to that in Scotland, if you exclude the bills of the leading firms in Glasgow and some of the other large towns. The trade paper in most of the English provincial towns is also inferior; but in many of these places the bankers never think of charging less than 5 per cent. The Bank of England does not discount bills of more than three months' currency. They make advances on longer-dated paper; but when holders of such bills wish to discount them they take them to the bill-brokers. Discount brokers' rates for 'short remitted bills' are almost always lower than the Bank minimum—perhaps a quarter per cent. under on the average—and even fine three months' trade bills are generally a shade under the Bank rate. But when you consider the amount of four and six months' bills which are also taken in the London market at higher rates, I am inclined to think that the average of the whole business done may be about a quarter over the Bank rate. The current rates for Bank and other bills, in the London market, of the various currencies, published weekly in the *Economist*, &c., are generally pretty near the mark—perhaps being rather under sometimes for four and six months' bills. But, of course, their figures can give no idea of the proportions of the different classes of paper." What the comparative rates of discount in the English provinces may be there are no means of ascertaining. The rates of discount of the Scotch Banks are uniform in town and country, and at all the offices of the Banks.

It will be observed in the first year of the above Table (1868), that the rates of discount on the various classes of bills in the Scotch Banks did not vary throughout the year, and our figures might have so far been curtailed but for the necessity of marking that the Bank of England minimum had changed during the year. When the Bank of England minimum falls to 2 per cent. and under, the Scotch Banks do not follow the ½ per cent. reductions and advances of that state of the London money-market; and on the other hand, as will be seen from the last year of the above Table (1872), when the Bank of England minimum is on the ascending scale, and reaches 5 to 7 per cent., the rates of discount on all classes of bills in the Scotch Banks are greatly equalized, and local bills obtain an advantage of which they seem somewhat unduly deprived when the Bank of England minimum is on the low and descending scale. Thus in 1872, though the higher rates of discount prevailed only in the latter part of the year, the average rate of discount on local three months' bills was precisely the same as on London four months' bills, and only 8/4 per cent. above the average Bank of England minimum. This policy of the Scotch Banks becomes still more marked when the Bank of England minimum rises above 7 per cent.—*R. S.*

AS

d Dr

1879

1,681,4

758,6

545,5

650,6

1,393,5

	1865	1869.	1872.	1865.	1869.	1872.	1865.	1869.	1872.
Bank of Scotland,	£6,448,727	£8,384,957[1]	£8,583,783	£553,160	£510,644	£617,832	£681,091	£912,256	£1,681,41[illegible]
Royal Bank of Scotland,	8,127,742	8,340,601	9,580,177	311,091	704,210	801,639	394,310	434,836	738,60[illegible]
British Linen Company,	6,886,804	7,110,460	7,431,671	444,343	308,303	318,130	276,501	458,032	515,5[illegible]
Commercial Bank of Scotland,	7,086,834	7,841,610	8,642,390	697,423	715,884	861,591	330,432	378,161	650,64[illegible]
National Bank of Scotland,	7,205,107	8,178,148	9,611,700	670,075	378,310	804,833	310,326	917,098	1,393,58[illegible]
Union Bank of Scotland,	7,771,567	8,519,690	8,719,957	379,201	508,008	884,213	231,043	380,014	318,60[illegible]
Aberdeen Town and County Bank,	1,221,033	1,690,746	1,348,087	134,801	144,913	175,337			
North of Scotland Bank,	1,716,127	1,815,371	2,069,508	212,629	243,073	326,330			...
Clydesdale Banking Company,	4,378,710	5,319,943	5,670,517	408,170	463,018	505,838	163,592	171,131	304,5[illegible]
City of Glasgow Bank,	4,446,365	6,015,341	6,613,343	620,397	618,659	681,340	541,180	611,833	868,5[illegible]
Caledonian Banking Company,	694,548	773,700	891,724	83,256	84,897	91,027			
Central Bank of Scotland,	954,134[1]	...		53,310[1]					
	£57,140,620	£63,580,811	£64,390,257	£4,930,946	£5,300,943	£6,348,360	£2,668,881	£4,296,319	£6,761,0[illegible]

NOTE.—(1) These Figures apply to the Year 1866, no previous publication of Accounts having apparently taken place. (2) [illegible] the Central Bank of Scotland, [illegible] always made up at the close of business on Saturday, while the Annual Balance may take place between Exchange days.

ASSETS.

	Banking Advances.			Stocks and other Securities.			Bank Premises.	
	1865.	1869.	1872.	1865.	1869.	1872.	1865.	1869.
Bank of Scotland,	£5,458,607	£7,390,467	£8,389,414	£390,532	£190,911	£174,389	£125,386	£170,213
Royal Bank of Scotland,	8,206,985	8,300,757	9,306,537	974,245	970,645	827,160	112,032	107,764
British Linen Company,	5,926,964	6,958,490	7,125,385	992,163	707,768	445,670	123,977	118,204
Commercial Bank of Scotland,	6,179,293	7,099,769	8,091,170	859,659	801,205	535,964	94,640	106,581
National Bank of Scotland,	6,737,303	7,479,689	9,110,559	435,107	916,442	610,485	101,765	128,375
Union Bank of Scotland,	7,507,548	8,176,391	8,198,100	270,624	440,671	416,528	172,484	158,428
Aberdeen Town and County Bank,	1,182,031	1,095,310	1,349,717	...			28,510	27,063
North of Scotland Bank,	1,687,528	1,721,353	1,919,768				8,616	18,344
Clydesdale Banking Company,	5,191,737	5,468,731	5,667,860				96,348	113,196
City of Glasgow Bank,	4,812,807	6,204,779	6,684,971				202,620	214,229
Caledonian Banking Company,	854,037	939,528	740,691				15,353	23,018
Central Bank of Scotland,	1,103,518	...	...	...		...	16,662	...
	£51,878,548	£61,095,698	£66,660,488	£3,925,539	£4,037,640	£3,010,031	£1,091,564	£1,187,111

IV.

RATES OF INTEREST PER CENT. CHARGED, AND RATES OF INTEREST PER CENT. ALLOWED, BY THE SCOTCH BANKS, ON CASH ACCOUNTS AND OVERDRAFTS, AND ON DEPOSIT RECEIPTS AND DEPOSIT CURRENT ACCOUNTS, IN 1872, AS FOLLOWING THE BANK OF ENGLAND MINIMUM RATE OF DISCOUNT.

DATES.	Bank of England Minimum Rate of Discount.	Rate of Interest charged by Scotch Banks on		Rate of Interest allowed by Scotch Banks on		
					Current Accounts.	
		Cash Accounts.	Overdrafts.	Deposit Receipts.	Monthly Balance.	Daily Balance.
January 1,	3	4½	5	2	1½	1
April 4,	3½	5	5½	2½	1½	1
,, 11,	4	5	5½	3	1½	1
May 9,	5	6	6½	4	2	1
,, 30,	4	5	5½	3	1½	1
June 13,	3½	5	5½	2½	1½	1
,, 20,	3	4½	5	2	1½	1
July 18,	3½	5	5½	2½	1½	1
September 18,	4	5	5½	3	1½	1
,, 26,	4½	5½	6	3	1½	1
October 3,	5	6	6½	4	2	1
,, 10,	6	6½	7	4½	2½	1¼
November 9,	7	7	7½	5	3	2
,, 27,	6	6½	7	4½	2½	1½
December 12,	5	6	6½	4	2	1

V.

STATEMENT OF PAID-UP CAPITALS, RESERVE FUNDS, DIVIDENDS, AND PRICES OF STOCK OF THE PRINCIPAL SCOTCH BANKS.

[The Capital of each of the Banks under-named is Consolidated into £100 Stock.]

When Established.	Name of Bank.	Number of Branches	Capital Paid-up.	Reserve Fund.	Dividends Paid.			Prices of Stock.		
					1860.	1870.	1872.	1860. 28th Feb.	1871. 28th Feb.	1872. 31st Dec.
			£	£				£	£	£
1695	Bank of Scotland, . . .	75	1,000,000	300,000	8	11 & 1 bonus	12	200	269	286
1727	Royal Bank, . . .	87	2,000,000	400,000	6½	8	8½	145	184	192
1746	British Linen Company, .	55	1,000,000	350,000	9	11 & 2 bonus	11 & 2 bonus	214	266½	276½
1810	Commercial Bank, . .	91	1,000,000	383,257	10	12 & 2 bonus	12 & 2 bonus	220	287	289
1825	National Bank, . . .	77	1,000,000	342,000	9	13	13 & 1½ bonus	180	281	299¾
1830	Union Bank, . . .	109	1,000,000	312,000	9	12	13	171	248	280
1838	Clydesdale Banking Company,	74	900,000	300,000	7½	11 & 1 bonus	11 & 1 bonus	137½	225	257½
1839	City of Glasgow Bank, . .	117	870,000	280,000	4	9	10	83¼	184½	208½

VI.

PROPORTIONS OF CAPITAL AND COIN RESERVES TO NOTES ISSUED IN MONTH ENDING 7TH SEPTEMBER, 1872.

Capital.	Name.	Authorized Circulation.	Actual Circulation.	Coin Reserves.	Capital for each Pound Note Issued.		Coin for each Pound Note Issued.	
					Authorized Circulation.	Actual Circulation.	Authorized Circulation.	Actual Circulation.
£		£	£	£	£ s. d.	£ s. d.	£ s. d.	£ s. d.
1,000,000	Bank of Scotland, . .	343,418	607,655	331,406	2 18 3	1 12 11	0 19 4	0 10 11
2,000,000	Royal Bank of Scotland, .	216,451	642,289	539,313	9 4 9	3 2 3	2 9 10	0 16 9½
1,000,000	British Linen Company, .	438,024	513,101	150,821	2 5 8	1 18 11	0 6 11	0 5 10½
1,000,000	Commercial Bank, . .	374,880	708,658	434,906	2 13 4	1 8 3	1 3 2	0 12 3¼
1,000,000	National Bank, . . .	297,024	534,527	347,490	3 7 4	1 17 4	1 3 5	0 13 0
1,000,000	Union Bank, ...	454,346	720,858	387,365	2 4 0	1 7 9	0 17 1	0 10 8¾
182,000	Aberdeen Town & Co. Bank,	70,133	175,079	120,501	2 11 10	1 0 9	1 14 4	0 13 9
320,000	North of Scotland Banking Co.,	154,319	281,280	144,744	2 1 5	1 2 9	0 18 9	0 10 3½
900,000	Clydesdale Bank, . .	274,321	483,961	257,490	3 5 7	1 17 2	0 18 9	0 10 7½
870,000	City of Glasgow Bank, .	72,921	550,868	551,928	11 18 7	1 11 7	7 11 5	1 0 0½
125,000	Caledonian Banking Co., .	53,434	95,284	58,929	2 6 9	1 6 3	1 2 0	0 12 4¼
		2,749,271	5,313,560	3,324,893				
	Six Irish Banks, . Total,	6,354,494	7,242,081	2,942,760				

VII.

CHARTERED AND UNCHARTERED SCOTCH BANKS.

THE Chartered Banks of Scotland, a few years ago, had various legal privileges of a minute though important character, which were not possessed by the Unchartered Banks, or Banks of later origin, that had been constituted in the ordinary form of Joint-Stock Companies. The chief of these were (1) the right of suing, and of taking and holding securities, as corporate bodies; and (2) the right of holding in deposit all moneys required to be lodged in Bank by public and private Acts of Parliament, and more especially by the Pupils' Protection Act, the latter embracing the funds of minors, or pupils as they are termed in Scotch law. It was grievous to the Unchartered Banks to have large sums either intercepted or withdrawn from them, by mere force of ancient privilege, against the will and interest of the parties compelled so to act, and often, indeed, by their own directors and shareholders, in order to be deposited with the Chartered Companies. Under a statute of the 7th and 8th of Victoria, charters of incorporation might be obtained by any banking company, but only on conditions, such as preventing it from making advances on or purchasing any portion of its own stock, publishing a *monthly* account of its assets and liabilities, and renewal of its charter every twenty years, which would only have been an exchange of one series of disabilities for another. It is difficult to say how long this venom of inequality would have been allowed to operate in the Scotch banking system had it remained a matter affecting only the Scotch banking companies themselves. Parliament after Parliament, and Cabinet after Cabinet since 1845, have almost worshipped the whole arrangement made by the Act of that year as regards the Scotch Banks, and have never been disposed to look into the plainest matter of grievance arising therefrom, as if in fright lest they might discover some error of legislation still more portentous. But the great progress of joint-stock enterprize in almost every branch of industrial and commercial life led, in 1862, to a general statute, entitled "The Companies Act," whereby any joint-stock company, by registration, under general conditions, could obtain the privileges of corporate and chartered bodies. The Unchartered Banks in Scotland immediately availed themselves of this statute, passed through its prescribed forms of registration in common with a mass of other companies of entirely different calibre, and in this way the disabilities of Unchartered Banks in Scotland existing before 1862, as regards the right of suing, the difficulty of keeping securities available on any change of trustees, and the deposit of moneys under Acts of Parliament, have been almost wholly, if not wholly, removed. The question in its chief point—the deposit of money—came before the Supreme Court of Scotland in case of "petition Sheppard" in March, 1864, and was decided entirely in favour of the Unchartered, but, under Companies Act 1862, now registered Scotch Banks.

There is a difference in the licence duty paid for each branch office of the Banks in Scotland, which is of little or no moment save for the principle involved—viz., of the law seeming invidiously to encourage the opening of branches by one banking company as compared with another. The general rule adopted in 1844-45 seems to have been that any banking company that had been paying four licences for branches should not be required to take out any more than four; but that banking companies, not so situated, should have to take out licences for each branch office, £30 each—a rule tolerable enough probably at the time, but sure to become more unjust every year afterwards. And by the 13th clause of the Act of 1845, all Banks in Scotland, save the Bank of Scotland, the Royal Bank, and the British Linen Company Bank, are required to return the names of their partners every year, and to have the same advertised in the newspapers at their expense; which requirement, in its distinctive application, has no practical meaning whatever—for which, indeed, the excepted Banks themselves would not give the Chancellor of the Exchequer the smallest coin of the realm to-morrow, if asked—and that might consequently be allowed to pass unnoticed among much worse follies of legislation, but for the inuendo it conveys that all Banks in Scotland, save the three excepted ones, are existing and acting all the time under the grave and laborious suspicion of the British Monarchy and the Imperial Parliament!

The difference on minor points of privilege between Chartered and Unchartered Banks in Scotland has all but vanished, not from any attention given by the Legislature to this question in its special banking relation, but from the force of developments outside the banking sphere. It is now being discovered that there are important differences of privilege between the Chartered Banks themselves. The National Bank of Scotland, for example, has found nothing in its Charter to prevent, or that has prevented, its actual opening of an office in London for the discharge of banking business; whereas the Royal Bank of Scotland, whose Charters go back to a more ancient date than the Charter of the National, finds that it cannot do what the National has done. There is nothing in the question whether a Scotch Bank is to have an office in London or not, that involves any cardinal principle of banking, currency, issue, or anything else, on which philosophers and law-makers are divided. It is simply a question of bank administration in its merest detail—*i.e.*, a Scotch Bank being under the necessity, in its regular course of transaction, of having large funds in London, and of having a bank correspondent in London for the discharge of its functions, it becomes a matter of financial calculation whether it can do this business more profitably through a London Bank or through an office in London of its own. Such a matter as this should not have been left in any doubt by the law of the country. But, in the deep somnolency of the Legislature on the banking question, and its reverence for all that was arranged by the Banking Acts of 1844-45, there is no course left to the Scotch Banks, one after another, as circumstances determine, but to apply by private Acts of Parliament for the most common rights, not only of their profession, but of ordinary trade and labour.

The Royal Bank has given statutory notice of a Bill for the Session 1873, in which it is proposed to enable the company to transact banking business in any part of the United Kingdom, saving always, of course, that bugbear in England—the issue of bank-notes anywhere out of Scotland. The Bank of Scotland has also given statutory notice of a Bill, the main object of which is to increase the capital stock to any amount not exceeding £3,000,000, the increased stock to be issued from time to time. The present capital stock of the Bank of Scotland is £1,500,000, of which £500,000, though issued, has not been paid up; and it is hardly probable, therefore, that there is any intention of calling up £3,000,000 save by a very gradual and remote process. One result of this Bill, however, if passed, is that, supposing even any doubt to exist as to the unlimited liability of the partners of the Bank of Scotland, their liability would be extended to the amount of capital stock issued, whether paid-up or not. The increase of the capital stock of banking companies in proportion as their business and responsibilities extend, is an object worthy of all promotion by legislation. The opposite course of gathering round small and stationary banking capitals increasing millions of deposits and discounts, and dividing 25, 30, and other wild rates of annual profits among the partners—which has become much the rule in England since 1844—is both dangerous in tendency and reprehensible in principle.

VIII.

REPLIES OF A SCOTCH BANKER TO QUESTIONS BY "THE SUPERIOR COUNCIL OF COMMERCE OF FRANCE."

THE Superior Council of Commerce of France, in the State Inquiry to which prominent reference has been made in this volume, issued a list of Queries to the Scotch Banks. The following example of these Queries, and the Replies made to them by Mr. Charles Gairdner, Manager of the Union Bank of Scotland, exhibits both the nature of the inquiry as regards Issue in France, and the views with which it is met by gentlemen of practical banking experience in this country:—

ON PAPER MONEY.

What is the utility of paper money?

It is understood that the term "paper money" is intended to include bank-notes and any other forms of obligation, bearing no interest, and payable to bearer on demand.

Paper money has its origin and chief utility in its superior convenience as compared with the coin which it represents.

It has also an important utility in so far as by diminishing the quantity of coin in circulation it economizes capital.

It confers a third advantage in respect that the amount of money in circulation in any country being a fluctuating quantity, an increase or diminution in the amount of paper money in circulation may take place without disturbing the stock of coin which forms the reserve.

Is the part played by paper money tending to become very important?

There is no particular tendency operating in Great Britain to make paper money more important.

Is it by issues of notes payable to bearer at sight, or by means of transfers, current accounts, cheques, &c., that credit has a tendency to extend?

It is *not* by issues of notes payable to bearer at sight, nor by any other form of obligation payable on demand that credit has a tendency, to any appreciable degree, to extend.

The tendency of credit to extend arises mainly through the commitments of merchants, manufacturers, contractors, and others, the settlement or accomplishment of whose transactions is postponed.

Can the employment of paper money take an indefinite extension? If not, in what limits shall it be confined?

Paper money cannot take an indefinite extension. The amount of money (whether paper or coin) at any time in circulation is the aggregate amount contained *in the pockets and tills of the whole people.* This may be more or less according to circumstances: but as long as the paper is convertible into the coin which it represents, each individual will regulate for himself the amount retained for his own purposes; and it follows, that the aggregate amount in circulation is regulated by the requirements, or the convenience, or, it may be, the whims, of the community at large.

ON THE CONDITIONS OF A GOOD PAPER MONEY.

Under what conditions does the employment of paper money present no inconvenience?

The only condition that is at once essential and universal is that it be convertible into coin at the will of the holder. Other regulations may be required for the safety and convenience of particular communities, but these must be ascertained with reference to the circumstances of each case.

Is the constant convertibility of notes indispensable?

Undoubtedly so.

Does the unity of the Bank note promote the circulation of it?

The unity of the Bank note involves the supposition of there being only one bank of issue. This again of necessity involves that non-issuing banks shall keep a stock of notes procured from the single bank of issue. As this would not be necessary were all banks free to issue notes (as is the case with the existing Banks in Scotland), it follows that the "unity of the bank-note" increases the *apparent* circulation by the amount of the note reserves of the non-issuing banks.

What are the inconveniences and advantages of the plurality of banks, whether general or of limited circumscription?

This question appears to be in other words: "What are the inconveniences and advantages of freedom as compared with monopoly?"—for the non-plurality of banks *is* monopoly.

In reply, it may be stated that the arguments in favour of freedom in trade apply equally to freedom in banking, and, further, that in England and Scotland the principle of freedom in banking is now all but universally accepted. A difference of opinion exists as to the propriety of allowing all banks to issue notes, but in Scotland the right to do so is regarded as an integral and important part of the business of banking.

The advantages conferred by the system of banking pursued in Scotland are seen—

(1) In the facilities afforded to the public by the establishment, throughout even the most remote districts, of branch banks. At present there are nearly 700 banking offices in Scotland, emanating from 12 parent Banks.

(2) In the economy of capital so effected,—it being the universal practice of people even of the most moderate means to lodge their money with the Banks. The cash deposits in Scotland approach 60 millions sterling. The population is about three millions.

(3) In the allowance of interest by the Banks on all the money held by them from the public.

(4) In the advantages afforded to the industrious classes throughout the country by means of loans and advances.

(5) In the perfect security afforded to the public,—there never having been an instance of a Joint-Stock Bank in Scotland failing to pay its debts in full; and the cases in which, in former times, the failure of a private bank involved loss were extremely rare.

(6) In the manner whereby, *through being free*, the banking institutions of the country have been able to adapt themselves to the changing circumstances of the country. The private banks, which formerly conducted a large proportion of the business of the country, had paid-up capitals of small amount and a very limited number of partners. These have all now been absorbed into Joint-Stock Banks, the amount of whose paid-up capitals varies from £100,000 to £2,000,000, and each

bank includes in its list of partners from 500 to 1500 individuals. In this way the security afforded to the public has kept pace with the demands of a constantly increasing commerce.

As opposed to these advantages, it is not known that there are any inconveniences to state arising out of the plurality of banks.

ON THE ESTABLISHMENTS WHICH ISSUE PAPER MONEY.

Is there advantage or inconvenience in separating the Issue Department from the Discount Department?

There does not appear to be any sound principle to justify the separation in question, and the experience of its working by the Bank of England has not proved it to be of any practical advantage, but, on the contrary, it has created on many occasions serious complications.

If the notes of the Bank of France were made a legal tender, as is the case of those of the Bank of England, would it have the effect of promoting the circulation of them?

No.

What number of signatures ought a bank to require for its true security in the discount of bills?

Security is not to be ensured by the number of signatures to a bill, but by the exercise of a sound discretion as to the parties and the cir cumstances of each case.

Ought the issue of notes to be limited? Ought the issue to be proportionate to the metallic reserve of the capital?

(1). No.

(2). It is not correct to say that the issue should be proportionate to the metallic reserve of the Bank,—but rather that the metallic reserve ought to be proportionate to the *character* and *amount* of the liabilities of the Bank, whether upon notes or upon other forms of obligation, and this is a mode of stating the case not sufficiently attended to and considered.

ON BANKING OPERATIONS.

At what level ought to be maintained the metallic reserve of the Bank of France in order to secure the convertibility of the notes?

There is no fixed rule can be stated in answer to this question. Every Bank ought to know the character and amount of its own liabilities,—keeping constantly in view that the deposits equally with the notes are payable in coin, and that in times of pressure a demand for gold and silver is more likely to arise from a withdrawal of deposits than from a diminution of notes in circulation.

It is also to be kept in view that Paris and London are the natural bullion marts of France and England; because, in Paris and in London the exchange operations with foreign countries are chiefly conducted.

It follows that the Banks in these cities (and notably the Bank of France and Bank of England) hold the chief bullion reserves of all the Banks in the two countries, and these reserves are accessible to any Bank which holds the obligations of the bullion-holding Banks.

The *character*, therefore, of the liabilities of Banks in Paris and London differs essentially from that of the country banks—from whom coin or bullion, in large quantity, is seldom demanded,—and the metallic reserve that may be adequate and proper for the one forms no guide to that which is essential to the safety of the other.

What are the causes which tend to reduce or augment the metallic reserve, and the means to be employed to maintain the level of it?

The causes that affect the metallic reserve may be classed under three heads:—

(1). The natural increase or diminution of gold and silver coin in active circulation.—*i.e.*, in the pockets and tills of the people.

(2). Hoarding. This may be either from ignorance or from want of confidence in the Banks.

(3). Receipts from or payments to foreign countries.

The means capable of being employed by Banks to counteract these influences, are as regards the—

(1). The issue of bank-notes of such denomination as will meet the particular demand of the time. The prudence, however, of having recourse to this expedient must always be considered with reference to other circumstances besides the question of the metallic reserve.

(2). The removal of the causes of hoarding in so far as it may be possible to do so.

(3). The raising or depressing of the rates of interest and discount.

What is the part played by, and the destination of, the capital of the Bank? Ought the capital to be increased? What would be the effects of the increase?

The capital of the Bank is a fund contributed by those who are to enjoy the profits of the business, as a protection or guarantee to the creditors of the Bank.

Assuming that the capital is sufficient in amount to secure entire confidence in the stability of the Bank, there is no advantage to be gained by its being increased.

BELL AND BAIN, PRINTERS, 41 MITCHELL STREET, GLASGOW.

THE SOUTHERN STATES SINCE THE WAR.

1870-71.

By ROBERT SOMERS.

MACMILLAN & CO., LONDON AND NEW YORK.

OPINIONS OF THE PRESS.

From the "EDINBURGH REVIEW" (July Number, 1872).

The author set out from Washington in the autumn of 1870, and travelled over the whole South, everywhere noting the commercial and industrial condition and resources of the country, and gathering an immense mass of the most valuable information. His volume is the most complete account yet given to the public of the condition and prospects of the Southern States since the war. Mr. Somers was eminently qualified for the task of estimating from actual observation what those resources were. A man of business, thoroughly familiar with the cotton trade, and completely at home on all questions of labour, production, capital, and culture, he knew exactly what to observe, and how to test his observations so as to make them valuable. The obstacles to Southern prosperity are moral, social, political, and industrial, not natural. The trail of an evil institution was over all the paradise; and, though the institution has passed away, is over it still. The intelligent observation of Mr. Somers has, however, enabled us to make a clearer estimate than was possible before of the industrial resources by which the great natural gifts of the South are being developed; of the progress which has been made in the commercial and social reconstruction of the country; and of the obstacles which political difficulties still put in the way of a full restoration of peace, plenty, and prosperity.

From the "MANCHESTER COURIER."

Mr. Robert Somers is a tourist of a kind not too common in these latter days. He has travelled with an object, and he has taken pains to tell his story in the fullest, clearest, and simplest manner. There has been no rushing through the country in order to get over as much ground in as little time as possible, and what is perhaps better still, Mr. Somers is good enough to refrain from re-hashing newspaper articles and blue-books, after the fashion which a writer followed who once discoursed of "Greater Britain." The object our author had in view was that of giving an account of what has been done in the Southern States since the war, of the amount of success which has attended the attempt to introduce a new system of government, of the prospects of success which attend the cotton culture, and of the probabilities of the future development of the country. In carrying out his inquiries Mr. Somers was somewhat unusually favoured.

It is scarcely necessary to say that Mr. Somers being an Englishman, and a man of strong common sense, is a free-trader, and as such is disposed strenuously to condemn the protectionist policy which is dominant in the States. He does not professedly trace the war to the conflict between the two financial theories, but from various indications scattered throughout his book, we gather that he is by no means disposed to accept the Northern pretence that the war was one wholly for the extirpation of slavery. . . . Be this as it may, the war has left behind it a cruel state of things.

. . . .

Our quotations have been somewhat lengthy, but we have after all done no more than dip here and there into the pages of a very interesting and valuable contribution to public knowledge on American questions. No one who really wishes to understand the condition of the Southern States can afford to dispense with Mr. Somers's work, and no one who desires revolutionary changes after American models in our Constitution ought to pass over this most interesting description of the original.

From the (London) "MORNING POST."

In prosecuting his investigations Mr. Somers had the advantage of a letter from the Foreign Office, commending Her Majesty's Consuls to render him such assistance as they could properly afford, and of letters of introduction from private friends to various other sources of information in the States. The results of his observations he now presents to the public in the form of a considerable volume, containing many interesting notes and facts, which naturally go to support the conclusions at which he has arrived, but which are intended also to enable readers to form their own opinions upon the subject. The author disclaims having any bias in the matter, and states in his preface that the inquiry "has been accomplished without connection with any association, mercantile or political." One of the points to which he calls particular attention is the effect of the existing tariff on the Southern States. The tariff of the United States, always more or less protectionist, he observes, has, under the financial exigencies entailed by the late war, "attained a prohibitory and vexatious rigour which is without parallel, and gives the United States the curious distinction of being—China or Japan scarce excepted—the most anti-commercial country in the world." Of the effect of this state of things on the South, Mr. Somers gives a lively picture. . . . Mr. Somers also offers some observations on the system of farming in the cotton States of the South, contending that as the owners can no longer depend upon property in slaves to give to the plantations that permanence of value and regularity of crop which they enjoyed before the war, it has now become an object of the first importance, alike to the good of the country and to the future cotton supply, that some regular system of rotation of cropping should be carried out, so as to develop all the best qualities of the soil, and attain the great ends of permanent profit and improvement: to do, in short, for farming in the cotton States of the South, under negro emancipation, what rotation and green cropping have done for farming in England and Scotland under free-trade. . . . With regard to the system of free labour, Mr. Somers has come to the conclusion that on the whole it has been attended with a reasonable amount of success; and, while admitting that there are substantial grounds of grievance with regard to the undue political elevation of the coloured people, says he can scarcely recall an instance in which any planter or other employer of negro labour has not said that the result of emancipation in its industrial bearings has been much more favourable than could have been anticipated, or who has not added an expression of satisfaction that slavery, however roughly, has been finally effaced. There are many other points of interest in Mr. Somers's book to which attention might be directed did space permit, but we must refer the reader to the book itself, which is well worth perusal.

From the (London) "DAILY NEWS."

A book of direct testimony and precise information concerning the social and industrial condition of the cotton-growing States since the American Civil War is likely to be very useful. His evidence is of substantial value, both for the guidance of commercial speculation or financial enterprise, and the formation of a sound political opinion. We derive much encouragement on the whole from the account given by Mr. Somers of the aspects of the South ten years after the attempted secession which provoked the great Civil War.

From the (London) "GLOBE."

The inquiry was of the first importance, and in the course of it Mr. Somers has noted down many things well worth reading. The book too much resembles a series of notes jotted down in a traveller's journal of a visit to each separate State; though this, if it makes the pages more difficult to read, also gives an appearance of truthfulness and accuracy to the narrative; and certainly many of the facts are valuable aids towards forming an opinion as to how far the Southern States are likely to make the vast progress that is expected of them during the next ten or twenty years.

From the (London) "SPECTATOR."

This volume is the work of a laborious and careful observer. Mr. Somers spent six months in going through the Southern States of the American Union, noting down facts and impressions as he went along. As an Englishman, he probably possessed facilities for obtaining information which would have been refused to a Northerner, while he had no bitter recollections of the past to affect his judgment. It is impossible to summarize briefly the results of an inquiry extending over so vast and various a tract of country; but, on the whole, the result seems to have been satisfactory. Mr. Somers thinks that the great question of labour is being solved satisfactorily.

It is interesting to observe that the "share system," which here has been so slow to come into existence, and which is still the rarest of exceptions, has grown up in the Southern States almost simultaneously with the system of free labour. Mr. Somers does not, indeed, express himself very favourably about it; but he allows that the majority of opinions is against him, while it is evident that he disapproves of the principle involved in the arrangement.

The political aspect of the Southern States is that in which they make the least favourable impression on an observer. Possibly the remark might be extended to their Northern neighbours. But negro supremacy, through the necessary consequence of emancipation, has had a disastrous effect. How could it be otherwise? Let any one think what would be the state of an English county if it was suddenly committed to the government of the agricultural labourers. The legislatures of some of the Southern States seem to be, if possible, more corrupt and certainly less dignified than is—or we hope we may say was—the Legislature of New York. Some of the details of Mr. Somers's observations are very interesting. On *The Battery* at Charleston there was not a single carriage to be seen except "the handsome buggy of a dry-goods man from the north." The loss of Paris from two sieges has been nothing like that. Indeed, the figures of the loss caused by the Civil War are staggering in their amount.

From the (London) "SATURDAY REVIEW."

The name of the publishing house under whose auspices this volume appears will be regarded, not without reason, as a sufficient guarantee for the absence of anything like a bias against the Northern States or the Republican party, as an assurance that Mr. Somers's evidence is that of a witness who, if not impartial, is at least in nowise hostile to the Federal cause or to the authors of the existing system of government in the South. To candid and unprejudiced minds, indeed, the internal evidence of fairness will suffice; for very few writers, in describing such a state of things as has prevailed in the Southern States since their conquest, would be able to preserve that judicial calmness of temper, that absolute avoidance of strong language, that strict abstinence from needless comment, and that careful adherence to observed facts, which distinguish every chapter and page of Mr. Somers's work. Yet, though this description of the Southern States since the war is studiously confined to an account of the writer's own observations, and is marked by an indifference of tone which is sometimes almost startling, its effect is to confirm nearly all that has been written by rational advocates of the South in defence of the conquered, and in condemnation of the conduct of the conquerors; and the impression left upon the reader's mind is the stronger because the author has evidently no such intention, and many of the most important parts of his evidence come out incidentally, and almost parenthetically, by way of explaining the facts immediately under his notice.

The author traversed nearly the whole of the cotton and sugar region, as a diligent and accurate observer, with a view to note its commercial prospects and material resources rather than its political condition; and it is only in its effect on the former that he is brought to take account of the latter. His description of the different States, and of the several districts into which each State is divided by natural peculiarities, of their physical and social characteristics, of their agriculture and manufacture, of their minerals—chiefly coal and iron—and the facility of their extraction, is most careful, interesting, and valuable; and it has seldom occurred to us to peruse a book of travel, or an account of a foreign country, in which the author had so successfully contrived to tell all that is worth knowing without becoming tedious or trivial, and to leave out all that is trifling or insignificant, while making a judicious selection of such minor incidents as help to give the readers a better idea of the institutions, scenes, or people whereof he writes.

From the (London) "GUARDIAN."

Mr. Somers is a quiet, sensible writer, who is backward, perhaps too backward, in giving us his own views and experiences. His book would have been more lively, though not essentially better, if he had instructed us more fully as to the object of his journey and his own personal adventures. He takes no definite standpoint, but leaves his readers free to make whatever use they please of his observations. He was a keen observer of cotton crops, and the way of growing them. He has likewise some brief but pertinent remarks on the land question in Virginia, and the advantages offered by that State to middle-class emigrants from England. He institutes a statistical comparison between the effectiveness of the sugar-making apparatus employed respectively in Louisiana and Glasgow, and in his remarks on Danks' patent puddling apparatus, which he found at work at Chattanooga, anticipates some of the conclusions since arrived at by the Commission of the Iron and Steel Institute. We should guess that Mr. Somers travelled in the Southern States with some special regard to commercial and mechanical subjects; but he is far too intelligent a man willingly to confine his observations during five or six months of locomotion to any merely technical field, and readers of various tastes will find in his pages an abundance of useful and agreeable gleanings.

From the "SCOTSMAN."

In this book Mr. Somers gives us an account of what he saw in, and what he learned about the Southern States of America, during a visit of several months in the end of 1870 and the beginning of 1871. Let it not be supposed, however, that the volume is simply a piece of book-making of the ordinary kind done by most people who visit the United States. It has no pretensions to solve in half-a-page great problems which have puzzled and distracted a continent. It is a book in which an intelligent and practical observer sets down the result of his inquiries and observations, and desires to know what is the condition of the Southern States. Mr. Somers has apparently had no preconceived theories on any subject in connexion with the States, and, therefore, unlike a good many people who have been to America and written books, and a good many more who have not been to America and have written books, he has not had any difficulty in making facts square with prejudices. His book is a storehouse of information, statistical, agricultural, and otherwise, and at the same time it is never dull.

From the "MANCHESTER GUARDIAN."

Mr. Somers throws more light upon the condition of the free negro and his place in the labour market than any observer we have hitherto met with.

Of the undeveloped mineral wealth of the South he speaks so highly that had not science already recorded the fact as true, it would seem but the romance of a visionary. To the capitalist his book offers innumerable suggestions, and we should hope that they will not be offered in vain, although by its restrictive commercial policy the Government of the United States is doing everything it can to retard the development and progress of the country.

Of the physical beauties of the South, of its delightful climate, Mr. Somers descants most pleasantly; and his book is both pleasant and instructive reading, and not wanting in humour of a quaint kind to enliven its more serious import. Both in its subject and its treatment it is highly commendable, and we rejoice to find that a region almost deserted by the literary traveller has found so capable an exponent as Mr. Somers.

From the "MANCHESTER EXAMINER."

We have much pleasure in calling the attention of our readers, general as well as commercial, to this important and interesting volume, the result of the author's observations during a somewhat extended tour of the Southern States in the autumn and winter of 1870-71.

The work is calculated to interest both the general and commercial reader, and though in Lancashire the information and statistics connected with the cotton cultivation, and the effect of the actual fiscal policy of the United States on the agricultural condition, must render this book pre-eminently valuable to all connected with the manufacturing interest, its lively narratives and vivid descriptions of men and manners will make it generally acceptable as a book of travel.

On the whole, Mr. Somers is very hopeful for the future of the South, and he tells us that the planters themselves are the most forward to bear testimony to the success of the free-labour system. The book is in all respects interesting.

From the (London) "MINING MAGAZINE AND REVIEW."

Virginia, the Carolinas, Georgia, Alabama, Mississippi, Louisiana, and Tennessee, were one after the other visited and investigated by the author of this thoughtful and successful work; and the information acquired is communicated in a style which is unassumingly interesting and graphic. We find ourselves easily initiated in the complex mysteries of cotton prospects and negro politics, and learn to realize the vastness of these mighty countries, an adequate conception of which, as Mr. Somers says, can only be attained by actual travel. . . . Exquisite little bits of word-painting every now and then set before us vivid pictures of the beautiful and remarkable scenery passed through. No mean observer of material facts, while he was keenly observing crops and calculating tariffs, the geological features of the country, as well as the natural beauties, nowhere escaped the eye or baffled the descriptive powers of the traveller. . . . But the intrinsic value of the work lies in its skilful presentation of data from which we may estimate the recuperative powers of these States. Capital and men are, we hear, now-a-days on all sides desiderated in the South no less than in the great West. . . . But the already known and probable resources of the Southern States are not so familiar—hardly indeed suspected; yet a careful reader of the pages under review will bethink himself that for those who are content to combine a little capital and industry, and patiently develop wealth from the plainer workshops, rather than amass it at once in the uncertain treasures of nature; the land of Virginia, the coal and iron of Alabama and Georgia, offer more inducements than the placers and silver ledges of the Rocky Mountains.

From (London) "ENGINEERING."

After spending many years in Glasgow as the editor of a daily newspaper, Mr. Somers resolved to seek a change of scene and employment for a time; and accordingly he betook himself to the Southern States of America, where he travelled and resided during the winter of 1870-71. His keen powers of observation were there abundantly called into requisition, and in the volume before us we have the results of his observation and inquiry. As he had so long moved and mixed among a great manufacturing and commercial community, having extensive dealings with every part of the civilized world, it was but natural to expect that in selecting such a place of resort for a season as the Southern States, his mind was bent in a great degree upon taking stock of the industrial resources of the country, bearing in mind the fact, doubtless, that few travellers in that part of the New World have ever devoted any particular attention to the subject which to him had many attractions. When the industry of the Southern States of America is spoken of, we rarely think of anything else but the cultivation of cotton, sugar, tobacco, wheat, maize, and rice, forgetting all the while, or, more likely, not knowing that there is in the country a great abundance of mineral wealth, which only awaits capital, enterprise, and commercial and technical capacity to turn it to good account.

We cannot lay down the "Southern States Since the War," without thanking Mr. Somers most cordially for giving us such a useful and and interesting book on a theme which in many hands would have proved "stale, flat, and unprofitable," but which has afforded him an opportunity of displaying his keen powers of observation, his enlarged views of public policy, and his great ability as a clear and vivid descriptive writer.

From the "MEMPHIS DAILY APPEAL."

Mr. Somers tries and often succeeds in doing us justice, and describes especially our plantation life with an honest pen. There are not wanting too, passages in which the author discovers a bias for the South. These are born of the sympathy that cannot fail to be evoked of any man who has a brain to comprehend, and a heart to yield to the stories of our great calamities of war and Radical thieving and crime. It would be impossible, as even Greeley of the *Tribune*, and Bowles of the Springfield *Republican*, confessed, for any heretofore man of ordinary observation to travel in the South and fail to note the marks of war and Radical crime, without expressing profound regret that a country so new, so susceptible of growth, and that, in the hands of its present population, has done so much for civilization, should be not only retarded in its march, but shorn of its wealth to feed the most infamous gang of political prostitutes that ever defiled public opinion. Mr. Somers has not failed either to describe what he saw of this sort of thing, or to condemn it. But not on that account do we commend the book to our readers. It is generally fair and candid, and devoted almost wholly to the South and her staple, will be read with avidity, North as well as South, especially by those who are interested in the growth or sale of cotton.

From the "NEW-YORK EVENING MAIL."

We have found few more capable and clear-sighted observers than Mr. Robert Somers, whose work on "The Southern States since the War, 1870-71," with map, we have from Macmillan & Co. We have reason to be profoundly grateful to any one, who, from external vantage-ground, can observe so widely, accurately, and usefully, and report so well. We cannot name any home work which gives so much valuable information in detail as to the material elements of wealth and the new conditions of life in the several Southern States, while it is also simply interesting as a record of travel. The author hesitatingly points out some of our economical mistakes, and especially the wrong done to our people by our tariff, "which has attained a prohibitory and vexatious rigour which is without parallel, and gives the United States the curious distinction of being—China or Japan scarce excepted—the most anti-commercial country in the world." He shows that this is from no merely British point of view; and we commend the work generally to all economists, thinkers or writers, editors, and business men, who would be thoroughly posted as to that section of our country which is now demanding just consideration.

From the "NEW-YORK WORLD."

Mr. Robert Somers's "Southern States since the War" is by far the best book written on the changed relations and the actual condition of the South since 1865—just such a work, in fact, as might be expected from a canny Scot who came to see things for himself, and brought a fine faculty of observation, a cool intelligence, and perfect impartiality to the difficult task.

From the "RURAL ALABAMIAN."

The perusal of this work has given us unusual pleasure. In the outset we had a strong curiosity to see how a highly educated and practical man, from a foreign country, would handle topics of immense concern to us, which had elicited so much angry discussion in the United States. We have finished the perusal, and must say that no more just, able, impartial and independent umpire has delivered his opinion upon them. . . . . . We predict for the book an extensive sale both in Europe and America.

www.ingramcontent.com/pod-product-compliance
Lightning Source LLC
Chambersburg PA
CBHW032138230426
43672CB00011B/2378

* 9 7 8 3 3 3 7 1 2 0 0 3 0 *